Boundless Grandeur

The Christian Vision of A. M. Donald Allchin

Boundless Grandeur

Edited by
DAVID G. R. KELLER

Foreword by
ROWAN WILLIAMS

Introduction by
METROPOLITAN KALLISTOS WARE

PICKWICK *Publications* · Eugene, Oregon

BOUNDLESS GRANDEUR
The Christian Vision of A. M. Donald Allchin

Copyright © 2015 Wipf and Stock Publishers. All rights reserved. Except for brief quotations in critical publications or reviews, no part of this book may be reproduced in any manner without prior written permission from the publisher. Write: Permissions, Wipf and Stock Publishers, 199 W. 8th Ave., Suite 3, Eugene, OR 97401.

Pickwick Publications
An Imprint of Wipf and Stock Publishers
199 W. 8th Ave., Suite 3
Eugene, OR 97401

www.wipfandstock.com

ISBN 13: 978–1–4982–0319–7

Cataloguing-in-Publication Data

Boundless grandeur : the Christian vision of A. M. Donald Allchin / edited by David G. R. Keller, with a foreword by Rowan Williams and an introduction by Kallistos Ware

X + Y p. ; 23 cm. Includes bibliographical references.

ISBN 13: 978–1–4982–0319–7

1. Allchin, A. M. 2. Anglican Communion. 3. Christian union. I. Keller, David G. R., 1937–. II. Williams, Rowan, 1950–. III. Kallistos, bishop of Diokleia, 1934–. IV. Title.

BV599 K45 2015

Manufactured in the U.S.A.   06/22/2015

For Donald
Friend, mentor, colleague.

I Donald
cyfaill, cynghorwr, cydweithiwr

"For the things which belong to the story of Jesus
are not yet completed."

Donald Allchin

Contents

Part Two: Donald Allchin and the Orthodox Church

Part Three: Donald Allchin's Ecumenical Dialogue and Theology

Part Four: Donald Allchin as Interpreter of Anglican Tradition and Theology

Part Five: Donald Allchin and the Welsh Spiritual Tradition

Editor's Note

" . . . in every generation, she [wisdom] passes into holy souls, and makes of them friends of God, and prophets."[1]

Donald Allchin (1930–2010) was an ordained priest in the Church of England, an historian, and theologian. After a four-year curacy in a parish in Kensington from 1956 to 1960, Donald became Librarian at Pusey House, Oxford. During the 1960s he developed a substantive interest in Eastern Orthodox Churches and became friends with the Orthodox theologians Vladimir Lossky and Dumitru Staniloae and the Russian historian Nicolas Zernov. Donald was an active member of the Society of St. Alban and St. Sergius promoting Anglican-Orthodox dialogue and later became the editor of its journal *Sobornost* until 1977. From 1968 to 1973 he was warden to the Sisters of the Love of God, an Anglican contemplative order in Fairacres, near Oxford. During this period he became a friend of Thomas Merton, visiting Gethsemane Abbey in Kentucky and conducting a lively correspondence. From 1973 to 1987 Donald was residentiary canon at Canterbury Cathedral where he developed an interest in the Welsh spiritual tradition. Donald returned to Oxford in 1987 to become director of the St. Theosevia Center with a focus on learning and dialogue between Eastern and Western Christian spirituality. In 1994 he moved to Bangor, North Wales and immersed himself in the poetry, saints, and holy places of the Welsh spiritual tradition. He remained there as professor in theology and Welsh until 2010 when he returned to Oxford and died later that year.

1. Wisdom of Solomon 7:27.

Donald Allchin was also a friend of God. He found God's presence and boundless grandeur everywhere and in every person he encountered. Without trying, Donald could be fully present in places, conversations, and relationships and at the same time make connections with other diverse yet complementary topics and persons. His endless curiosity and delight in life gave birth to an eclectic range of interests and academic investigations. Donald's gift of friendship was contagious. He could draw people from a variety of backgrounds and interests into a collegial network of collaboration and mutual support. All of this flowed from Donald's prayerful experience of God. The life of the Trinity was the template for Donald's awareness and celebration of the unity of all creation and human life. At the same time he knew that the resurrection of Christ brings both the opportunity for transformed human life and the responsibility to mend and transform broken human lives and institutions.

The chapters, poems, and memoirs in this book represent what Donald's friendship and mentoring have brought forth in the lives of the contributors. The book is an example of his ability to bring people together, even after his death, and it testifies to Donald's influence and contributions to the life of the world. Here you will meet poets, historians, bishops, archbishops, monks, priests and lay persons, scholars, professors, and writers. You will taste the rich ecumenical dialogue between Donald's Anglican heritage, the Eastern Orthodox Churches, the Roman Catholic Church, and churches of the Reformed Traditions, including Donald's friendships and correspondence with Thomas Merton and the Romanian Orthodox theologian Dumitru Stăniloae. Readers will gain insights into Donald's interpretation of the Anglican Tradition and his emphasis on the value of monastic solitude and community for the lives of modern Christians. And last, but certainly not least, you will enter Donald's journey into the lives, poetry, saints, and holy places of the Welsh spiritual tradition. And this is only a taste of his legacy. In Donald's words, *"For the things which belong to the story of Jesus are not yet completed."*[2]

2. Allchin, *Participation in God*, 1.

Foreword

When I first learned that my doctoral supervisor at Oxford was to be Donald Allchin, I was pleased but slightly surprised; I had associated him up to that point with his work on the Anglican monastic revival, and I was planning to study contemporary Eastern Orthodox theology. The surprise didn't last, of course. Not only did I discover the unique breadth of Donald's acquaintance with the Orthodox world, I learned never to be surprised at the depth and range of Donald's interests. At the end of our first hour of (nominal) supervision, during which we had discussed Orthodoxy, Merton, Wales, David Jones, John Wesley, and much else besides (even, briefly, my proposed research), he said with that characteristic beaming smile, "Well! This is all turning out even better than we could have hoped." What I think he meant was that he was always delighted by the chance of conversation that roamed anarchically around the wide world of Western and Eastern Christian civilization and glad to find someone who was equally happy to let it do so—even if they could not begin to match his energy, appetite, and capacity to make connections.

As many have said, that capacity was one of his greatest gifts: allowing you to link up some insight from a modern Episcopalian literary critic with an aphorism from sixth-century Syria, a Welsh elegy, and the notebooks of some out-of-the-way Tractarian; and linking up people with the same imaginative gusto ("You know x, of course? No? Really? Oh, you *must* meet . . ."). Thinking about all sorts of things and persons that have been intellectually, spiritually, and emotionally precious to me over the years, I am quite taken aback to recall how many of them I owe to Donald: from an introduction to some of Merton's lesser-known work through to the manuscripts of Vladimir Lossky that formed the main matter for my doctoral research, from the philosophy of Christos Yannaras to the poetry of Denise Levertov, and the later Geoffrey Hill (whose *Tenebrae* I first picked up in Donald's house in Canterbury). It is Donald's eye and ear that I realize picked out for me so much that gave lasting nourishment and joy.

In 1973 I went with him on a visit to Paris to meet an assortment of mostly Orthodox friends, and was delighted and amused to see that the reaction to him of these Franco-Russians was so like the way in which he was received and welcomed in the UK—the affectionate exasperation at his utter impracticality, the awe at the breadth of his interests, the intense warmth of appreciation and gratitude for his spiritual luminosity. His unselfconscious enthusiasm and sheer enjoyment of his friends and his faith never seemed to vary from one cultural context to another, and the response was always the same. And, it must be said, his willingness (untypical of the English) to converse in fluently rickety and English-accented French (or indeed Welsh) never failed to consolidate the affection he won.

One of those Orthodox friends remarked on that visit as he greeted him, "Pas encore évêque?" "Not a bishop yet?" And that reminds us of another feature of Donald's ministry: he managed to be close to many powerful and influential figures in the church, near the heart of the Anglican Establishment in Oxford and Canterbury, yet supremely uninterested in church politics, let alone a "career" in the church. He once quoted to me a remark made to him by (I think) David Edwards when both were young clergy: "You'll be fine when you're Dear Old Father Allchin—but what are you going to do until then?" In the event, he found innumerable things to do, and none of them required any particular hierarchical meal ticket. It was part of the "monastic" quality of his contribution to the church. He came close a couple of times to committing himself to the monastic calling in the traditional sense; but (surely rightly) recognized his charism as being more to do with living on the edge of the institution in a rather different way—even more insecure in many respects, but simply a visible presence on the edge of the church's "business" world, reminding people of other and more fruitful explorations to be had, if only they would turn to the larger horizon. Unfussily compliant (mostly) with the rules around intercommunion and the like, he nevertheless behaved in so many respects as if the divisions between churches had already been healed. He was never an ecumenical negotiator; always an ecumenical witness. To be with him in that context was to recognize that in some profound sense he was right and the divisions *had* been healed—not by our ingenuity and good will but by the abiding, inexhaustible presence of grace. Like a few others of his generation, he embodied a style of Anglican identity that succeeded in being utterly and humbly hospitable just because it was fundamentally confident and unworried. It does no harm to be reminded that this was once possible; and perhaps still is, by the grace of God.

The essays in this book present a wonderfully rounded picture of Donald in so many settings, so many conversations. For those who knew him, they will rekindle not only memories, but shared enthusiasms; for those who didn't, they should open up a world of new and startling possibilities for joining up the dots in theology and creativity and spiritual understanding. It is a welcome tribute to a loving and much beloved friend, and I hope it will make new friends for him and his vision of the church and the kingdom.

Rowan Williams
former Archbishop of Canterbury; currently Master,
Magdalene College, Cambridge University.

Editor's Acknowledgements

One of Donald Allchin's great gifts was creating communities of colleagues and friends who shared and contributed to his Christian vision of life. This book is an example of Donald's handiwork, even after his death. I am grateful for the encouragement and work of the fourteen other contributors, each of whom brings a unique perspective to Donald's life and vision. I am especially grateful for Esther de Waal who, as a close friend of Donald, helped me identify contributors and offered personal support along the way. My wife, Emily Wilmer, who was present when I shared the idea for this book with Donald, has been a patient companion and guide throughout this project.

Gladstone's Library in Hawarden, North Wales, is a place Donald Allchin loved. Thanks to the vision of the Warden, Peter Francis, the Allchin Archive is housed there and the staff of the Library, especially Peter, has given professional support to the development of this book. I was awarded a month-long residential scholarship in July 2014 to organize the editing process. Louisa Yates and Gary Butler digitalized part of the archive for contributors' access through the internet. The Library accepted an offer to host an initial book launch and seminar on Donald's life and work in November 2015. I'm grateful as well to Patricia Williams, a former Gladstone's Library librarian, and Mae Balchin and Alexandra Ross, two former interns at the Library, for their work in the early stages of organizing Donald's archive. Their assistance helped me in planning the scope of this book.

St. Theosevia Center for Christian Spirituality in Oxford, England, is a place that was dear to Donald Allchin's heart. He was Director from 1987 to 1994, offering courses and dialogue between Eastern and Western Christian spirituality. I appreciate the support of the current Director, The Rev. Dr. Liz Carmichael, who offered to host a Study Day at the Center to launch the book and give Oxford students, faculty, and the general public an opportunity to be more familiar with Donald's life and work.

Larry Todd Wilson, Founder and Director of Knowledge Harvesting, Inc. helped me design a format for the three hour-long interviews I conducted in 2007 with Donald Allchin at Gladstone's Library. It was part of an ecumenical effort to archive the spiritual wisdom of elders. Edited transcripts of these interviews are in the Appendix; they give the only known overview of Donald's life, thought, and work in his own words. I'm grateful to Suzanne Cahoon who transcribed the interviews from a digital recorder to computer documents which I have edited. Father Stephen Platt, Editor of the ecumenical journal *Sobornost* has given generous support to the project through access to issues and permissions to use copyrighted material. Dr. Paul M. Pearson, Director and Archivist of the Thomas Merton Center in Louisville, KY, provided links to resources on the Center's website that document the friendship and correspondence between Donald Allchin and Thomas Merton. Dr. Pearson gave permission to use material from the Center's *The Merton Annual*, including two addresses by Donald and one by Dr. Pearson. Peter Francis Barrett, retired Anglican Bishop of Cashel and Ossory in the Church of Ireland helped with communications between the editor and contributors and offered faithful support for the project. I am grateful to the staff of Pickwick Publications for recognizing the unique value of this book and to Dr. Robin Parry, my editor, who has provided timely, professional, and friendly support.

In March of 2010 Ann Shukman of Elshieshields Tower, Lockerbie, Scotland, a long-time friend and colleague of Donald's, invited me and my wife, Emily, to visit Donald who was staying with his caregiver, Ciaran, in her guest cottage. We stayed with Ann and it was during this visit that Donald endorsed the idea that has become *Boundless Grandeur*. I am grateful to Ann for her hospitality and encouragement. It was the last time Emily and I would see Donald and is a memory we cherish.

David Keller
The Feast of All Saints 2014

Permissions

The Editor and other contributors to *Boundless Grandeur* are grateful for permission to use material from publishers whose works have made this book possible.

Excerpts from the following works published by Darton, Longman and Todd are used with permission:

Allchin, A. M. *The Kingdom of Love and Knowledge: The Encounter between Orthodoxy and the West*. London: Darton, Longman and Todd, 1979.

Allchin, A. M. *N. F. S. Grundtvig: An Introduction to His Life and Work*. London: Darton, Longman and Todd, 1997.

Allchin, A. M. *The Joy of All Creation*. London: Darton, Longman and Todd, 1993.

Allchin, A. M. *Participation in God*. London: Darton, Longman and Todd, 1988.

Excerpts from the following issue of *THE WAY, a Journal of Christian Spirituality* published by the British Jesuits, Campion Hall, Oxford, OX1 1QS, (www.theway.org.uk), are used with permission:

"Spirituality and Welsh Poetry, 1930–80," in "Spirituality, Imagination and Contemporary Literature," Supplement to *The Way*. 1994.

Excerpts from the following work published by The University of Wales Press are used with permission:

Allchin, A. M. *Praise Above All: Discovering the Welsh Tradition*. Cardiff: University of Wales Press, 1991.

Excerpts from the following issues of *Sobornost incorporating Eastern Churches Review,* Journal of the Fellowship of St. Alban and St. Sergius, 1 Canterbury Road, Oxford OX2 6LU are used with permission:

Allchin, A. M. "The Holy Spirit in Christian Life" *Sobornost incorporating Eastern Churches Review* 5/3 (1966).

Allchin, A. M. "Michael Ramsey and the Orthodox World." *Sobornost incorporating Eastern Churches Review,* 10/2 (1988).

Ware, Kallistos. "Obituary: Canon Donald Allchin (1930–2010)." *Sobornost incorporating Eastern Churches Review* 33/1 (2011).

Excerpts from the following publications of The Thomas Merton Center at Bellarmine University, Louisville, KY are used with permission:

"Our Lives, A Powerful Pentecost: Merton's Meeting with Russian Christianity." *The Merton Annual*, 1998.

"'A very disciplined person' from Nelson County: An interview with Canon A. M. Allchin about Merton." *Merton Annual*, 17 (2004).

Excerpts from the following publications of The Thomas Merton Society of Great Britain and Ireland are used with permission:

"Can we do Wales then?" *The Merton Journal* 13/1 (2006a).

"Merton at Ninety" *The Merton Journal* 12/1 (2005).

Remembering Merton. A roundtable discussion between a few of Merton's friends—Tommie O'Callaghan, Donald Allchin, Jim Forest, and John Wu, Jr., chaired by David Scott at the Thomas Merton Society conference "Your Heart is my Hermitage," held in Southampton, 1996. http://www.thomasmertonsociety.org/panel.htm

"Donald Allchin and the Thomas Merton Society." *The Merton Journal* (2011).

Excerpts from the following work originally published by Faith Press are used with permission of the Executors of the Allchin Estate:

Allchin, A. M. *The Spirit and the Word: Two Studies in Nineteenth Century Anglican Theology*. Faith Press, Ltd., 1963.

Excerpts from the following work published by SPCK are used with permission:

A. M. Allchin and John Coulson, eds. *Rediscovery of Newman*. London: SPCK, 1967.

The cover photo of a sunrise at St. Non's Holy Well, near St. David's, South Wales, is used courtesy of David Keller. Photos of Donald Allchin and Thomas Merton and Donald Allchin and Dumitru Staniloae are used with the permission of Donald Allchin. All other photos are used with the permission of David Keller and Emily Wilmer.

The following permission for an additional excerpt from Seabury Press was not possible to obtain prior to publication:

Allchin, A. M., *The Living Presence of the Past: The Dynamic of Christian Tradition*. New Haven: Seabury, 1981. (Publisher is no longer in business. Copyright holder is unknown.)

Contributors

Ruth Bidgood was born and brought up in South Wales. She studied English at Oxford, then served in the WRNS in Egypt. She married and had three children. Her writing life in poetry and local history started in middle age, on her return from Surrey to live in Wales.

Ciprian Burca is a priest of the Romanian Orthodox Church. His current theological research is focused on the challenges and the perspective of modern Christian theology, spirituality, and ethics within the recent ecumenical context of the end of the twentieth century and the beginning of the twenty-first century.

James Coutts is a retired parish priest of the Church in Wales who served in urban, rural, and small town parishes.

Fiona Gardner is a psychoanalytic psychotherapist and a spiritual director. She is the UK International Advisor for The International Thomas Merton Society, has been very involved in The Thomas Merton Society of Great Britain and Ireland, and has presented papers regularly at both TMSGBI and ITMS conferences. She is an author and her latest book is *Precious Thoughts, Daily Readings from the Correspondence of Thomas Merton*. She is currently working on a book about Thomas Merton and the child-mind.

Kallistos Ware was born in 1934 and joined the Orthodox Church in 1958, becoming priest in 1966, and bishop in 1982. He is a member of the monastic brotherhood of St. John the Theologian on the island of Patmos, Greece and for thirty-five years (1966–2001) he taught Orthodox theology in the University of Oxford. He is Orthodox Co-Chairman of the International Anglican-Orthodox Theological Dialogue, and he is also a member of the

International Commission for Theological Dialogue between the Orthodox Church and the Roman Catholic Church. His best-known publications
are *The Orthodox Church* and *The Orthodox Way*. He is a co-translator of
three volumes of material from the Orthodox service books, and of four
volumes of *The Philokalia*.

David Keller, an Episcopal priest, has led retreats, seminars, and pilgrimages with Donald Allchin in the United States and the UK. From 1994–2002
he was the Steward of the Episcopal House of Prayer at St. John's Benedictine Abbey in Collegeville, MN and serves as Adjunct Professor of Ascetical Theology at the General Theological Seminary in New York City. He is
co-steward, with his wife, Emily Wilmer, of Oasis of Wisdom: An Institute
for Contemplative Study, Practice, and Living, based in Asheville, NC. He
is the author of *Oasis of Wisdom: The Worlds of the Desert Mothers and
Fathers*, Desert *Banquet: A Year of Wisdom from The Desert Mothers and
Fathers*, and *Come and See: The Transformation of Personal Prayer*.

Charles Miller met Donald Allchin as a teenager and remained a life-
long friend. He is Team Rector of Abingdon-on-Thames in the Diocese
of Oxford and has served parishes in the United States and England. He
has taught historical and ascetical theology and church history at Nashota
House, The General Theological Seminary, and Yale Divinity School in the
United States. His areas of special interest are seventeenth-century English
and twentieth-century Orthodox theology and spirituality, and Anglican-
Orthodox relations. He is the author of four books, *Praying the Eucharist*,
Toward a Fuller Vision: Orthodoxy and the Anglican Experience, *The Gift
of the World: An Introduction to the Theology of Dumitru Staniloae*, and
Richard Hooker and the Vision of God: Exploring the Origins of Anglicanism.

D. Densil Morgan is Professor of Theology at the University of Wales Trinity Saint David and was previously Professor of Theology, Bangor University, Wales. He was educated at the University of Wales and the University
of Oxford. Among his publications are *The Span of the Cross: Christian Religion and Society in Wales, 1914–2000*, *Barth Reception in Britain*, *The SPCK
Introduction to Karl Barth*, *Wales and the Word: Historical Perspectives on
Religion and Welsh Identity*, as well as books in Welsh on different aspects
of theology and modern church history. He co-authored with A. M. Allchin
Sensuous Glory: The Poetry of D. Gwenallt Jones.

Barry A. Orford was born in Manchester and ordained in the Church in Wales. He worked in North and South Wales and in Yorkshire. From 2001 until his recent retirement he was Priest Librarian and Archivist at Pusey House in Oxford. He now lives near London.

Geoffrey Rowell is an Emeritus Fellow of Keble College, Oxford, where he served as Chaplain and Tutor in Theology from 1972 to 1993, teaching theology, church history, and Christian spirituality in the University. He was Bishop of Basingstoke from 1994 to 2001 and Bishop of Gibraltar in Europe from 2001 to 2013. He is the author of several books, including *The Vision Glorious: Themes and Personalities of the Catholic Revival in Anglicanism,* published to mark the 150th anniversary of the Oxford Movement in 1993, and was co-editor, with Rowan Williams and Kenneth Stevenson, of *Love's Redeeming Work: The Anglican Quest for Holiness.*

David Scott is an Anglican priest, spiritual writer, and poet. A friend of Donald's for almost fifty years, he was much influenced by his guidance. They had a shared affection for poetry, religious communities, and Thomas Merton. The latter led to the creation of the Thomas Merton Society of Great Britain and Ireland. David's most recent collection of poems is entitled *Beyond the Drift: New & Selected Poems.* He has published five collections of his poetry and won the National Poetry Competition in the UK in 1978. In 2008 the Archbishop of Canterbury conferred on Scott a Lambeth Doctorate of Letters.

Martin L. Smith is a priest of the Episcopal Church and the writer of a number of widely read books exploring contemporary spirituality. After reading theology at Oxford, he was ordained in 1970, served for three years in parish ministry, and then entered the Society of St. John the Evangelist. He became a member of the American Congregation of SSJE in 1979 and took American citizenship. After serving as Superior of the American Congregation, he left the Society in 2002 and moved to Washington DC, where he has been on the staff of the United States Holocaust Memorial Museum and St. Columba's Episcopal Church. In retirement he travels widely to lecture, preach and lead retreats.

Patrick Thomas is Vicar of Christ Church, Carmarthen, and Canon Chancellor of St Davids Cathedral, Pembrokeshire. He is a former member of the Welsh Language Board and an honorary member of the Gorsedd of Bards. He has published books on a variety of subjects, including Welsh Celtic Spirituality, and worked with Donald Allchin and Densil Morgan on the volume *Sensuous Glory: The Poetic Vision of D. Gwenallt Jones.*

Esther de Waal is an Anglican lay woman who grew up in a Shropshire country vicarage and there had her first experience of history under the guidance of her father, who showed her the importance of recognizing the role of landscape and buildings, as well as the written word. This shaped her life, since it was the monastic remains at Canterbury that drew her to the Rule of St. Benedict, and the Irish High Crosses that first awakened her awareness of the Celtic tradition. Later her interest in the Cistercians, in Welsh religious poetry, and Thomas Traherne ensured that she and Donald continued to share those enthusiasms that had nourished their friendship since the 1950s. Esther and Donald edited *Daily Readings from Prayers & Praises in the Celtic Tradition.* She is the author of *Seeking God: The Way of St. Benedict.*

Rowan Williams studied theology in Cambridge and then worked on modern Russian Orthodox thought at Oxford under Donald Allchin's supervision. He has been a teacher of theology in Oxford and Cambridge, served as Bishop of Monmouth for ten years, three of those also as Archbishop of Wales, then as Archbishop of Canterbury from 2002 to 2012. He is now Master of Magdalene College, Cambridge.

Introduction

Kallistos Ware, Metropolitan of Diokleia

Donald Allchin's friend Thomas Merton has written some striking words that apply exactly to Donald himself.

> If I can unite *in myself* the thought and the devotion of Eastern and Western Christendom, the Greek and the Latin Fathers, the Russians with the Spanish mystics, I can prepare in myself the re-union of divided Christians. From that secret and unspoken unity in myself can eventually come a visible and manifest unity of all Christians. . . . We must contain all divided worlds in ourselves and transcend them in Christ.[1]

Donald did indeed come close to realizing within himself "the secret and unspoken unity" of which Merton was speaking. Christian reconciliation was the central theme that inspired his life. To a remarkable degree he united in himself Eastern and Western Christendom, Orthodoxy, Roman Catholicism, and the Anglican and Protestant worlds. He wrote scholarly works on monasticism in the Church of England and on the great Danish theologian N. F. S. Grundtvig. He was co-editor of a book on the hymns of John and Charles Wesley. He loved the land and the poetry of Wales. He numbered among his friends several of the leading theologians of the Orthodox Church, such as the Greeks Demetrios Koutroubis and Christos Yannaras, the Russian Vladimir Lossky and the Romanian Dumitru Stan-iloae. He was truly a bridge-builder.

1. Merton, *Conjectures of a Guilty Bystander*, 21. In this introduction I draw upon the obituary that I wrote on Donald Allchin in the journal of the Fellowship of St. Alban and St Sergius. Ware. "Obituary," 37–46. Used with permission.

Through this notable variety of interests—wide-ranging, yet without superficiality—Donald's life was marked above all by the quality of *fullness*. This was rightly emphasized by Archbishop Rowan Williams in the homily that he gave at the High Mass of Requiem and Thanksgiving held in Donald's memory in St. Mary Magdalen, Oxford, on January 12, 2011. "Emptiness," said Archbishop Rowan, "was not a quality of any desk, any room or conversation with which Donald was involved. And it is that fullness we are celebrating today, the fullness of a man and a mind and a heart receptive in a very rare way to whatever gifts the Father gave." The Archbishop went on to speak of Donald's "capacity for welcome, a spiritual and intellectual hospitality the like of which is rarely seen."[2] The contributions to this present volume, written from different points of view, illustrate exactly the receptive and outgoing generosity of Donald's "spiritual and intellectual hospitality."

Arthur Macdonald Allchin, to give him his full name—but to everyone he was known as Donald—was born in London on Easter Day, April 20, 1930, the son of a distinguished doctor. He was the youngest in a family of four, with two brothers and one sister. He was brought up as an Anglican. From 1943 to 1948 he was educated at Westminster School. In his first two years the school was still in Worcestershire, where it had been evacuated during the war, but in 1945 it returned to London, resettling as best it could in buildings that had been partially destroyed by bombing. In 1948 Donald entered Christ Church, Oxford, where he read Modern History, gaining his BA in 1951 with Second Class Honors. Although at this time most young men were required to do two years of "National Service" in the armed forces, Donald was exempted from this, presumably on grounds of health. Still remaining at Christ Church, he embarked on postgraduate research into the revival of the religious life in nineteenth-century Anglicanism. For this he was awarded the degree of BLitt in 1956. Today he would certainly have received a DPhil, but standards in those days were more demanding.

This led to his first published book, *The Silent Rebellion*,[3] a pioneering study that is still well worth reading, based on the original sources, both published and unpublished, and notable for the skill with which it places the Anglican monastic movement in its broader cultural context. Donald expressed particular admiration for Fr. R. M. Benson, founder of the Society of St. John the Evangelist (the "Cowley Fathers"). In common with all

2. Williams, "The sermon preached by the Archbishop," 46–47.

3. Allchin, *The Silent Rebellion*.

his works, the book was written in a fluent and elegant style that was easily readable. Yet here, as also in his other works, I sometimes wish that he had developed his theme with greater rigor and precision, pressing his argument to a more decisive conclusion. He was asking the right questions, but there was something deficient in the answers. It has to be said that Donald was not a systematic thinker. His main strength did not lie in dogmatic theology, nor did he ever study philosophy in any depth. He was at his best when writing imaginatively about the life of prayer, and when exploring in a free-ranging manner the interaction between spirituality and poetry.

In 1954 Donald entered Cuddesdon Theological College, outside Oxford, where he trained for the Anglican ministry. He spent eight months in Greece, from July 1955 to March 1956, as a Philip Usher Scholar, and during this time he visited Athos, Constantinople, and Jerusalem. He was ordained deacon in 1956 and priest in 1957. From 1956 to 1960 he was one the curates at the fashionable Kensington parish of St. Mary Abbots. This was his only experience of parochial work, for he never served as priest-in-charge of any parish. While firmly rooted in the High Church tradition, he was not an extreme Anglo-Catholic.

In 1960 Donald moved back to Oxford, spending nine years as Librarian at Pusey House. During this time he developed close links with the Sisters of the Love of God at the Convent of the Incarnation, Fairacres, Oxford. In 1967 he succeeded the well-known spiritual director Fr. Gilbert Shaw as Warden of the Community, a position that he held for twenty-seven years until 1994. In the words of one of the nuns, Sister Rosemary, "He used sometimes to say that his relationship to SLG provided a thread of continuity through the changes of his life, and he gave something of the same to us." Another women's community of which he served as Warden from 1986–2008 was the Anglican Society of the Sacred Cross at Tymawr in Wales. Although himself far from being a recluse, he took a particular interest in the eremitic life, and acted as guide to several solitaries. He organized a memorable conference on the hermit life during September 29–October 4, 1975 at St. David's in Wales; the proceedings were published two years later by Fairacres Publications under the title *Solitude and Communion*.[4]

Among the research students at Oxford whom Donald supervised was the future Archbishop of Canterbury, Rowan Williams. Rowan's thesis on the theology of Vladimir Lossky, for which he was awarded a doctorate in 1975, has unfortunately remained unpublished. It is a work of great

4. Allchin, ed. *Solitude and Communion.*

brilliance, in no way superseded, and it is much to be hoped that it will eventually see the light of day. There is a story told of Rowan's time as Donald's student—I cannot vouch for its accuracy—that after a few weeks Donald told Rowan that there was nothing further that he could teach him. Be that as it may, in his preface Rowan thanks his supervisor for "unfailing help and encouragement," and speaks of the "many insights" that Donald provided through his personal acquaintance with Lossky.

From 1973 to 1987 Donald was a Residentiary Canon at Canterbury Cathedral. The relatively large house that was assigned to him (since then, pulled down) enabled him to provide a home for his elderly parents. "Residentiary" is perhaps not totally appropriate as a description of his life during those years, for he was frequently absent from Canterbury at conferences and speaking engagements. He was, for example, a visiting lecturer at Nashotah House, Wisconsin, and also at General Theological Seminary and at Trinity Institute in New York. In 1973, with the establishment of the International Anglican-Orthodox Joint Doctrinal Commission, Donald was an obvious choice as one of the delegates, and he continued to play a highly positive part in the dialogue until 1984. The two Agreed Statements produced by the Commission during those early, creative years—the Moscow Statement of 1976 and the Dublin Statement of 1984—owe much to his expertise and discernment.

In the anonymous obituary in *The Times* on December 31, 2010, it is asserted concerning his years at Canterbury, that Donald did not enjoy his time at the cathedral. This is strenuously denied by some who knew him well at this time. Admittedly, cathedrals these days are complex organizations, and Donald was far from being a natural administrator. But he valued the monastic past of the cathedral and its choral tradition, although he was doubtless less at home with its civic role. Incidentally, there is another misleading statement in *The Times* obituary, when it said that Donald possessed "private" financial resources. He may have received a small inheritance from his parents, but he was never well off financially. His way of life, without being ascetic, was modest and simple.

In 1987 Donald returned once more to Oxford, to become the first Director of the St. Theosevia Center for Christian Spirituality. Here Donald was in his natural element, for the purpose of the Center is to build bridges between Eastern and Western ways of prayer, and this was a cause very close to his heart. The Center, at 2 Canterbury Road, is closely associated with the nearby ecumenical House of St. Gregory and St. Macrina, dedicated to work for Christian unity, and also with the Orthodox community worshipping in the adjacent church of the Holy Trinity and the Annunciation. At St. Theosevia's Donald organized an exciting program of day conferences, while from time to time the Center also sponsored seminars of a more academic character, bringing together senior members of the university.

In 1994 Donald returned to Wales, a land to which he had long felt strongly attracted. He was a keen admirer of the Welsh poet and artist David Jones, as also of other poets who have enriched the literary tradition of Wales in the last two hundred years, such as Ann Griffiths, Gwenallt, Saunders Lewis, and R. S. Thomas. Settling in Bangor, North Wales, he was made an honorary professor at the University of North Wales. By the end of his life he had become fluent in the Welsh language.

As his health deteriorated, Donald planned to return to Oxford. But a house in Bangor will not buy one in Oxford, and so he moved to Woodstock, some eight miles distant. Before he could settle into his new home, he had to be transferred to the John Radcliffe Hospital in Oxford, and here he died shortly before Christmas, on December 23, 2010. Donald, it has been rightly said, never acquired the art of cooking and housekeeping, and in his later years he was fortunate to be looked after by his friend Ciaran.

Donald neither desired nor received high office in the Anglican Church, for he was essentially a free spirit. At one time he was invited to become dean of a major English cathedral, but he declined the offer. It was a wise decision. He would have had oversight of a staff of more than sixty persons, and this he would not have enjoyed; and he would have been required to remain in one place, whereas he was always by inclination a wanderer. The possibility was mentioned more than once that be might become a diocesan bishop in the Anglican Church of Wales. That would have suited him better, as his gifts of preaching and of pastoral care could have been put to good use. In the end, however, nothing came of this.

While sociable, with an outstanding gift for friendship, he remained unmarried. In our numerous conversations, on no occasion did he imply that he had ever seriously envisaged marriage. In a notebook that he kept, entitled "A Book of Prayers," found after his death, he inserted a piece of paper dated December 20, 1957, with the words, "O Lord, if it be thy will, grant me the grace to serve thee in a life of poverty, chastity and obedience. Amen." This suggests that, around the time of his priestly ordination, he made a private vow of celibacy. This he kept throughout his life. He may also have thought, particularly during the 1950s, of entering a religious community, but he never did so. Throughout his life, however, he followed a disciplined pattern of daily prayer and regular almsgiving.

Donald was a prolific writer, the author or editor of some twenty-two books. The most substantial among them were the two works already mentioned, *The Silent Rebellion*, and his monograph on Grundtvig.[5] Danish Lutherans have assured me that, in their opinion, this is the best work on Grundtvig in any language, not excepting Danish; and this is indeed high praise, in view of the jealous pride with which Grundtvig's fellow-country-men extol his memory. Many of Donald's other works were collections of talks and of occasional essays rather than systematic expositions of a single topic. But all of them abound in original ideas and illuminating insights. A recurrent theme in his writings is the sacred in nature, one of his works being entitled characteristically *God's Presence Makes the World*.[6]

No account of Donald's life would be complete that did not emphasize his love of poetry. When asked what a speaker should bring to an audience, his immediate and simple advice was: "Give them poetry, poetry, poetry!" This leads me to recall how, when I was at Westminster School, during my first year as a "Junior" in 1947–48, Donald was the Monitor in charge of the communal room to which I was assigned. It was the custom at the end of the school year for each Senior to give a book to one of us Juniors, as a reward for the "fagging" that we had done (not that Donald ever made heavy demands on us, nor did he exercise his right as a Monitor to impose corporal punishment). At that time, although only aged thirteen, I took a precocious interest in philosophy. We were allowed, during the periods of evening "prep," to read a book of our choice when we had completed our work, but we had to secure permission from the Monitor in charge. On one occasion, so Donald used to remind me—I myself had forgotten about this—I went up to Donald and asked him, "Allchin, may I read Kant's *Critique of Pure Reason*?" Donald, however, when he approached me about the book that he proposed to give me, said firmly and even severely, "I shall not give you a book of philosophy: I shall give you some poetry." What he gave me was in fact *The Oxford Book of English Verse*—not at all a bad choice, as it introduced me to a wide range of poetry with which I was unfamiliar. As I write, I have the very same copy before me now, in which he has put

5. Allchin, *Grundtvig*.

6. Allchin, *God's Presence Makes the World*.

a quotation from Chaucer as his inscription: "Know thy contree, look up, thank God of al!"

From the Welsh poets whom he loved Donald quoted in particular the opening words of a poem by Ann Griffiths, "Wonderful in the sight of angels . . . ." Truly, a sense of wonder was one of his most attractive characteristics. It was his openness to the dimension of wonder that led him to feel an especial affinity with the seventeenth-century mystical poet Thomas Traherne. He was a founder-member of the Traherne Association, established in Hereford some twenty years ago, and he was a faithful attender at its annual conferences.

The concentric eddies of Donald's many interests and enthusiasms were ever expanding. Donald liked to use the phrase of Ann Griffiths, "We are keeping house amidst a cloud of witnesses," and his own noetic domicile had no lack of denizens. He was at home in many worlds. In addition to his links with Eastern Orthodoxy and Danish Lutheranism, he had plenty of Roman Catholic friends. He was much influenced by André Louf, Abbot of Mont des Cats, and while at Canterbury—with the support of the Dean and Chapter—he arranged for regular visits by monks and nuns from Bec, as well as from Mont des Cats and Chevetogne, who stayed in the precincts and shared in the liturgical life of the cathedral. Another Roman Catholic friend was Thomas Merton, whom Donald met during visits to the Abbey of Gethsemani in 1963, 1967, and 1968. Their initial conversation moved slowly until they discovered a shared appreciation for the Shakers: "That got us going," Donald recalled, "and from that moment we never stopped . . . . There was a kind of quicksilver quality about the conversation." When the Thomas Merton Society of Great Britain and Ireland was founded in 1993, Donald became the first President, and continued as such until his death. His ecumenical outreach also embraced the Methodists, and the book on the hymns of the Wesleys that he edited with Professor H. A. Hodges appeared under the evocative title *A Rapture of Praise*.[7] In his book *We Belong to One Another* he explored links between Methodists, Anglicans, and Orthodox.[8] He also had a warm devotion to the Mother of God, and was a supporter of The Ecumenical Society of the Blessed Virgin Mary.

Donald's book on Mary was entitled *The Joy of All Creation*,[9] and this choice of title is significant for at least two reasons. First, it underlines

7. Allcinn and Hodges, *Rapture of Praise*.
8. Allchin, *We Belong to One Another*.
9. Allchin, *The Joy of All Creation*.

Mary's cosmic role, which is of great importance to Orthodoxy, and to which Donald was deeply sensitive. Secondly, it emphasizes the element of joyfulness that the presence of the Mother of God communicates to Christian liturgy and life. Joy was certainly a *leitmotif* throughout Donald's talks and writings. Some people felt that he spoke too often of joy, but for me his words rang true. He had, moreover, the precious gift of sharing this joy with others. I recall how, when at Oxford in 1960–61 as I was writing my book *The Orthodox Church*,[10] I frequently came to a halt, baffled and discouraged. I used to walk down from the House of St. Gregory and St. Macrina to Pusey House, where Donald was librarian. If I was lucky I found him at home, although that was by no means invariably the case; for throughout his life Donald was usually not in the place where he was expected to be. Half-an-hour's talk was enough to break my writer's block. He did not usually offer specific advice. But his personal warmth, his infectious enthusiasm, his vision, and his sense of wonder, were enough to overcome my hesitations and to give me a sense of direction. I returned home knowing exactly what I wanted to say and how I was going to say it. That was typical of Donald's influence upon those around him. In his own inner life he experienced times of discouragement, yet to others he was a life-enhancer who communicated light and encouragement.

One of the titles that Orthodox Christians ascribe to the Holy Virgin is "Mother of Unexpected Joy." That is exactly what Donald brought into my life and into that of many others: unexpected joy. It is my hope that readers of this book who did not know Donald personally will discover through the pages that follow something of the enthusiasm and visionary joy that marked his life. May the Kingdom of Heaven be his!

10 Ware, *The Orthodox Church.*

Give them some poetry
i.m. Donald Allchin

by David Scott[1]

1

When first we met I saw a lightness off the ground in him;
the air of outside, high up, the world all sides of us,
had space to breathe the meeting into life.
A meeting that would last both in and out of time,
and all this as I saw it. It may quite well
be fixed inaccurately, but the height and the space
at the first, is sure. He in a cassock. I not.
He just back from America; I coming to the end
of school. I liken it now to other meetings,
other heights, grander and more biblical,
keen not to miss the precedents, and the connections:
Mt. Alverna, say, or wherever light takes over from the dark.

---

1. This poem was first Published in *Beyond the Drift: New and Selected Poems,*
Bloodaxe Books, David Scott, 2014. Used with permission of the author.

2

Of the world he was not; born somehow
to have that extra inch or two which left him in the air.
So many ideas that others could organise,
which they did, and happily, on the whole.
He liked his spirituality corporate;
serving solitaries, he was not one himself.

3

Our common thread was Merton,
that English-American-Nowhereboy. Donald,
returning from Kentucky met the monk
the day that Martin Luther King died,
which left a generation seathing, grieving.
I with a volume of some early Merton poems
newly spread with gravy from reading them
at meals and a term away from A-Levels.
From America, Donald wrote about an emptiness
of saints, and of a space unfilled by holiness.

4

Through all the years he came by saints and scholars;
scholars and writers and poets; and religious and hermits,
and poets: and rarely by children, but once he came by Lucy
in her cot, whose heart was not yet strong, and he prayed
and I saw him unusually paternal, and now she bikes up
mountains, and down again, in Wales.

5

And then came Wales for him, and how fresh it looked
upon the page away from English tightness.
He was forever inviting us to "do Wales,"
and got the words from Merton: "Lets do Wales," said Merton,
Donald did Wales avidly: so many poets, so many saints,
so many friends. Bardsey, in its distance, in its beauty,
a metaphor for death, for passing from one realm
to another. The journey had begun.

6

The handwriting turned frail.
The phone call said he was enjoying Traherne.
I said,
I was about to conduct a retreat.
He said:
"Give them some poetry."

The Rev. Canon David Scott is a Church of England priest, poet, playwright, and spiritual writer.

PART ONE

Donald Allchin's Life

"I was born on Easter day. Then I realized, as a child, that Easter was not going to come on my birthday again until I was 75, which was a little bit of a damper. One of things that influenced me at that time, thinking of the fact of having been born on the day of the Resurrection, is that as soon as I came across Christianity where the Resurrection was emphasized, I felt immediately attracted. As a child I was fascinated by history and thought I wanted to be an historian."[1]

Almost sixty years later Donald proclaimed: "In Christ all creation is raised up into the possibility of new life. In the coming of the Holy Spirit, a communion, a sharing of life comes into being which crosses over the gulf of death and makes the world one with the world to come. Time and space are no longer barriers to communion, they become its channels. Death itself is no longer supreme in human affairs. When we pray through Christ and in the Spirit we are caught up into his victory over death and enter into a communion of love and knowledge which unites us with those who are farthest from us."[2]

1. Donald Allchin. An Interview with David Keller, July 11, 2007. See Transcript 1 in Appendix.

2. Allchin, *Praise Above All*, 59.

CHAPTER 1

Arthur Macdonald Allchin (1930–2010)

A Personal Tribute

Barry A. Orford

Priest Librarian 2001–14

Pusey House, Oxford

Notwithstanding his baptismal names, Father Allchin was always Donald to his friends and acquaintances. His career was a remarkable one, embracing among other things a Canonry of Canterbury Cathedral, the care of the St. Theosevia Center for Christian Spirituality in Oxford, and visiting lectureships abroad. From Pusey House's viewpoint he must be considered one of our most distinguished Priest Librarians.

One of four children, Donald Allchin was a Londoner. He was educated at Westminster School, where one of his teachers was Robert Llewelyn, the priest and writer on spirituality who later had a rich ministry at the Julian Shrine in Norwich. Another friendship which started at school was that with a younger boy, Timothy Ware, who joined the Orthodox Church, was ordained, and received the name Kallistos. Metropolitan Kallistos spoke movingly at Donald's funeral of their long and uninterrupted friendship.

It would seem that Donald's interest in the church and spirituality started young, because he recorded that at school he was encouraged by

Father Llewelyn to read the *Spiritual Letters* of the noted authority on mysticism, Evelyn Underhill.[1] He commented that the picture of her inside the book reminded him of one of his aunts. She was a writer to whom he returned frequently over the years, and on whom he wrote with discernment.

From Westminster School Donald came to Oxford, where he was a member of Christ Church. After graduation he proceeded to his BLitt, and with that good fortune which seemed to attend his life he was supervised by the Regius Professor of Ecclesiastical History, Claude Jenkins. While at Christ Church it must have pleased Donald to be in close proximity to the house where Dr. Pusey had lived, and he told me delightedly that on one occasion Professor Jenkins had referred to the familiar small doorway in Tom Quad as "Dr. Danby's house—Dr. Pusey's, as was," almost, said Donald, as if Dr. Pusey had left the house only a few weeks before.

More than once I tried to persuade Donald to write down his recollections of Claude Jenkins, one of Oxford's legendary eccentrics, who survives in several hilarious pages of Eric Mascall's autobiography,[2] but alas, he never did. A volume containing his memories of Jenkins and others of the important figures he had known would have been valuable indeed. Let me, then, record a story which Donald told me about his supervisor. Jenkins' learning was enormous but unsystematic, and he published little more than an occasional article. A book that did see the light of day was a small study of the Victorian theologian F. D. Maurice. All of the publisher's copies were destroyed during a World War II air raid, causing Jenkins to say Donald, with some satisfaction, "You see? I'm not *meant* to publish anything."

I have wondered whether a part of Claude Jenkins' legacy to his pupil was the gift of untidiness. The professorial abode in Christ Church was stuffed with books from ground floor to attic, stacked in tottering towers filling all available spaces including the bath. (It is still possible to buy a postcard showing the entrance hall with its mountains of volumes on the floor and rising up the staircase.) Those who knew Donald's houses in later years will have received an accurate impression of Jenkins' residence, and the similarity was not confined to his home.

1. Underhill, *Letters*, 1951.
2. Mascall, *Saraband*, 1992.

Donald's study in Bangor, North Wales. Photo courtesy of David Keller.

At some point Donald contrived, by means unclear to me, to pass his driving test. The inside of his car, at least when I knew it, was an extension of the clutter of his house.

To be a passenger in Donald's car was to have your faith in guardian angels (your own and his) increased tenfold. I remember an occasion in North Wales when he drove us from Bangor to find lunch near Beaumaris. All through the journey a large spider swung lazily from the driving mirror. At no point did we go above thirty miles per hour, and usually we were somewhat below it, which meant that we quickly acquired a lengthy tail of irate motorists who could not pass us on the winding road. Donald, holding forth on some aspect of Welsh folk singing, was unaware of any problem.

The subject of Donald's BLitt thesis was the revival of religious communities in the Church of England in the nineteenth century. The Regius Professor may have derived a certain wry humour from the topic—Donald remembered Jenkins saying to a departing visitor, "Here comes Allchin with his nuns" as his student came into view—but the result was published in 1958 as *The Silent Rebellion*.[3] It was a ground-breaking study, and half

3. Allchin, *The Silent Rebellion*, 1958.

a century later it remains an indispensable contribution to the history of Anglican religious communities.

Three years ago, when Archbishop Rowan Williams awarded Donald the long overdue honour of a Doctorate of Divinity, I was able to contribute to the citation another story involving Claude Jenkins, who once said to Donald, "The trouble with you, young man, is that you *enjoy* life too much." Certainly Donald enjoyed life greatly. He enjoyed meeting people and was endlessly interested in what they might be studying or doing. He enjoyed travelling and he enjoyed good food. (The latter, it must be said, contributed to a marked increase in his girth in mid-life.) He was, in the best sense of the word, an *enthusiast*, constantly finding new material in areas which interested him and showing unexpected connections between them. Awarding Donald his DD, Archbishop Rowan hit the mark when he said, "Jenkins probably did not know that Donald Allchin had been born on Easter Day. It may or may not be consequential that his theology is one of the resurrection rather than of the passion. He is one of life's natural encouragers who fosters, both in his writings or in personal encounter, the theological virtue of *hope*. This gift of compelling enthusiasm and imaginative sympathy has enabled Donald to perceive illuminating likenesses between such unlikely pairs as Maximus the Confessor and Richard Hooker, Ann Griffiths and Elizabeth of Dijon, Solzhenytsyn and Pantycelyn, Evelyn Underhill and the Italian Sorella Maria.[4] Here we see something, not only of the breadth of his interest and scholarship, but also of an essential—perhaps *the essential*-quality of his mind. In Donald we celebrate a bridge-builder; one who connects and sees connections."

My first sighting of Donald was when I was an ordinand at St. Stephen's House, Oxford, at that time still in Norham Gardens. He was one of the speakers in a course of lectures on spirituality, and he addressed us on Julian of Norwich. I regret that I cannot remember what he said, except that one of Julian's visions was rather frightening, but he appeared almost the archetypal Anglican cleric, smooth, pink, and neat in a Sarum cassock. We disrespectful students were more impressed by the redoubtable Mother Mary Clare from Fairacres, who came to speak on the Carmelites and put everyone, including our principal, in their place.

4. Ann Griffiths (1776–1805) and William Williams of Pantycelyn (1717–91) were notable Methodist hymn writers, the latter familiar from his hymn, "Guide me, O thou great Redeemer," translated from his Welsh original. Ann Griffiths was the subject of one of Donald's best contributions to Welsh studies, *Ann Griffiths, the Furnace and the Fountain*, originally published in 1976 and reprinted in a revised form in 1987.

Some years later, when I was a curate in the Monmouth diocese, our clergy conference was held in Oxford, and Donald lectured to us. By this time his interest in things Welsh was well known, and I remember his beginning with a few words in Welsh. Later still, when I was a member of the Community of the Resurrection in Mirfield, he was invited to lead our community retreat. There was a general feeling that what he gave us was excellent material, but not really food for a retreat. The reason for this became clear shortly afterward, when many of the words he had spoken appeared in his book, *Participation in God*,[5] a fascinating study of the doctrine of *theosis* (deification), and its place in the Anglican tradition, not least in the writings of Dr. Pusey.

I came to know Donald personally when he lived in North Wales, in Bangor, during the 1990s. An uphill walk from the railway station led to the rather down-at-heel house in Snowdon View Terrace where Donald lived amid the clutter previously described. In due course his brother Bill, a highly respected psychologist, came to live in the adjoining house. ("We'll have an Allchin enclave," said Donald cheerfully.) Donald acted as my supervisor for both my Master's degree and my Doctorate. By then the clean-cut, youthful looking clergyman had become a bulky, slightly dishevelled figure, whose long hair gave him a somewhat bardic appearance. He was an excellent supervisor, insisting on written material being submitted regularly and making insightful comments on what I wrote. He struggled hard to make me keep my eye on the wood rather than on particular trees, and drew my attention to sources I should otherwise have missed. However, a session with Donald could never be restricted simply to the matter in hand, and it was inspiring to listen as he talked about the people, the books and the experiences which stocked his mind.

His decision to move to Bangor must have surprised many, but it is not difficult to see why he did it. He found there not only the stimulation of a university setting, but one which had lively departments of Theology and Welsh Studies. It was exceptional for an English scholar to set to work studying Welsh, but Donald did it with vigour and must have relished the opportunity to soak himself in the living Welsh ethos. He claimed to me that he could not really speak Welsh, but certainly he could read it well and he entered into fruitful dialogue with scholars of Welsh language and literature, among them Professor Bedwyr Lewis Jones, whose relatively early death was a great loss to Welsh studies, and Professor Densil Morgan,

5. Allchin, *Participation in God*, 1988.

with whom he wrote a book on the poet Gwenallt. This volume was one of a series of books in which he tried to make his fellow Englishmen (and, it must be said, not a few natives of Wales) aware of the amazing riches and durability of Welsh culture, not least its spiritual heritage. He did not stop at theory, however. He was keen to revive the tradition of pilgrimage which had once flourished in these islands, and so he was influential in establishing Bardsey Island, off the Llyn Peninsula, as a place to be visited by those seeking quiet and solitude. No less important was his involvement with the restoration of the church and shrine at Pennant Melangell which in recent years has seen a remarkable growth in the ministry of healing. His guide books to Bardsey and Pennant Melangell are concise, informative and inspiring.

**Donald Allchin at the entrance to the church and shrine at Pennant Melangell.
Photo courtesy of David Keller.**

It was inevitable that Donald should be sought out by those interested in the study of "Celtic Spirituality." Here he was keen but cautious. The sentimental cult of nature has too often crept into this area, and Donald was anxious that what was said of the spirituality of the Celtic church should have a firm grounding in history. After I had joined the Chapter of Pusey House Donald twice came to stay in our guest room. On the second occasion he was recovering from a bout of illness. As a result he had lost a lot of weight, which suited him, and he seemed more tired, but the enthusiasm was still there and as always his conversation ranged widely over topics which interested both of us. He presented me with copies of pamphlets which he had published recently, and characteristically he gave a copy of one of them, which was on a Welsh subject, to our Welsh-speaking Sacristan. He had asked me a while before whether I thought he should gather together for publication some of the essays on Tractarian themes which he had written over the years. I wished very much that he should, but in the event he never did so. There must be a huge accumulation of material which Donald did not publish in book form, and I hope that a discerning literary executor will set to work to make some of it available to us.

Two or three years later it came as a surprise to me to discover that Donald had left Bangor and was living near Oxford, and I began to hear disquieting rumours suggesting that all was not well with him. When I learned that he had been taken to hospital in Oxford, I went to see him. He was clearly in some confusion about his surroundings, but he answered readily when I asked him about people he had known and books he had read. Subsequent visits revealed a rapid deterioration in his physical and mental condition, however, and his death just before Christmas was in every way a blessing.

This is not the place to attempt a critical estimate of Donald's writings. He said to me that he had come to the conclusion that the essay was his natural length, and I think this was true. Almost all his books have their origins in occasional papers and lectures, the notable exceptions being his first book on the Religious Life and his later studies of the Danish theologian Grundtvig (for which he had learned Danish) and the Welsh spiritual tradition which he examined in *Praise Above All*.[6] When the latter book appeared I was asked to be one of its reviewers, and I remember voicing a concern that because there was such an emphasis on praise and joy it seemed sometimes that the cross and human suffering were not

---

6. Allchin, *Praise Above All*, 1991.

allowed their due weight. I would revise that opinion now, but there is no question that Archbishop Rowan was right in describing Donald's theology as primarily one of the Resurrection. It was this outlook which made him particularly sympathetic to the spirituality of the Eastern church, and the distinguished Orthodox theologians Vladimir Lossky and Dumitru Staniloae were friends of his. During his last weeks in hospital a photograph of Fr. Staniloae with a young Donald Allchin had a place near his bed, and Donald spoke with some pride of his association with him.

Donald was someone who could be described as "Anglican to the core" but there was nothing insular about his Anglicanism. He was one of a number of theologians who have sensed similarities of approach between Catholic-minded Anglicanism and Orthodoxy. From an early age he was a member of the Society of St. Alban and St. Sergius, which works to foster Anglican-Orthodox relations. Although he had many Roman Catholic friends, notably the famous Cistercian monk, Thomas Merton, I felt that Rome did not speak to him in the way that Orthodoxy clearly did. On the other hand, he stood apart from both traditions when he came to support strongly the ordination of women to the priesthood.

The monastic life was a continuing concern of Donald's, and he worked closely with the Sisters of the Love of God at Fairacres in Oxford and with the sisters of the Society of the Sacred Cross at Tymawr, near Monmouth. I do not know whether he had ever considered the Religious Life as his vocation, but he never joined a community. Probably he was too free a spirit to be confined by monastic institutions, greatly though he valued them.

Of Donald's time as a Priest Librarian at Pusey House I cannot write. He never told me in detail of those years which stretched from 1960 to 1969. He served under Father Hugh Maycock, another builder of book piles and paper mounds which choked his rooms. Donald always spoke of Father Hugh with enormous affection. It is easy to see why they should have complemented each other, given their wide interests and the breadth of their reading. In 2002, when Father Davage and I were preparing a collection of essays on the Principals of Pusey House to honour Father Philip Ursell on his retirement, I asked Donald to write the chapter on Father Maycock. After some coaxing, the necessary pages appeared in manuscript. (Typing was not an Allchin skill.) A passage toward the end of the chapter says as much about Donald as it does about Father Hugh:

> The precariousness of existence, the mystery and absurdity of tragedy and waste and evil, these were things he would not and could

not ignore. They raised questions with which he never ceased to wrestle, but ultimately they could not quench his joy. For him there was endless wonder in the prodigality of the universe . . . .

His life, so apparently filled with human interests, his numerous friends of all ages, the volumes of biography and literature, history and astronomy, philosophy and theology which lined the walls of his room and overflowed onto the floor, all these ultimately had their deepest significance for him in God.[7]

In due course scholars will get to work on Donald's published legacy. But however great the value of his writings—and I believe Donald's work to be of vital importance to a Church of England desperately impoverished by a lack of knowledge of its own theological heritage—it is the man himself who will stay with those of us privileged to have known him. As Archbishop Rowan pointed out, Donald was almost a one-man ecumenical movement, and his ecumenism was based not on laborious meetings of eminent divines but on the call to share in the worship of God, who is the source of our ultimate unity. Alas, it is not easy to see how such a mission as Donald's could flourish in today's bureaucracy-stifled church, yet never was there a greater need for a Donald Allchin to call us to raise our eyes to the heavens while celebrating the things of earth. If *glory* was the word ever on the lips of Archbishop Michael Ramsey, then *praise* is the word always to be associated with Donald. The title of his book *Praise Above All* comes from a poem by the eighteenth-century poet Christopher Smart, and it captures the essence of Donald's spirit and his message:

> Praise above all—for praise prevails
> Heap up the measure, load the scales,
> And good to goodness add:
> The gen'rous soul her saviour aids
> But peevish obloquy degrades;
> The Lord is great and glad.[8]

---

7. Orford and Davage, *Piety and Learning*, 84.

8. Allchin, *Praise Above All*, quoted in Acknowledgements, xiii.

CHAPTER 2

In His Face Was Prayer
Reflections on a Friendship with Donald Allchin

The Reverend Canon James Coutts
Canon of St. Woolos Cathedral and Rural Dean of Monmouth, Retired.

Part of what everyone owes to Donald is his gift of creating and main-taining friendship. We first met in the early seventies when I was on retreat at The Convent of the Incarnation at Fairacres in Oxford. He invited himself to stay at our Vicarage in rural mid-Wales and when I prevaricated, explaining that we were expecting the birth of our third child at around the time he proposed, he cheerfully replied, "But I shall come to help." As we got to know him we discovered that any kind of domestic skill was beyond him.

In that parish was a very old church, founded according to legend by St. David and later served as curate by the Rev. William Williams, "Pantyce-lyn," the great hymn writer and evangelist. This building was quite unlike the churches of Ealing, Oxford, or Kensington with which Donald was familiar. Like so many Welsh country churches celebrated by R.S. Thomas, it had survived long centuries of rough weather and poverty, tucked away and clinging against the hillside. Although it was outside the modern vil-lage that had grown up around the railway station, it was here that everyone was buried and it was the spiritual reservoir for all the villagers—Church, Chapel, even the three local Roman Catholics. It was empty of prestigious family monuments and tombs, empty of impressive furniture, empty to give space for the local community to approach the numinous, the "beyond words," the presence of the saints, the presence of God. In words Donald used to recite:

> Christ's sacrifice is a marriage
> and here in the marriage of the Eucharist
> the family of faith is brought together.
> (Priodas yw aberth Crist
> Ac yma, ym mhriodas yr aberth
> Y mae undod teulu'r ffydd).

Donald truly lived a eucharistically orientated life. I used to wonder whether he ever had doubts? Apart from his referring to Father Zossima, I never picked up references to Dostoevski. Certainly he could not cope with situations of conflict.

From then on, Donald always came to stay with us three or four times each year, sometimes bringing with him distinguished academic theologians. On one occasion I took him, as on separate occasions I took Mother Mary Clare S.L.G. and Father Roland Walls, on his first visit to St. David's Cathedral. From those visits came the conference in 1975 on the Solitary Life: participants stayed with the Sisters of the Community of St. John the Evangelist (founded in Dublin) and included Dom André Louf, abbot of Mont-des-Cats: we sang the "Salve Regina" in the Trinity Chapel, probably for the first time since the Reformation.

When Donald holidayed with us we would explore these hidden, spiritual resources for the local communities' prayer and encounters with holiness—Patrishow, Llanthony, Capel-y-Ffin, Llanelieu, Llanvillo, Craswall Priory, Rhulen, Maes-yr-onen, Nevern, Mwnt—all "rooms with a view," where the visitors' books are filled with appreciation for the non-threatening, aesthetic, peace-restoring gifts shared both with those who only pass by as well as with their faithful local congregations. We also visited Vaughan's grave (where Donald subsequently preached at a Commemorative Service) and Traherne's Credenhill. Like Traherne, Donald was a "rapturous" person and he became ever more devoted to him. Forays across the border also took us to Abbey Dore, St. Margaret's, and Kilpeck.

The old church of St. David, Llanwrtyd stands in a hidden but friend-filled valley (which one of those born there described as "being like heaven"—fel y nefoedd). Here Donald discovered a profound and long admiration for the local poet and historian Ruth Bidgood. In the church there were copies and translations of poems about St. David and Pantycelyn by David Gwenallt Jones. Together we explored his poetry, also that of Waldo Williams, Euros Bowen, Saunders Lewis, James Nicholas, and of course the hymns of Pantycelyn that "brought the cradle, the cross and the empty tomb" to the mining valleys and small-holdings of Wales. Donald had a particular respect for those who "sang theology," having previously written about the Danish evangelist Grundtvig and going on to promote enthusiastically the writings of Ann Griffiths.

Donald always gave us an inscribed copy of his latest work. In one of these he had written a quotation from James Nicholas:

> Yn ei gwedd y mae gweddi
> Disgwyl hwyr yn disgleiro drwdi.
> Y dwyn y Tad ynot ti.

> In his face there was prayer.
> There glow'd through him a waiting for what is coming.
> In you is the Father's gift.

CHAPTER 3

Homage & Gift

Intercession with Donald in the Communion of Saints

The Rev. Canon James Coutts and Dr. Esther de Waal

Nid oes ffin rhwng deufydd yn yr eglwys; yr un ydyw'r eglwys fil-wriaethus ar y llawr, a'r eglwys fuddugoliaethus yn y Nef, a bydd y saint yn y ddwy-un eglwys.[1]

(There is no division between the church struggling on earth and the church gathered by the Shepherd into heaven; and the saints live together in this undivided church.)

S urrounded by the prayers of Mary, the praise of all creation and of the saints, let us pray with them to the Father of Christ our Lord:

1.

Born on Easter Day 1930, Donald continued as a child of the resurrection. These intercessions today, while they center on our friend and brother

---

1. Waldo Williams, "Pa beth yw dyn?" in *Dail Pren*, 67.

in Christ, look beyond his earthly life to the sure and certain hope of the resurrection.

But now, as we reflect on the fullness of that earthly life, giving thanks for what he meant to so many and for what he achieved in so many spheres, our prayers are not only gratitude for what Donald has shown us, but for the grace that we may continue faithful to the legacy that he has left us.

2.

We thank God for the giftedness of Donald's family, in which we can see something of the universal character of his own life. For Raymond, in his dedication to the search for truth, who used his skills to enlarge and deepen the horizons of knowledge. For Betty, dedicated to working in the wounded society of South Africa. For Bill, who overcame his war experiences in Japan to exercise his healing powers, not least his understanding of the power of forgiveness. Donald showed his very immediate concern with those who need our help and understanding in his long connection with L'Arche, where he was the Anglican Theological Advisor to its international community.

> *God suffers in those who suffer, taking their pain into Himself. But God heals in those who heal, in those who show by their actions that they share God's own perception and understanding of things.*[2]

3.

We thank God for the world of academic scholarship which shaped Donald: at Westminster, Christchurch, and Cuddesdon, seen in his research into the history of Anglican Religious Communities. Here we saw what was to become one of his lifelong passions: their vital role in the life of the church

> *The object of all Religious Societies is to gather up and, as it were, focus the love which ought to animate the whole body of the Church Catholic.*[3]

---

2. Allchin, *Participation in God*, 71.

3. R. M. Benson, quoted in Allchin, *The Silent Rebellion*.

4.

We thank God for Donald's continual sense of *"an underlying unity which has not yet been appreciated"*[4] and for the friendships he cultivated with Religious Communities. He knew and loved Fairacres and Tymawr, but also Bec, Bose, Mont des Cats, Chevetogne and several more. The circle was continually widening, and recently he had come to know Sr. Sorella Maria of Campello. These monastic friendships crossed space and time as he explored the common ground which they shared through creative conversation and correspondence.

Amongst these friends was Thomas Merton, whom he was instrumental in making more widely known in this country and whose words, which conclude our prayer and our thanksgiving are also a summation of Donald's reconciling life:

> *If I can unite in myself the thought of Eastern and Western Christendom, I can prepare in myself the reunion of divided Christendom. From that secret and unspoken unity in myself, can eventually come a visible and manifest unity of all Christians.*[5]

5.

We thank God for Donald's knowledge of the Orthodox Church and world; his commitment to opening our eyes to their riches. He loved his Orthodox encounters in Paris, on Mount Athos and in Romania alongside other places, making available what he had discovered and experienced there through the spoken word, in conferences and lectures, and in the written word in an outpouring of articles and pamphlets:

> *What is a compassionate heart? It is a heart on fire for the whole creation, for humanity, for the birds, for the animals, for demons and for all that exists. Such a person offers up prayer full of tears.*[6]

---

4. Allchin, *The Spirit and the Word.*

5. Merton, *Conjectures of a Guilty Bystander,* 21.

6. Allchin. *Heart of Compassion,* 9.

6.

We thank God for the way Donald used his linguistic skills to write about the Danish theologian Grundtvig. In particular, with Charles and John Wesley, he delighted in the hymns:

> *God grant his holy angels bright,*
> *His heavenly armies to watch around and protect us.*
> *May they go with us on the way*
> *And bring us home along the right path,*
> *And bring us from the vale of tears,*
> *Into the glad house of heaven.*[7]

7.

We thank God for Donald's undying love for the Anglican tradition, shown in his devotion to the Anglican Divines. He always wanted to share his current discoveries and enthusiasms with us, so that as his interests never stood still, we watched in recent years his deepening affection for Thomas Traherne:

> *Your enjoyment of the world is never right, till every morning you awake in heaven; see yourself in the father's palace; and look upon the skies, the earth and air as celestial joys: having such a reverend esteem of all, as if you were among the angels.*[8]

8.

We thank God for the many places which nurtured Donald's life, giving him the opportunity to express and to enjoy the gift of friendship. Pusey House and the St. Theosavia Centre in Oxford; Canterbury; Bangor and not least, the great number of Conferences and Retreat Houses, amongst which in particular, St. Deiniol's (now called Gladstone's Library) which houses his archive and library. In America: the Cowley Fathers, General Theological Seminary New York, and Nashotah House; not forgetting our own homes.

---

7. Quoted in Allchin, *N.F.S. Grundtvig*, 302.

8. Allchin, *Landscapes of Glory*, 4.

"The interpenetration of people and place takes a very special form in the case of those whose lives are shaped by the practise of prayer and praise."[9]

9.

We thank God for Donald's love of Wales: its landscape and language and for his rejoicing in the Celtic Saints especially on Bardsey and in Pennant Melangell. But he also told us about its poets: Ann Griffiths, Gwenallt, R. S. Thomas, Ruth Bidgood and many more. *"He was aware that we were 'keeping house amidst a cloud of witnesses.'" Beth yw gwladgarwch? Cadw ty mewn cwmwl tystion"*

We picture the merriment in heaven as he goes to join the angels and saints: his laughter and his infectious enthusiasm ringing out, as we recall the ending of one of Ann Griffiths' hymns: *"O am aros yn Ei gariad dyddiau foes: what happiness to remain forever in His love."*[10]

10.

Let us now keep silence to thank God for the love that God has given and shared with us in and through Donald's life-enhancing role in so many lives and especially, for the love and care that he himself received.

---

9. Allchin, *Praise Above All.*
10. Allchin, *Ann Griffiths,* 26–27.

PART TWO

Donald Allchin and the Orthodox Church

"I got into this thing called The Fellowship of St. Alban and St. Sergius in my late teens. There I met Antony Bloom, who afterwards became famous. He was a very powerful person who impressed you with his absolute authenticity—given this Orthodox Christianity. There I met a man called Vladimir Lossky who was undoubtedly the best theologian I had ever heard. I was in my 20s and 30s. I became great friends with his sons and his two daughters. I was the eldest in that Lossky family, and I was very much the youngest in my own, so it became a kind of second family for me."[11]

Later, when Donald was forty-eight he wrote: "And surely the Orthodox Church is right when it sees the incarnation of the Word, not as an isolated, single event, but as a revelation of God's love which wills to redeem and transfigure the whole created universe. The person of Jesus of Nazareth in whom all the fullness the godhead dwells is to be the focal point from which the divine presence is to radiate out into the world, and bring the Church into being. The presence of God is to be found throughout the life of the Church."[12]

11. Donald Allchin. An Interview with David Keller, July 11, 2007. See Transcript 1 in Appendix.

12. Allchin. *The World Is A Wedding*, 134.

CHAPTER 4

Father Donald and the Orthodox Church

Kallistos Ware, Metropolitan of Diokleia

The late Cardinal Suenens summed up the aim of the ecumenical movement in words that are both simple and profound: "In order to unite, we must first love one another; in order to love one another, we must first get to know one another." This process of getting to know one another—slow and often disappointing—needs to be carried out at many levels: through official dialogues and international conferences, through contacts between local parishes, through the exchange of theological students, and through the publication of books, whether learned or popular. Yet perhaps more important than any of these is the cultivation of what may be called "ecumenical friendships"—direct contacts face to face, person to person, across church boundaries. Without a firm foundation in such friendships all our other endeavours towards Christian reconciliation are in danger of proving rootless, abstract and theoretical. They will lack the dimension of Martin Buber's "I-and-Thou."

Among the various "ecumenical friendships" in my own life, much the most important, as well as the longest-lasting, has been my friendship with Donald Allchin. He was one of my earliest friends. I first came to know him in the autumn of 1947, when I arrived at the age of thirteen as a King's Scholar at Westminster School, London, and was assigned to the communal "Election Room" of which Donald, four years older than me, was in charge as Monitor. Our friendship extended from then until his death in 2010.

Four years make a vast difference in the hierarchy of an English boarding school. Yet, although I was in awe of Donald, I never found him a daunting and authoritarian figure. On the contrary, he was kindly and approachable, a luminous presence in my first year at public school, and such he remained throughout the sixty-three years of our spiritual companionship. I was an Anglican when we first met, but my reception into the Orthodox Church in 1958 did not involve any interruption in our friendship.

It was through Donald that I gained my first personal encounter with the Orthodox Church. As secretary of the leading society in the school, the Political and Literary Society—"Pol. and Lit. Soc.," as it was known—he had invited the Russian theologian from Oxford, Dr. Nicolas Zernov, as one of the speakers. This must have been in the early part of 1948. For some reason that I do not now recall, I asked Donald to be allowed to attend the meeting. In a slightly stern tone he answered that "Juniors" such as myself were not usually admitted to meetings of the Society, and that he needed to consult the members of the committee. Next day, with a gentle smile, he told me that it had been agreed to allow an exception in my case on this occasion. Alas! I cannot now remember even a single word that Nicolas said.

I am not sure when and how Donald first became interested in Orthodoxy. Certainly, as we have just seen, this interest extended back to his schooldays, and it was always one of the most important elements in his life and work as an Anglican Christian. In May 1948 he joined the Fellowship of St. Alban and St. Sergius, which is specially dedicated to Anglican-Orthodox *rapprochement*, and he remained a life-long and highly active member, serving as editor of the Fellowship journal *Sobornost* from 1960 to 1977.

In a notebook kept by Donald at a retreat that he attended in September 1948, just before going up to Oxford, he gave a revealing summary of his viewpoint. "At any rate as far as ritual is concerned," he wrote, "I am *not* an Anglo-Catholic, but a sort of Protestant-Orthodox combination. The awful uncertainty in an Anglo-Catholic Mass of what is going to come next is extraordinarily distracting. Furthermore, the insistence on the adoration of the Consecrated Elements, the concentration of the whole of the Eucharist into the moment of consecration, is not to my mind right." At once he went on to apologize for being judgmental: "I started off determined not to criticize, and there we are."

Donald belonged throughout his life to the High Church Anglican tradition, but—as is clear from the passage just quoted—he was not an

Anglo-Catholic in any narrow or partisan sense. Indeed, ecclesiastically he was never a "party" man; his sympathies were too wide-ranging for that. The slightly odd phrase "a sort of Protestant-Orthodox combination" is surely significant. Already at the age of eighteen he felt a strong affinity with Orthodoxy, but he did not allow this—together with his High Church background—to make him reject the distinctive values of Protestantism. It might even be claimed that it was precisely his closeness to Orthodoxy that helped him to appraise in positive terms the Protestant strand within the Anglican heritage. What Donald said in his retreat notebook in 1948 remained true of his standpoint throughout his later life.

I began this chapter by speaking about the influence of ecumenical friendships, and about the part that my friendship with Donald has played in my own life. Personal friendships with Orthodox were certainly of decisive importance in Donald's discovery of the Christian East. First, however, it is right to mention in this connection a friendship that Donald had, not across church boundaries, but with a fellow Anglican, the Revd Peter Hammond (1921–99), author of what remains one of the most perceptive books on Greek Orthodoxy, *The Waters of Marah*.[1] Donald came to know Peter in the early fifties at Oxford. "What drew us together was our common enthusiasm for Eastern Orthodoxy," said Donald in the obituary that he wrote for Peter,[2] "and here . . . felt that I had everything to learn." Peter had spent 1948 to 1950 in Greece, and no doubt what he told Donald about his experiences there prepared the latter for his own visit to Greece in 1955–56. One of the things which Peter stressed in his writings, and which Donald also regarded as profoundly significant, was the way in which within Orthodoxy dogma and liturgy, theology, and personal piety are indissolubly linked. Donald believed that the disjunction between these things, which occurred in the later Middle Ages in the West, was one of the underlying causes of the Reformation. If Protestants, Anglicans, and Roman Catholics were to overcome the sixteenth century schism, then in Donald's opinion they needed the help of Orthodoxy in transcending this disjunction. What Orthodoxy at its best could convey to the West, so both Peter and Donald were convinced, was a sense of *wholeness*.

To turn now to Donald's friendships with Orthodox, the most important of these, particularly in his earlier years, was with the Lossky family, who introduced him to the world of the Russian emigration in Paris. He

1. Hammond, *Waters of Marah*.
2. Allchin, "Peter Hammond," 51.

first came to meet the Losskys at the conference of the Fellowship of St. Alban and St. Sergius that met from July 27 to August 17, 1949. (In those more spacious times the summer conference of the Fellowship lasted for a full three weeks; today it has shrunk to a meagre five days.) This was the first Fellowship conference that Donald attended, and he wrote an account of it in the Fellowship journal *Sobornost*.[3] Was this perhaps his first published work? Donald was immensely struck by the lecture delivered at the conference by the distinguished Russian theologian Vladimir Lossky (1903–58). As Donald wrote later, "It is difficult to convey the overwhelming impression made by the theology of Vladimir Lossky as we began to know it at first hand, above all through his regular presence at the Fellowship's annual conference . . . of course Lossky was not the only eminent Orthodox voice which we heard in those conferences. But for some of us at any rate it was the voice which most imperiously demanded our attention."[4]

In due course Donald, in collaboration with others—Peter Hammond was also a member of the group—worked on the translation of Lossky's master-work *La théologie mystique de l'Eglise d'orient* (1944), which appeared in English as *The Mystical Theology of the Eastern Church*.[5] To quote Donald once more, "It is difficult to convey the sense of revelation that this book gave to English readers at the time."[6] Significantly, the translators had great difficulty in finding a publisher; because at that time Orthodoxy was not widely known to the English public and was seen as marginal and eccentric. Yet in fact, during the fifty-seven years since it first appeared in English, the book has never gone out of print, and has been regularly republished on both sides of the Atlantic. Vladimir's wife Madeleine commented to me that the French style of the original was somewhat heavy, and she thought the work read much better in the English version.

Donald was a regular visitor at the Lossky family home on the Ile Saint-Louis in the centre of Paris. He was the friend in particular of the younger son of Vladimir and Madeleine, Nicholas, who studied for the BLitt. in Oxford during the mid-1950s. Donald acted as a crown-bearer or best man at Nicholas's wedding in Paris on July 14, 1962, and later, in 1984, he was one of the examiners at the Sorbonne of Nicholas's doctoral dissertation on the seventeenth century Anglican divine Lancelot Andrewes.

3. Allchin, "Abingdon Conference," 258–60.

4. Allchin, *Sobornost* 22/1 (2000), 51.

5. Lossky, *Mystical Theology*.

6. Allchin, *Sobornost* 22/1 (2000), 51.

Anglicans have often written about Orthodox thinkers, but it is not so usual for an Orthodox writer to return the compliment!

Among Donald's Greek friends, two call for particular mention: Demetrios Koutroubis (1921–83) and Christos Yannaras (born 1935).[7] In the tribute that Donald wrote in memory of the first of these, he concluded with words that recall the statement of Thomas Merton which I have quoted in my introduction to this present volume: "The life and prayer of such a man, who united in his own heart and mind England and Greece, Anglicanism, Orthodoxy and Catholicism, has much to say to us about the possibilities of reconciliation. It warns us against setting one thing against another too easily. It heartens us to think that the pattern of unity in diversity which is God's will for his people is richer and more unexpected than we have thought."[8] Just as Merton's words can be applied to Donald himself, so also what Donald says here about Koutroubis sums up his own ecumenical vocation. The phrase "unity in diversity" exactly describes the ideal by which he was consistently inspired.

In Donald's later years the most important of his Orthodox contacts was undoubtedly his warm friendship with the great Romanian theologian Dumitru Staniloae (1903–99). The role played in Donald's earlier life by his encounter with the Lossky family was fulfilled in the second part of his life by his many meetings with Staniloae.[9] They corresponded frequently with each other, and it is greatly to be hoped that these very interesting letters—along with those that Donald exchanged with other Orthodox such as Koutroubis—may eventually be published.[10]

In the obituary that Donald wrote on Staniloae, he said that he first came across his name at the end of 1958, when he read two long articles in the French journal *Istina*, published under the name "A Monk of the Orthodox Church of Romania" (the author was in fact Fr. André Scrima): "The articles which greatly impressed and intrigued me discussed at length the tradition of hesychastic spirituality in Romania from the fourteenth

7. Among the many writings of Yannaras that have appeared in English, perhaps the most significant is his programmatic work *The Freedom of Morality*.

8. Allchin, "A Vision of Unity in Diversity." *Sobornost* 6/1 (1984), 76–77.

9. Staniloae's greatest work, his *Dogmatic Theology*, has been published in English in six volumes under the title *The Experience of God*. Brookline, MA: Holy Cross Orthodox Press, 1994 to 2013.

10. The letters from Staniloae to Allchin are included in the Allchin Archive at Gladstone's Library, Hawarden, North Wales. The friendship and correspondence of Staniloae and Allchin are the subject of the next chapter in this book.

century to the present day. They spoke in some detail of the work of Fr. Dumitru Staniloae in creating a renewed Romanian version of the *Philokalia*." Donald noted the way in which Staniloae's Romanian *Philokalia* took account of Western critical scholarship and was related to the spiritual and psychological problems of the twentieth-century. "It was evident," wrote Donald, "that the editor of this work was a man in whose hands the tradition came to life."[11]

It was not until ten years later that Donald had the possibility of meeting Staniloae face to face. This was in January 1969 when on Donald's initiative, in company with another Romanian scholar, Fr. Ene Braniste, Professor of Liturgics at Bucharest, Staniloae was invited to give some lectures and seminars in the University of Oxford. The main substance of these was subsequently published in *Sobornost*.[12] Staniloae had spent the years 1958–64 in prison in Romania, and it is remarkable that the Communist authorities allowed him to travel to the West so soon after his internment. This was the first of several foreign visits that Staniloae made in the 1970s and 1980s. Much earlier he had studied in Paris in the 1930s, but with the establishment of the Communist regime in Romania the door to the west had for many years been closed to him. Donald deserves full credit for enabling Staniloae to become, in this way, widely known and respected in the West.

Writing of the impact that Staniloae had upon him, Donald remarked: "He was a strongly built figure with an impressive head. But one was immediately conscious that, full of joy and interest in life though he was, he carried a heavy weight of experience inside him. I always associated that weight with the five years he spent in prison." "In general he spoke very little about the prison years," Donald continued. "On one occasion in Oxford when someone introduced him rather grandiloquently, 'This is Fr. Staniloae, he is a confessor of the faith, he has been in prison,' he protested mildly, 'Don't mention it. All experiences in life are good.' And, turning to me, he said quietly, 'It was very difficult for my wife and daughter.'"[13] Just how difficult it was is evident from the fact that his daughter Lidia had been divorced by her husband since he was unwilling to be connected with the family of a prominent political prisoner.

---

11. Allchin, *Sobornost* 16/1 (1994), 39.

12. Staniloae, *Sobornost*, series 5, no. 9 (1969), 627–29, 652–73.

13. Allchin, *Sobornost*, 16/1 (1994), 39–40.

When asked what the prison years had taught him, Staniloae replied (so Donald recounted), "I realized that our theology had been too abstract and theoretical. We needed to be closer to people in our teaching, nearer to where they really are."[14] Commenting to Donald on what he saw as the worst effects of the Communist system, Staniloae said firmly, "There are two things. The first is the fear, the second is the lie."[15] Yet, despite the fear and the lie, Staniloae did not lose his gentle sense of humor, his feeling of hope and wonder. As he wrote to Donald in his hesitant English (usually the two communicated in French), "The reality seen in God is so deep and rich that we arrive never at end."[16] Donald saw this as "a summary of all his thought and life." To convey the impression that Staniloae made on him, Donald used in particular the word "luminous." I myself recall Staniloae in exactly the same way. Yet for him Christian joy did not in any way signify a facile optimism, for it went hand in hand with suffering and sorrow. He saw the cross and the resurrection as constituting a single mystery.

Staniloae had a deep reverence for human freedom and diversity. On one occasion he said to Donald, "There are as many kinds of love as there are human persons."[17] As a dominant element in Staniloae's theology, Donald noted in particular his insistence upon the nearness of God as well as divine transcendence. "He saw the glory of God shining out in all kinds of unexpected places," stated Donald. Staniloae believed that there was "a constant overlap" between heaven and earth, between eternity and time. His sense of God's presence in creation, of the created order as "God's word" to us, was well expressed in the title that he gave to one of his Oxford lectures, "The World as Gift and Sacrament of God's Love." This encapsulates admirably what Donald found most inspiring in Staniloae's theology, and indeed in Orthodox theology in general. As Donald put it in the title of one of his books, "*God's Presence Makes the World.*"

Before we leave the subject of the friendship between Donald and Fr. Dumitru, there is one further point that should be mentioned: Donald introduced Fr. Dumitru to the sisters of the Convent of the Incarnation at Fairacres in Oxford, of which he was Warden. This contact was greatly valued by Staniloae. "There is such a depth of perception, such a delicacy of understanding here," he said of a text written by one of the sisters, and it

14. Ibid., 40.

15. Ibid., 41.

16. Ibid., 44.

17. Ibid., 42.

applies more widely to what he found in Fairacres as a whole. "It is something the Church needs."[18] He approved of the way in which the nuns at Fairacres enjoyed the opportunity to study and to engage in intellectual work; and he regretted that such an opportunity did not exist for nuns in Romania. "He himself believed," said Donald, "that women had a distinct approach to theological and spiritual questions which was different from that of men."[19] Staniloae's approach, with which Donald was in full sympathy, resembles that of the Russian thinker Paul Evdokimov.[20]

Donald's links with Fr. Dumitru Staniloae, and more broadly with Romanian Orthodoxy, were reinforced when in 1977 he was awarded an honorary Doctorate of Divinity by the University of Bucharest. This was something that gave him particular pleasure. He also held a Lambeth DD.

Donald's deep love of Eastern Christendom raises the question: Did he ever think of becoming Orthodox? Once, when I asked him about this, he said in reply: "I will join the Orthodox Church when the Anglican Communion as a whole does so." I took him to mean that he did indeed see it as his calling to bring Anglicanism closer to Orthodoxy; but he was convinced that, so far from making an act of individual conversion, he ought to bear witness *within* Anglicanism to the truths revealed to him by the Orthodox tradition. I have a sincere respect for this "Anglo-Orthodox" vocation, even though I have personally followed a different course. Donald agreed here with other "Anglo-Orthodox" members of the Fellowship, such as Fr. Derwas Chitty, Professor H. A. Hodges, and Archbishop Michael Ramsey. Before becoming Orthodox, I discussed my prospective decision at some length with Donald. Always attentive to the variety of paths along which different Christians are guided by the Spirit, he did little to dissuade me. But he was greatly concerned *what kind* of Orthodox I would become, and strenuously warned me against the dangers of rigorism. The Orthodoxy that he admired was generous and affirmative. I remain grateful for his counsel.

It is difficult to find a single passage in Donald's writings that sums up in synoptic terms his appreciation of Orthodoxy. This was something that permeated all his theological explorations, even when he was dealing with an entirely different topic such as modern Welsh spirituality. In

18. Ibid., 43.

19. Ibid.

20. Evdokimov, *Woman and the Salvation of the World.*

the following text, "Michael Ramsey and the Orthodox Church,"[21] Donald is describing not his own convictions but those of Archbishop Michael Ramsey (1904–88), long-time president of the Fellowship of St. Alban and St. Sergius, with which Donald was also so closely associated. Yet the standpoint here expressed with such eloquence by the Archbishop was likewise that of Donald himself, and so this piece about Ramsey can also be taken as Donald's own *apologia fidei*. Here he indicates how Ramsey valued above all the manner in which Orthodoxy has held together in a single whole the three elements of doctrine, worship, and life. He speaks also of the way in which Ramsey appreciated the centrality of the resurrection in Orthodoxy, along with the "ascendant quality" of Orthodox eucharistic worship and the Eastern sense of the communion of saints. These were likewise primary themes in Donald's own spiritual vision.

Donald's friend and mentor Fr. Derwas Chitty (1901–71) used to insist that Orthodoxy is not something outlandish and exotic but "simple Christianity." That was exactly what Donald also believed.

> Just fifty years ago Michael Ramsey spoke to the Fellowship Conference at High Leigh on the subject of Anglican-Orthodox relations.
>
> "We think a lot about the tragedy of the Christian division, and it is only right that we should do so: the divisions between Canterbury, Constantinople, and Rome. But behind the outward divisions there is an inner schism between doctrine, worship and life."
>
> And that, he said, is as tragic, or more tragic, compared to the outward divisions themselves. The way in which we can bring together three elements in the division—doctrine, worship and life—is through Orthodoxy.
>
> "Orthodoxy . . . means not only the holding of right opinions, but also the expression of right worship and the living of right life. The three are bound so closely since it is the Lord's opinion, the Lord's worship, and the Lord's life that dwell in his people. And today, beneath our divisions and our sins, this Orthodoxy lies deep within us all."
>
> That, of course, is a very Anglican way of seeing it. It is a very Anglican conviction that this Orthodoxy is there. I think that

---

21. Allchin, "Michael Ramsey and the Orthodox World." *Sobornost* 10/2 (1988), 49–52. This article is part of an address to a conference of the Fellowship of St. Alban and St. Sergius in 1988. The segment begins with reference to an address given to the Fellowship by Michael Ramsey in 1938.

for both Roman Catholics and Orthodox that is more difficult to say, if possible at all. As for us Anglicans, perhaps we say it too quickly. But we are conscious of not being the *whole* Church. It is therefore easier for us to recognize that there is orthodoxy in others. Ramsey himself asks what Anglicans should gain from Orthodoxy. Somewhat more modestly, he asks if Orthodox can gain from Anglicans.

What of the future? is the question with which our president-to-be concluded his address. It was 1938. It was clear that a new war might soon break out. Hence ecumenism could no longer be the hobby of a few church scholars. It was becoming a matter of life and death; we lived in an age of martyrs. Ramsey spoke of the martyrdom of the Orthodox Church in Russia, which was reaching its climax in those years. He spoke also of the witness and martyrdom of Protestants in Germany. In the battle between the Church and Satan, he concluded, theology, worship and life are drawn together in a way that is not possible by other means. It is because of his theology that Niemöller is in a concentration camp. His presence there is an act of worship. And this is a life which few of us desire: nevertheless it is one which Christ and his disciples knew. In this conflict the Church is not only feeling the need of its outward unity: it is discovering its inner unity as well. When this happens, noted Ramsey, we know that Satan trembles.

Immediately after the war, SPCK published a pamphlet for the Fellowship, *The Church of England and the Eastern Orthodox Churches: Why their Unity is important*. Its author was Professor Michael Ramsey of Durham. Here he begins with the question of external schism. He is particularly concerned with seeing the divisions in historical perspective.

"I shall not shrink from making some very big claims, that our familiar divisions between Catholics and Protestants have their root in the original schism between East and West. In unity with the East there lies a remedy for many of the problems and perplexities of the whole Church. The Church of England has a special debt and obligation in the matter; the present crisis of Church and world summons our thoughts Eastwards."

Eastwards, also backwards in time:

"The lop-sidedness of Rome in the later Middle Ages led to the lop-sidedness of Luther and Calvin. The lop-sidedness of the Church of England in the eighteenth century encouraged the separation of the Methodists. But before and behind all the familiar tragedies of division there was the internal tragedy of the schism between East and West, a tragedy that meant that henceforth all

Christendom was maimed. The East and West sorely needed one another; ever since they went their separate ways neither has been able to present the wholeness of church life."

The schism between East and West is seen by him as the supreme tragedy, the parent tragedy of many later divisions in the Christian world.

It was a powerful statement. Michael Ramsey's is a position which is familiar to us: it is the position to which Pope John-Paul II constantly returns with his image of the body which has two lungs and needs both if it to be whole and healthy. But it remains a vision which is not accepted all that widely in the West.

One problem in particular worried Michael Ramsey. He spoke of his fear that we might try to create a merely English unity. "Here in England the thoughts of many are turning towards unity of Christians in our own land," he explained. "This is as inevitable as it is right. It would be disastrous if it were in terms of a sort of national Christianity, based on the lowest common measure of English religious sentiment, bearing no true relationship to the wider idea of one, holy catholic and apostolic Church."

In 1962 Archbishop Michael Ramsey addressed the University of Athens. Here he spelled out some of the things which in his mind the Churches of the West in general, and the Church of England in particular, have to learn from the Orthodox world.

First a vivid realizsation of the centrality of the Resurrection.

"How we meet it is that the heavens should rejoice, that the earth should be glad and that the whole world both visible and invisible should keep the feast when Christ is risen, the everlasting joy. All things are filled with light, both heaven and earth and earth and the places under the earth; all creation doeth celebrate the Resurrection of Christ. Easter brings the dawning of a new world. Nature shares in it together with mankind. These are the convictions with which the heart of Eastern Christianity throbs."

In a characteristic way, Michael Ramsey noted a difference of emphasis in the East and in the West. If in our Western sacramentalism we have thought of Christ coming to us by his presence in the Eucharist, the East swells far more on the lifting up of the bread, the wine and the worshippers into the heavenly places with Christ. This aspect of primitive Christianity comes into its own in the Liturgy of St. John Chrysostom: the ascendant quality of the Eucharistic presence.

Ramsey also spoke of the Eastern sense of the communion of saints. If Western devotion to the saints has sometimes seemed like an individualistic appeal to a heavenly intermediary, the Eastern attitude to the saints seems far more the natural corollary of the Church's family life. The saints, the departed, between whom the Orthodox are unwilling to make a rigid division, are one with us in Christ. The Orthodox pray both to them all and for them all, summoning them to join with their brethren on earth, giving glory to Christ, whose body and whose members are one.

These are three points which seemed vital to Michael Ramsey in his own discovery of Orthodoxy and which have brought a fullness into his understanding of Christian faith and doctrine, of Christian worship and sacrament, and of Christian life. All this, he insisted, was of vital importance for the Church in the world. For the inner life of the Church is seen in Orthodoxy (also, albeit differently, in Anglicanism) to be directly related to the whole of human history. Truth is one. And so the work of Christian thought cannot be isolated from the world of thought in general.

"While we discuss the theology and the Church life of Constantinople, Canterbury and Rome, there is around us the modern world, wherein is terrible rejection of divine truth and indifference to it. The task of unity among ourselves is inseparable from our bringing the everlasting gospel of God to the nations.

"What follows from this? There are at least two points. The first relates to modern scientific, technological culture.

"Can our theology ignore this scientific culture? I can think of theologies whose nature it would be to say, 'Yes, we can ignore it.' Such is not the nature of Orthodox theology, or of Anglican wherever the Orthodox spirit has influenced it. The divine Logos working in all the created world, the author of all truth, the inspirer of all knowledge properly so-called, is working within the scientific methods of our time. If we shrink from saying this, we may be in danger of being false to the teaching of the Fathers. If we do say this, then theologians will be conversing not only with one another in ecumenical exchange, but with every other academic discipline, not least those which seem more modern. The theologian will best teach when he is ready to learn, to receive, wherever the divine Wisdom is the teacher.

"So science and technology are not irrelevant to living out our Christian life and faith in their fullness.

"The second point is also concerned with the material world, the world of famine, poverty, distress and race discrimination.

"Here we can listen to the prophetic words of St. John Chrysostom. 'It is vain to come to the altar in the Eucharist unless we go out to find the altar which is identical with the poor brother. This altar you may see everywhere lying both in the lanes and marketplaces, and you may sacrifice upon it every hour. When you see a poor brother, reflect that you behold an altar.' St. Chrysostom knew the very rich and the very poor within his own city. Today there are countries relatively prosperous and countries of deep poverty. The succor of the homeless and the refugees is a very part of our search for unity in Christ."

For that unity requires to be sought at every level of life. Only so will it have firm foundations, and issue into lasting glory. "The task of unity among ourselves is [indeed] inseparable from bringing the everlasting gospel of God to the nations": so spoke our president, archbishop and spiritual guide.[22]

22. Allchin, "Michael Ramsey and the Orthodox World." *Sobornost* 10/2 (1988), 49–52. Used with permission.

CHAPTER 5

An Icon of True Communion

The Dialogue and Friendship of Father Donald Allchin and Father Dumitru Staniloae

Reverend Dr. Ciprian Burca
Romanian Orthodox Church

"It is only with the heart that one can see rightly;
what is essential is invisible to the eye."

ANTOINE DE SAINT-EXUPÉRY, *THE LITTLE PRINCE*

I have to start my humble contribution to this work dedicated to Fr. Donald Allchin with a confession. It concerns one of my dearest personal memories that determined me to gladly accept the kind invitation of Fr. David Keller to write about the special and iconic friendship between Fr. Donald Allchin and Fr. Dumitru Staniloae.

As a newly ordained priest, I had the chance to meet Fr. Allchin in person during a conference about Eastern Orthodox Spirituality held in the Italian monastery of Bose in September 2003. During one of the conference's breaks I took the courage to approach Fr. Allchin and once I said that I was a Romanian orthodox he instantly mentioned about his life-time friend Dumitru Staniloae, although it was almost ten years after the latter's passing away. His spontaneous smile and kind words about Fr. Staniloae were overwhelming. It felt like Fr. Staniloae was actually there with us. The interesting fact is that although I am Romanian I have not had the chance to meet Fr. Staniloae in person as I was blessed to meet Fr. Donald Allchin. It might sound odd but after the short yet intense discussion I had with Fr. Allchin I started to regard the theology and personality of Fr. Dumitru Staniloae in a whole new light and broader perspective.

It is not easy to point out the most relevant and profound aspects of the relationship between such complex personalities which left distinctive marks in the life of the church going far beyond any confessional limitations. I consider their sincere and prolific friendship a paradigmatic image of what Fr. Allchin calls "the kingdom of love and knowledge"[1] since once they have met, time and space did not succeed to separate them. This was a book in which Fr. Staniloae fully recognized himself as an orthodox theologian, considering it a great contribution to the spiritual renewal of the West and a needed impulse for the rapprochement between the West and Orthodoxy.

They both were men of strong convictions with the vocation of an authentic spiritual ecumenism, churchmen with deep living faith and courage who constantly praised and participated in God's love as communion through their love towards the others. Besides the correspondence which includes all seventy letters sent by Fr. Staniloae to Fr. Allchin (which are being kept in the Allchin Archive of Gladstone's Library), their encounter and meetings in England or Romania cover a period of almost two and a half decades. The relevance of this friendship represents an important part of the history of Anglican—Romanian Orthodox relationship.

1. Allchin, *The Kingdom of Love and Knowledge* (1979).

Donald Allchin and Dumitru Staniloae: Photo courtesy of Donald Allchin

From the obituary[2] written by Fr. Allchin for Fr. Staniloae we learn that the reputed Anglican theologian discovered the name of Fr. Dumitru Staniloae in two articles of Fr. Andrei Scrima published in the French Dominican Review *Istina* at the end of 1958 which treated in detail the Romanian Tradition of the hesychastic spirituality from the fourteenth century to the twentieth century and the Romanian version of *Philokalia*. The "Staniloae Philokalia" as it is also known was more than an enlarged version of the Greek one of St. Nicodemos the Hagiorite. All new added texts, notes, and commentaries, the critical approach and the relatedness to the problems and concerns of twentieth century drew the attention of Fr. Allchin. This aspect is very important because Fr. Staniloae, despite the fact he was a married priest, had a major contribution to the renewal of the monasticism in Romania which could be compared in terms of impact with the nineteenth-century recovery of monastic life in the Anglican Church that was studied in detail by Fr. Allchin in his work *The Silent Rebellion*.[3]

---

2. Allchin, "Dumitru Staniloae" *Sobornost* 16/1 (1994), 1.

3. Allchin, *The Silent Rebellion* (1958).

Therefore, we can say that the common interest they shared in monasticism, in fact in monastic spirituality, drew Fr. Staniloae and Fr. Allchin closer. His strong impression on the work of Fr. Staniloae was that "in his hands tradition came to life," tradition seen by Jaroslav Pelikan as "the living faith of the dead."[4] Perhaps this could explain why the volume edited by Fr. Allchin dedicated to the Romanian Orthodox spirituality and theology was entitled *The Tradition of Life: Romanian Essays in Spirituality and Theology*.[5] Before that the invitation addressed by Fr. Allchin to Fr. Staniloae to write an article for the *Sobornost* review about Orthodoxy in the autumn of 1968 became the motive of the first visit of Fr. Staniloae in England where he lectured at St. Stephen's House, Oxford, on January 23, 1969. Although the lecture was given in French, Fr. Donald translated and published it in *Sobornost* under the title "Some Characteristics of Orthodoxy."[6] Somehow what Fr. Scrima had started in *Istina* review, Fr. Allchin continued in *Sobornost*. Fr. Allchin would later return the visit spending a quite long time with Fr. Staniloae in Bucharest and Sibiu. All these proved to be the signs of a life-time and memorable friendship that has always seen in the broader perspective of the rapprochement between the Anglican and Romanian Orthodox Church.

Speaking of the correspondence between them it could be roughly divided in two parts: the letters from the seventies and the ones from eighties. Obviously these letters are extremely important for their documentary value but they could picture only partially the depth of the relationship between these two distinguished churchmen. Fr. Allchin's impression after meeting Fr. Staniloae personally was that "one was immediately conscious that full of joy and interest in life he was, he carried a heavy weight of experience inside him."[7]

Although they first met through their work, this did not stop Fr. Staniloae to sense the personality of Fr. Donald Allchin and his kindness, openness, and interest in Orthodoxy. In the second letter, for example, Fr. Staniloae deeply touched by the generous hospitality he enjoyed during his staying in Oxford as well as by "the familiar spiritual atmosphere" created on this occasion wrote full of confidence: "My conscience tells me that I

---

4. Pelikan, *The Vindication of Tradition*, 65.

5. Allchin, *The Tradition of Life* (1971).

6. Staniloae, *Some Characteristics of Orthodoxy*, 627–29.

7. Allchin, *Dumitru Staniloae* , 1.

have a friend in you, a heart which beats for me and this strengthens me."[8] We should also add here that Fr. Staniloae's meeting with the Sisters of the Love of God from the Convent of the Incarnation, Fairacres in Oxford moved him and imprinted deeply in his soul, greeting them on every occasion through Fr. Allchin.

It might sound strange but Fr. Staniloae used to call another theologian "Father" only if he felt that he was in communion with that person. During the next few months of 1969 Fr. Allchin had translated from French some other lectures and essays of Fr. Staniloae: "Tradition and the Development of Doctrine"[9] and "The World as Gift and Sacrament"[10] publishing them in the same *Sobornost*. Moreover he wrote regularly articles about Romania, Romanian theology, and the Romanian Orthodox Church in *The Church Times*. Undoubtedly one can say without the fear of being wrong that Fr. Allchin is the one of those who made tremendously concentrated efforts so that theology and personality of Fr. Staniloae, and Romanian Orthodox spirituality and history would be known and appreciated in the Anglican world. On the other hand, Fr. Staniloae constantly encouraged and sustained the publication of Fr. Allchin's lectures and articles in the main Romanian periodicals such as *Romanian Orthodox Church* and *Theological Studies Review*, also striving to improve his English language proficiency to honour and better understand his friend. For instance, the translation of the two lectures given by Fr. Allchin at the Theological Institutes from Bucharest and Sibiu were published in *Romanian Orthodox Church* in the same year. As a certain sign that their friendship grew fast Fr. Staniloae did not hesitate to suggest that he considered Fr. Allchin like a brother in Christ, evoking the words of David in Psalm 133:1 to describe the time they had spent together, as we can read in the fifth letter sent from Cologne on the November 14, 1969.

In another letter dated December 6, 1969 we can see Fr. Staniloae's vivid interest in the Anglican theology and philosophy of J. L. Austin (1911–60) and E. L. Mascall (1905–93). The first was White's Professor of Moral Philosophy at Oxford University, philosopher of language, developer of the theory of speech acts, and who became known especially for the William Lectures given at Harvard in 1955 and later published under the title

8. All letters mentioned or quoted in this chapter are from the Allchin Archive at Gladstone's Library in North Wales.

9. Staniloae, *Tradition and the Development of Doctrine*, 652–61.

10. Staniloae, *The World as Gift and Sacrament*, 662–72.

How to Do Things with Words. It seems that Austin inspired Staniloae to better picture the inner connection between word and act by emphasizing the fact that the word is simultaneously sign, sound, memory, and light. The latter, Professor of Historical Theology at King's College, London and supporter of neo-Thomism, approached the relationship between the order of creation and sacramental order form a new perspective, which intrigued Fr. Staniloae. Both of them had a great impact on the spirituality of the twentieth century. One could trace some significant influences of these two thinkers in Fr. Staniloae's theology of creation, influences which could be the subject of a relevant research work concerning the theological legacy of the Romanian theologian. Moreover, it seems that Fr. Staniloae was interested in Mascall's Mariology. This proves that Fr. Staniloae did not have at any time the intention—despite the restrictions, censorship, and the harsh communist oppression—to write only for his fellow Romanian.

Many of the books of the Anglican theologians or philosophers that were always kindly provided by Fr. Allchin helped Fr. Staniloae to make his voice heard in the context of the theological debates and discussions of the last century. He was aware of many of the challenges, transformations, and mutations of the post Vatican II theology and their direct consequences for the ecclesial life in the West and East-West relationship. From the twelfth letter sent by Fr. Staniloae on the May 1, 1970 we learn that Fr. Allchin facilitated the presentation of some theological ideas of Fr. Staniloae by Professor George Every during a BBC show.

In the same year he enjoyed the hospitality of the Sisters from Fairacres Convent where Fr. Allchin was warden for a long time. Finding himself in the middle of a dynamic community in which the intellectual matters were not at all overlooked, Fr. Staniloae was struck by the depth of perception and the delicacy of understanding hidden in some of the unpublished meditations one of the sisters confided him.[11] He has always considered that women's distinctive approach to theological and spiritual questions was something the church needed. On that occasion Fr. Staniloae gave a lecture about the role and significance of the cross and the meaning of the suffering in Christian life. Actually, the publication of this lecture by SLG Press in 1970 as *The Victory of the Cross* was a saga in itself.[12] Fr. Staniloae was distressed by the thought that this subject was very sensitive and would agitate the censors since this text was banished from publication in

---

11. Allchin, *Dumitru Staniloae* , 1.

12. Staniloae, *The Victory of the Cross.*

Romania. Although Fr. Allchin wrote a preface saying that the text was the result of both Fr. Staniloae's lecture given at Fairacres and the subsequent discussions, this was only partially true. What has been published was in fact the English translation of the text Fr. Staniloae brought with him from Bucharest with some small annotations. The well-known English diplomacy paid off. By carefully avoiding any references to the conflict between the communist regime and the Orthodox Church "a luminous and profound piece of Staniloae's theology was made available to readers in the English-speaking world."[13] Anyway, one could read between the lines if interested. Overall this literary sensitivity best portrays their epic friendship.

The landscape, the magnificent cathedrals he visited, and the warmth and kindness of the Sisters of the Love of God from Fairacres literally overwhelmed Fr. Staniloae determining him to say, full of gratitude, in the fifteenth letter, dated September 7, 1970 that although "I returned home . . . it feels like I have another home in England, that is a community of souls who really love me." Fr. Staniloae considered England, the Fairacres Convent, and Oxford in particular, his second home. He would mention this journey many times in the future correspondence with Fr. Allchin. Based on this unique experience of fraternal love he would later write on December 20, 1970, "The friendship in Christ truly belongs to God and there is definitively something divine in it. It is [in] the image of the Holy Trinity and it has [reflects] the relationship of the divine persons." Despite a rather busy 1971, with many and long travels in Germany, Ethiopia, or Italy, the letters exchange continued. The letter from January 21, 1971, shows that Fr. Staniloae was not very pleased with the trend of the Romanian orthodox theology at that time hoping, through the election of Antonie Plamadeala as Patriarchal Vicar, for a renewal of the Romanian theology, so that it would be more opened towards the world and more focused on the spiritual aspects of life. Fr. Staniloae received many of Fr. Allchin's letters through Fr. Plamadeala. In the letter from February 1971 Fr. Staniloae thanked Fr. Allchin for the proposing him as one of the vice-presidents, although as distant, of the Fellowship of St. Alban and St. Sergius. This nomination could be regarded as recognition of Fr. Staniloae's theological contribution in ecumenical context and it definitively marked a new stage of the Romanian-Orthodox-Anglican dialogue.

The twentieth letter sent on April 9, 1971 is significant not only because of its "paschal tone" but also because of its salutation and finale. It

13. Allchin, *Staniloae*, 1.

was the first time that Fr. Staniloae called Fr. Allchin "My Dear Brother Donald." This letter is important also because it reflects the most intimate feelings of Fr. Staniloae regarding his own experience of the infinite joy of the Lord's resurrection.

He wrote:

> The certainty of our own resurrection based on the Lord's Resurrection fills us with joy. This is [ultimately] our only true joy which fills all with joy. All is merry in the world and in our live because of the joy of Resurrection. There would be only sadness [in the world] without Resurrection. We are joyful because we all shall be one in Christ, the perfect whole, through our resurrection [in Him]. That means that our love will be also perfect. Looking for our resurrection, unity, and perfect love in Christ we foretaste this love and joy. Let us embrace one another having our faces enlightened by the light of Resurrection. Please send my best regards to the sisters and soul friends in Christ from the Fairacres Convent. Let us rejoice together of the certainty of our resurrection and unity in Christ.

This year was shadowed by the fact that Fr. Staniloae did not receive the books and brochures sent by Fr. Allchin. This could have been a repercussion of the Romanian communist censorship because of publication of *The Victory of the Cross*. It was something ordinary in those days in Romania. The openness of one towards the other was complete. In the twenty-third letter Fr. Staniloae did not hesitate to ask Fr. Allchin to bring him to Bucharest a medicine for treating his eye condition. The last letter, dated December 16, 1971 has a particular theological relevance because it comprises, besides the Christmas wishes for Fr. Allchin and the sisters form Fairacres, some theological insights on the Maximian theology gathered in his own study of *Mystagogy* by St. Maximus the Confessor, and some short but profound prayers. "The reality seen in God is so deep and rich that we arrive never at end. May God grant us the grace of love for the created and uncreated reality, the thirst of knowledge and longing for unity." Fr. Staniloae would visit again Fr. Allchin in England at the beginning of May 1972. In another letter from the same year dated March 16 Fr. Staniloae confesses "I treasure each meeting with you as a feast because of the light and warm purity which irradiates from your soul. I am also glad to learn that you always approach new themes of a wide and lively theology."

From the twenty-eighth letter sent on May 12, 1972, after his visit to Oxford and London and long awaited reunion with the sisters from

Fairacres Monastery, we can see that Fr. Staniloae also met there Fr. Kallistos Ware and the Zernov family to whom he sent kind regards through Fr. Allchin. The Christmas letter dated December 9, 1972 is even more touching "I feel like we are always in a special spiritual communion. And this is possible only in Christ, from whom comes all love among people. Together forever is my never ending spiritual desire." At the beginning of 1973 Fr. Staniloae congratulated Fr. Allchin for his new appointment as Canon of Canterbury Cathedral hoping that would also improve the Romanian-Orthodox Anglican relationship. The presence of the young student Alan Scarfe (the future bishop of Iowa of Episcopal Church) starting in 1973 to pursue his doctoral studies at Theological Institute of Bucharest under the supervision of Fr. Staniloae fully confirms this improvement. This year also marked the retirement of Fr. Staniloae from the Theological Institute of Bucharest. However, he continued his work with the doctoral students. Unfortunately all the plans for a meeting in the autumn of 1974 failed because of some Fr. Staniloae's family problems. Moreover, he had to decline an invitation to Canterbury the following year.

We could consider the year 1977 the year of great accomplishments for both theologians. In January Fr. Allchin was awarded the title of Doctor *honoris causa* by the Theological Institute of Bucharest at the same time with the late patriarch of the Romanian Church, Justinian. On this occasion he delivered a very interesting lecture "Trinity and Incarnation in Anglican Tradition," published subsequently by SLG Press.[14] He also reviewed the book of W. Nyssen, a German Catholic theologian who wrote about the significance of mural paintings of Moldavian monasteries, in *Fairacres Chronicle*. *The Treatise of Orthodox Dogmatic Theology* of Fr. Staniloae was already in print and he continued to publish his *Philokalia*. In a letter dated July 9, 1977 we find, although somehow indirectly some very interesting information. It seems that Fr. Allchin was the first one who suggested to Fr. Staniloae that his Dogmatics should be translated in English. The way Fr. Staniloae tried to comfort Fr. Allchin for the loss of his father is moving "I fully share the grief and sorrow that you and your beloved mother are experiencing. May God comfort you by giving you the certainty that we all shall be reunited in the everlasting joy of Christ endless love." In the Christmas letter from the same year Fr. Staniloae wrote after reading the Fr. Allchin's study about Trinity and Incarnation "I saw again that our vision on these fundamental aspects of doctrine was identical." Fr. Allchin

14. Allchin, *Trinity and Incarnation.*

was impressed by the special spiritual sensitivity of Fr. Staniloae, shaped by the way he perceived the reality of the nearness of heaven and earth and his constant positive attitude and flexibility despite all the hardships he had experienced in life. Seeing the glory of God shining out in all kinds of unexpected places, Fr. Staniloae used to say that "the world is God's world and gift to us."[15] For him the natural beauty and the human achievements (a creative synthesis between the divine inspiration and human effort) should be seen only together, always reflecting one another.

In 1978 Fr. Allchin kindly provided a copy of the English translation of St. Athanasius work *Contra Gentes* and *De Incarnatione* by R. W. Thomson, a work Fr. Staniloae used for his own translation of the text in Romanian. In the fifty-second letter dated April 21, 1978, once asked by Fr. Allchin to pray for his mother who was in a poor health condition, Fr. Staniloae revealed with a great sensitivity his deepest thoughts about maternity. "We are praying for your beloved mother. Mother is the connection to infinite love. She is the living proof of God's existence."

In the last letter from 1978 Fr. Staniloae, thanking Fr. Allchin for the dedication of his last book on Christian Spirituality,[16] described the unifying power of love which comes from Christ, the source of the true and infinite love. "Our greatest joy on earth and in Heaven is love. I feel your love and this brings me a great joy. If we love one another and we are being loved by the others then we have found Life." It is very interesting that Fr. Allchin chose the wedding as the most suitable image of his vision of the world, despite the fact that he was unmarried. Another aspect of his theological vision which he shared with his friend is the way he always argued the preeminence of love over knowledge; true knowledge always comes from love. Based on this preeminence Fr. Staniloae showed in his *Dogmatics* that the knowledge of God could never be some kind of reductive, abstract speculation but the outcome of a personal and communitarian experience of Trinitarian God who unceasingly calls us to live as sons and daughters of the Father, brothers and sisters in Christ, the incarnated Son of God being vivified by the Holy Spirit.

Fr. Allchin and Fr. Staniloae would meet again in Bucharest at the end of October 1980. It was a very short meeting because Fr. Staniloae had to travel in Germany to be awarded a prize for his theological contribution by

15. Allchin, *Dumitru Staniloae*, 1. See also Staniloae. *The World as Gift and Sacrament*, 662–72.

16. Allchin, *The World Is a Wedding* (1978).

the Theological Faculty of Tübingen. In a letter sent in August 1981 Fr. Staniloae expressed his heartfelt gratitude for Fr. Allchin's contribution to His Excellency Robert Runcie, Archbishop of Canterbury's decision to grant him the Cross of St. Augustine. On this occasion Fr. Staniloae reiterated his strong belief that both the Anglican and the Romanian Orthodox Church had undeniable roles as mediators for divergent Christian traditions. Fr. Staniloae's English proficiency has constantly improved and apparently his surveillance by Romanian secret police somehow eased since he was able to speak with Fr. Allchin even on the phone. Nevertheless there were hard times. Fr. Allchin wrote "The whole situation was one in which the Church was under constant supervision on the part of government. The secret police were everywhere and foreign visitors came under particular scrutiny. One's host was always conscious of the possibility that conversations might be bugged."[17] Paradoxically the safest place for discussions in Romania of that time was in the street. That is why in their case "the habit of discussing things as one walked became deeply ingrained."[18] Fr. Staniloae was awarded the Cross of St. Augustine, one of the highest distinctions of the Anglican Church. The solemn event finally took place in October 1981 at Canterbury Cathedral after Fr. Allchin made all the necessary travel and accommodation arrangements for Fr. Staniloae and his beloved daughter Lidia. Fr. Staniloae would always remember with great joy the time he spent together with Fr. Allchin and the sisters from Fairacres in Oxford and then in Canterbury.

After 1981, ill and weakened, Fr. Staniloae would write to his friend only once a year. He would write to his friend that he felt like his life and work in this world was coming to an end. In the letter dated July 10, 1984 Fr. Staniloae expressed again his unreserved joy after receiving the last book of Fr. Allchin *The Joy of All Creation*,[19] which the former considered to be a representative picture of Anglican devotion to the Holy Mother of God. The next letter dated May 18, 1985 actually includes a very short yet substantial review Fr. Staniloae made to a book[20] by E. Charles Miller. He wrote "It gives me a great joy to see a young man who follows in your steps, working for the rapprochement between Anglicanism and Orthodoxy and striving to emphasize the actual spiritual kinship between the great Anglican theo-

---

17. Allchin, *Dumitru Staniloae*, 1.

18. Ibid.

19. Allchin, *The Joy of all Creation* (1984).

20. Miller, *Toward a Fuller Vision* (1984).

logians he refers to and Orthodoxy. I particularly enjoyed his assertion that the Anglicanism is that spiritual *space* through which Orthodoxy could have access to the Western Christianity." Later on Charles Miller would write what Fr. Allchin described as an admirable, "lucid and well-balanced" introduction to the work of Fr. Staniloae.[21] The volume, dedicated to Fr. Allchin, is still considered an important guide to the work of Fr. Staniloae. Left alone with his wife, Mary, Fr. Staniloae experienced a continuous deterioration of his health condition during the following years. As usual he did not hesitate to share with his friend the most intimate concerns regarding his daughter and nephew who had left for Germany asking Fr. Allchin to help and protect them in any way he could. In all letters of Fr. Staniloae the formal and informal tone always mingles.

The last letter dated January 20, 1990 (immediately after the fall of the communists) remains the only letter known so far that Fr. Staniloae wrote in freedom, without any restrictions. Cherishing the feeling of love and admiration Fr. Allchin has always showed for Romanian people, for its capacity of self-sacrifice, endurance of oppression which stemmed from a profound and delicate spirituality, Fr. Staniloae openly described the communist régime as being both tyrannical and monstrous. As a conclusion of this fruitful friendship Fr. Staniloae wrote to Fr. Allchin "You gave me the chance to discover and experience the gentleness and nobleness of the English People. Each nation has its own wonderful originality." We could consider that the special relationship which these men of love had was an insightful image of true spiritual communion of humans in Christ for whom it is more important to give than to receive; a communion which is love manifested as harmonious unity in diversity. According to Fr. Allchin, during one of their discussions Fr. Staniloae said to him "There are as many kinds of love as there are human persons."[22]

In the Autumn of 1993, Fr. Staniloae—the one who believed that the fullness of this world and space would be taken up into a greater fullness of eternity,[23] whose open and inclusive vision about the centrality of the Orthodoxy in the Christian world did not prevent him from being always interested in and willing to learn and to accept from the Western Christianity, despite his critique of certain aspects of the Western theology—would

21. Miller, *The Gift of the World* (2000).

22. Allchin, *Dumitru Staniloae*, 1.

23. Ibid.

follow his wife in eternity. We like to believe that Fr. Allchin joined them in the kingdom of the infinite love of the life-giving Trinity.

Maybe these words are not enough to express the depth of such an exemplary and unique friendship between two great spirits, a friendship in Christ, which grew step by step as a child under the eyes of his loving parents, but at least it could be considered an icon of true communion of which our world is in such a need nowadays.

PART THREE

Donald Allchin's Ecumenical Dialogue and Theology

"One of the principal ways in which I think of transformation, in the sense of growing into the life which comes from God, is in relation to unity and diversity. The real transformation is that God brings us together into one. In doing so we don't become monolithic and rigid. On the contrary, our different gifts and our capacities for relating to other people all develop too. It is always with transformation a matter of both unity and diversity; that is my fundamental answer to the term."

". . . Christian unity is central to my being a person of faith. In the last twenty years I have been thinking gradually that Christian unity is only the beginning. From there, we have to go on to interfaith unity—that all of the major religions should listen, understand and love one another, and understand what the Almighty is saying to all of them, together. All of that has developed very rapidly in the last ten years (1997 to 2007)."[24]

---

24. Donald Allchin. An interview with David Keller, July 12, 2007. See Transcript 2 in Appendix.

CHAPTER 6

Enlarge My Heart

Donald Allchin and the Exploration
of Christian Traditions

Geoffrey Rowell

Emeritus Fellow of Keble College, Oxford
Bishop of Gibraltar in Europe, 2001 to 2013

T he great Anglican poet-priest of the seventeenth century, Thomas
Traherne, wrote in his *Centuries of Meditation,* that "love has a mar-
vellous property of feeling in another."[1] This was certainly true of Donald
Allchin, who was himself an admirer of Traherne, and who regularly
attended the annual Traherne celebration at Credenhill just outside
Hereford, where Traherne had been the parish priest. With a deep sense of
the ecumenism of the Spirit, Donald had an intuitive ability to enter into
different Christian traditions, cultures and languages, and discover their
riches and what they could contribute to a wider and deeper understanding
of the Christian faith and the dynamic of tradition (the title of one of his
books)[2] whereby that faith was handed on from one generation to another.

---

1. Traherne, *Centuries of Meditation,* 1 sec. 52
2. Allchin, *The Dynamic of Tradition.*

I have in my library a personally inscribed copy of *A Rapture of Praise,*[3] the anthology of the hymns of John and Charles Wesley which he edited with Herbert Hodges, then Professor of Philosophy at Reading University, and who shared with Donald a love for the Orthodox tradition. Donald wrote on the fly-leaf of this book words from one of the Wesley hymns:

> Enlarge my heart to understand
> the mystery unknown.

These are words which might be taken as summing up the theological and spiritual task in which Donald was engaged for the whole of his ministry. He would have rejoiced that Wesley's words had in an earlier generation resonated with Teresa of Avila, when she heard in the psalms of the daily office, the words *Thou hast enlarged my heart*—words that pointed her to a prayer that was not a mechanistic repetition of formulaic phrases but an allowing the Spirit of God to catch her into the spring of living water. As Wesley again put it much later in *Jesu, lover of my soul!*

> Thou of life the fountain art,
> Freely let me taste of Thee,
> Spring thou up within my heart,
> Rise to all eternity!

But my first encounter with Donald Allchin was not in the context of the Wesleys and their hymns—and particularly their eucharistic hymns—but of the first Newman Symposium to be held in Oxford in 1966. This was a significant event, growing out of the conferences which Abbé Nicolas Theis had organized from Luxembourg. It brought Newman back to England, to Oxford, and to Oriel, and was marked by the presence of Archbishop Michael Ramsey, coming straight from his significant meeting with Pope Paul VI in Rome, during which Pope Paul had taken the episcopal ring from his own finger and placed it on Archbishop Michael's in a dramatic ecumenical gesture. Donald edited the proceedings of the Symposium with the lay Catholic theologian, John Coulson, whose book, *Newman and the Common Tradition* had explored the literary roots of Newman's theology and reflected on the consequences of this for Catholic theology following Newman's conversion. It was published as *The Rediscovery of Newman,*[4] and in two major sections examined the sources of Newman's power and the

---

3. Allchin, *A Rapture of Praise.*
4. Allchin and Coulson, *Rediscovery of Newman.*

development of his influence—in continental Europe, in the Free Church-
es, and in the Second Vatican Council. Donald Allchin made a particularly
original contribution in a major paper on "The Theological Vision of the
Oxford Movement" in which he drew significantly on the unpublished
Lectures on Types and Prophecies, which Pusey had delivered in 1836, and
which Newman had attended. The manuscript of these *Lectures* is in the
Pusey House archive, but they had lain there neglected, until Professor
Alf Härdelin of the University of Uppsala had made use of them for his
significant study of Tractarian sacramental theology, *The Tractarian Understanding of the Eucharist.*[5] Donald immediately recognized how important
these *Lectures* were as providing a major key to the theological vision of
the Oxford Movement, though he did not know Newman's later comment
to Pusey that Pusey's patristic typological understanding of Scripture was
the only real riposte to the subjective deconstruction of the New Testament
by David Friedrich Strauss in his *Leben Iesu.* As Donald wrote in his paper,
there were "two central elements in the Tractarian vision of the world and
of God":

> First that *everything* created shouts the glory of its Maker, whence
> follows the need to bring all human knowledge, activity, and ex-
> perience into relation to God's revelation of himself, and secondly,
> that at the moment of recognizing the utter transcendence of God
> we also experience his agonizing nearness, and that this nearness
> is such that though all the resources of the human mind and heart
> must be summoned to its apprehension, in the end no words can
> express it. It must be known in life. For a moment they saw the
> whole transfigured by uncreated light, and man in its midst caught
> up into an awe-full union with the divine. And that vision, which
> certainly owed much to Wordsworth, was understood by them
> finally in terms which they had learnt from the Fathers, and above
> all from the Greek Fathers, This meant that a vision of an aesthetic
> origin could be integrated into a larger view of things, which
> would do justice not only to man's perception of beauty, but also
> to his moral and intellectual apprehensions This was a view which
> centered upon the mystery of the Incarnation, seen as providing
> the key both to the sacramental understanding of the universe,
> and to an understanding of the Church wholly centered upon the
> person and work of Christ, the redeemer. In the mystery of the In-
> carnation of the Son of God, in his death and resurrection, we see

5. Härdelin, *The Tractarian Understanding of the Eucharist.* See especially chapter 2,
"The Sacramental Principle and the Nature of the Church," 60–107

the full height and depth of the miraculous interchange between God and man, and the full extent and scope of the operation of God's glory, gathering together all things created, making them instruments and vehicles of the divine presence.[6]

Donald described the outstanding feature of Pusey's *Lectures* was "their romantic quality" and their stress on the imagination. He endorsed Härdelin's observation that the Tractarians "were fighting on a double front; on the one hand against rationalist anti-dogmatism, and on the other against the intellectualism of older orthodoxy."[7] As Donald goes on to comment on the major themes of Pusey's *Lectures:*

> There is the conviction that clarity and immediate intelligibility are qualities dearly purchased in reflection on divine things; that God reveals himself in images which strike us forcibly almost in proportion to our inability to capture or define them fully; that everything in this world can be a type or symbol of heavenly realities; and that the whole history of God's dealings with his people foreshadows and is prophetic of his revelation of himself in Christ. Finally there is the belief that to try to make a rationally intelligible and complete system of God's ways will inevitably lead to a narrowing and limiting of our apprehension of them.[8]

Pusey's conviction that "biblical revelation is given through the use of types, symbols and sacramental actions" anticipates, as the present Principal of Pusey House, Dr. George Westhaver, has argued in his in-depth study of Pusey's *Lectures,* the theology of later thinkers such as Henri de Lubac and Austin Farrer, as well as current rediscoveries of the significance of both patristic exegesis and the place of the imagination in human understanding.[9] As Donald presciently put it:

> One of the most important elements in the Tractarian vision of the Christian faith, and one which still has great relevance today, is the way in which it involved a rediscovery of the sense of Scripture and Tradition alike, a new insight into both sacrament and prophecy. For . . . Pusey is sure that without an understanding of the essential role played by type and sacrament in the process of revelation, we shall be false to revelation itself, losing our awareness of it as a gift

6. Coulson and Allchin, eds., *Rediscovery of Newman*, 53–54
7. Härdelin, *The Tractarian Understanding of the Eucharist,* 56
8. Ibid., 58
9. Westhaver, *The Living Body of the Lord.*

from God, into which we are called to enter, and instead transforming it into a mere conceptual scheme of our own devising.[10]

Pusey's vision—and that of the Oxford Movement—was one to which Donald often returned, as we can see in the concluding lecture in *The Dynamic
of Tradition*, where he writes of John Keble, and of Hooker (whose *Works*
Keble edited) behind him, that in Keble we find "the patristic view of the
world itself as the sacrament of God's providential care, a view which is not
afraid to affirm that God is present in all things."

> He makes it clear that in this world we are not simply dealing with
> material copies of ideal archetypes. The picture is more dynamic
> than that. Objects and events are seen as meeting places; places
> where man can come out of himself in return to meet God, finding
> his daily life to be full of occasions for making over to God the
> happenings of everyday. The moral implications of this vision are
> as clear as its aesthetic consequences.[11]

Donald, like Michael Ramsey, was a theologian of transfiguration. The
Christian faith was not just a set of ideas but a participation by grace in
the Divine life. Our calling was to be transformed from glory into glory.
He found this theme in the Fathers, in Orthodoxy, in the Tractarians, and
in the Wesleys. In the introduction to the selection of Wesley hymns, *A
Rapture of Praise*, published in the same year in which he delivered his
lecture on Pusey's *Lectures on Types and Prophecies*, which he wrote with
his fellow-editor, Herbert Hodges, he spoke of where we must begin, "with
God's love for us." This is a love "which is infinite, inexhaustible, unfathomable, wholly undeserved, wholly generous and self-giving. It evokes in us
a response of love, both towards God and towards one another for God's
sake, so that in the end the true divine love, which only God can give, is
more and more shed abroad in our hearts as our resistance to it weakens;
until at last, being wholly freed from sin, we are wholly filled with pure
love." "Love is not merely one of God's attributes, it is his very nature"—as
John Wesley powerfully wrote in his hymn *Wrestling Jacob—Come, O Thou
traveller unknown! His nature and His Name is Love.*

For men to be filled with love is to be fashioned into the image and
likeness of God:

> Love, thine image, love impart!

10. Härdelin, *The Tractarian Understanding of the Eucharist*, 67–68

11. Allchin, *The Dynamic of Tradition*, 38

> Stamp it on our face and heart!

It is to become partakers of the divine nature:

> Heavenly Adam, Life divine,
> Change my nature into thine.

It is to be re-created:

> Thy creature, Lord, again create
> And all my soul renew.

It is to re-enter Paradise:

> My heart, thou know'st, can never rest
> Till thou create my peace,
> Till, of my Eden repossessed
> From every sin I cease.[12]

Donald noted specifically amongst the Wesleys' hymns, their Eucharistic hymns, collected in their *Hymns on the Lord's Supper,* which was re-published nine times after it first appeared in 1745. Allchin notes that these eucharistic hymns are "equalled perhaps only by the sacramental hymns of N. F. S. Grundtvig in Denmark," about whom he wrote a major study. But, if this was one parallel for him, he noted another, in Symeon the New Theologian, the Byzantine "Mystic of Fire and Light," at the turn of the first millennium. "There are indeed remarkable similarities between some aspects of [Symeon's] teaching and that of John and Charles Wesley. There is a strange similarity between the situation in which he [Symeon] lived and the response he made to it, and the situation of the Wesleys."[13] In writing of Symeon, Donald quotes a comment of Ernest Rattenbury on the Wesleys as equally applicable to Symeon: "His theology of is an account of truth realized in personal experiment and experience . . . his soul and mind are supplied, not from cisterns, but from springs; his teaching was not merely of a school, but of a genuine experience of life—the divine life."[14]

At the end of the introduction to the hymns that follow in *A Rapture of Praise* Donald notes that on the day of his conversion experience (May 28th, 1738) John Wesley had been reading from 2 Peter the words that

---

12. Allchin and Hodges, *A Rapture of Praise,* 20

13. Allchin, *The Kingdom of Love and Knowledge,* 39

14. Ibid., 50, citing Rattenbury, *The Evangelical Doctrine of Charles Wesley's Hymns,* 85, 87.

speak of God's "exceeding great and precious promises, even that we should be partakers of the divine nature" (2 Pet 1–4).

> This teaching, so basic to the whole life of the Eastern Church, seems to have been with John Wesley, consciously or unconsciously, throughout his ministry, and it is to be found in Charles Wesley's hymns with an insistence which is rare in Western Christendom. . . .
>
> Thy kingdom come to every heart,
> And all thou hast, and all thou art.
>
> These declarations that the end of man is to live in union with God are not incidental in his writings, nor are they literary exaggerations. They give us the clue to understanding his whole life, which was an ardent longing after a "perfect love," to which in this world he never attained. They are fundamental to the whole attitude revealed in his hymns with their eager expectation of the fullness which is yet to come, and their constant sorrow over the awareness of the sin which still remains. They go some way to explain the otherwise surprising fact that with very few exceptions his Ascension hymns are much finer than his Resurrection ones. For with him the meaning of Easter is swallowed up in the splendor of the Ascension, in which the King of Glory has with great triumph exalted his only Son to his kingdom in heaven. He prays that we too may ascend there in heart and mind, so that the Holy Spirit may exalt us unto the same place whither our Saviour Christ is gone before.[15]

If the hymns of the Wesleys were seen as expressing a theology which reflected that of the Eastern Fathers and of a Byzantine mystic like Symeon the New Theologian, the Danish theologian, educationalist and hymn-writer, N. F. S. Grundtvig (1783–1872) also kindled Donald's imagination, and led to a major study, *N. F. S. Grundtvig: An Introduction to His Life and Work* (1997).[16] There can be few who have become fluent in Danish, as Donald did, in order to study Grundtvig, whereas many have done so in order to read Kierkegaard in the original.

Donald had come to Denmark to stay with a Danish family as a seventeen-year-old schoolboy in 1947, and during that time not only had he learned some Danish and become acquainted with the Danish church and culture, he had also been taken to the Grundtvig Church in Copenhagen. This was clearly the beginning of a lifelong fascination with Grundtvig,

15. Allchin and Hodges, *A Rapture of Praise*, 48–49

16. Allchin, *N. F. S. Grundtvig*

whose thought Donald came to believe would have had a much greater influence had Grundtvig written in English or German and not his native Danish. He had first intended to write substantively on Grundtvig in 1960, out of the conviction that Grundtvig needed to be presented to the English-speaking world. In the end all that appeared were two articles in the *Eastern Churches Quarterly*, the first on "The hymns of N. F. S. Grundtvig," and the second on "Grundtvig's translations from the Greek."[17] But his interest in Gruntdvig continued and twenty years later, in *The Kingdom of Love and Knowledge*, with its concern for Orthodoxy and the West, he saw Grundtvig as important in this context, including in that book a chapter on Grundtvig—"N. F. S. Grundtvig: The Spirit as Life-giver."[18] In that chapter he wrote that it was Grundtvig's sermons and hymns that were at the heart of his teaching and theology. "His is a theology of praise and proclamation. He created a body of liturgical hymns, hymns for the festivals and for the sacraments, which are without parallel in Protestant Christendom. His is a theology, moreover which is expressed primarily in images and not in concepts."[19] As Donald had found in the Tractarians so also he found in Nikolai Grundtvig—"he came to think of the world around him as no more than a shadow, an image of an eternal and heavenly reality to which, occasionally the poet's genius might give him access. He felt, and was to feel all his life, an aching longing for that heavenly and eternal world which here we know only in shadows, shadows which are indeed most tantalizing when they are most beautiful and apparently real."[20] He noted how, as Grundtvig's Eucharistic theology developed, the Eucharistic gifts "precisely because parts of [the] material creation" were fitted "to partake of the glorious reality they convey." "It is the Spirit who brings together earth and heaven, human and divine in a new unity," so that "the chalice of human life and joy is also the chalice of God's love, which unites earth and heaven, and builds up the holy city into a union of love."[21] The Eucharist is not just a past remembrance, nor even simply a present reality, but is orientated to the future. "In the Eucharist the heavenly and the earthly are fused together in

17. Allchin, "The Hymns of N. F. S. Grundtvig," *Eastern Churches Quarterly* XIII (1959) 129–43; "Grundtvig's Translations from the Greek," *Eastern Churches Quarterly* XIV (1961–62) 28–44.

18. Allchin, *The Kingdom of Love and Knowledge*, 71–89.

19. Ibid., 72.

20. Ibid., 82

21. Ibid., 84

the power of the Spirit, as a sign that the whole earthly creation is called to share in the final transfiguration of all things, when the union of earth and heaven which here we know in faith will be fully and openly revealed."[22]

Donald's major study of Grundtvig was intended "to present Grundtvig to the English-speaking world." It was, he said, the first time that "someone neither Danish nor Scandinavian [had] attempted to make an extended presentation of Grundtvig's life and work." It was a major achievement, succeeding through the clarity of its presentation and the rich and well-ordered quotations from Grundtvig's sermons and hymns. Grundtvig's theology, as Donald summed it up was "a theology of praise and proclamation, a doxological and kerygmatic presentation of the faith, with ecumenical implications which need to be explored."[23] Grundtvig's theology was also an ecclesial theology. Christianity is not a theory derived from the Bible and then elaborated by professors. Christianity exists in the one church, "grounded in the apostolic confession of faith and in the sacraments of the Gospel. . . . We cannot build the Church on the Bible alone, still less on the interpretation of individual experts. It is in the life of the Church and in the sacraments of the Church, in which God is present and at work, that we hear God's word addressed to us and discover what true Christianity is."[24] For Grundtvig the life of the church is "not a thing which exists in this world alone, It includes the Church triumphant in heaven. The idea of the communion of saints is a vital aspect of this mysterious reality."[25] In this stance Donald notes Grundtvig anticipates Florovsky's affirmation that there the ecumenism in time is no less significant than the ecumenism in space.[26]

In his concluding epilogue, Donald identified what he called seven tentative conclusions, which are not only true of Grundtvig but of Donald himself, with his ability for "feeling in another" and for discerning a wider and deeper Christian perspective in Christian contexts and cultures different from his own Anglican roots. It is worth summarizing these briefly.

(1) Grundtvig's view of humanity "is radically collaborative and interdependent. . . . He sees the relationship society as the only truly human society, for human beings find themselves only when they find that their life is rooted in the life of God, three in one."

22. Ibid., 84.

23. Allchin, *N. F. S. Grundtvig*, 1.

24. Ibid., 106

25. Ibid., 110

26. Ibid., 111

(2) "He is man who speaks to the situation of a world which is deeply perplexed by the strength and persistence of feelings of national identity. We thought we had left these things behind, but they now come back to us to in frighteningly irrational and destructive ways." Grundtvig is a man who takes these questions of national awareness with the utmost seriousness. He knows how important these questions are, and how much human beings need the sense of belonging and identity which active participation in a national community can give. But he sees that nations, no less than individuals, only function properly when they function in a collaborative and interdependent way. The nations have need to work with one another and to respect one another's differences; they too discover themselves in discovering their neighbors.[27] (What Donald writes about Grundtvig has roots not only in the two Great Commandments, but also in the words of St. Anthony from the time of the Desert Fathers, "Our life and our death are with our neighbour.")

(3) Grundtvig saw the inseparable connection of national identity with the importance of language and the differences of languages. He believed passionately that "languages are among the greatest of God's gifts to humanity, and that each one has its own specific beauty and excellence" so that "it is saddening and perplexing to see how little time, energy and thought our society is willing to spend on learning to appreciate the languages of others, and to understanding the full meaning of their diversity and difference."

(4) Grundtvig not only valued differences between people and languages, but even more "values and affirms the possibilities of communion and unity within the human family."

> As a priest, a preacher and a pastor in the Church of Christ he is passionately concerned for the unity and integrity of the Church through time and through space. He is . . . one of the major ecumenical prophets of the nineteenth century. His insights could be of direct use in our problems today.
>
> His wonderful sense of the poetic, many-layered nature of language, his feeling for the living presence of the past, in and through the vicissitudes of history, point towards a church which is one in its freely accepted diversity. This "poetic-historic" view of things provides a sovereign antidote to temptations towards

---

27. Ibid., 308

authoritarian and literalist systems of whatever kind, which seek to reduce all to unity by decreeing uniformity.[28]

(5) "The strongly poetic nature of Grundtvig's theology is also to be seen in his awareness that the whole living world, and not humanity alone, is involved in the drama of God's self-disclosure. For him the earth too is made in God's image. In opening themselves to the divine realm men and women find that their sense of bodily solidarity with the natural world is strengthened and not weakened. It is not only a solidarity in death; more deeply it is a solidarity in transfiguration and resurrection."[29]

(6) Grundtvig's vision, moreover, is one which takes up themes characteristic of the primal religions which have a significance for contemporary environmental dilemmas.

(7) "Grundtvig's view of the Christian faith is constantly crossing the barriers between Catholic and Protestant, and between East and West in the Christian world. It is highly unitive. His vision of God's purpose is not restricted to the drama of sin and redemption, however vital that may be. Rather, he thinks in terms of a purpose of love which begins in creation, grows through the transfiguration of the things that are made, and comes to the fulfillment of that purpose in the revelation of God's kingdom, or, as he loves to say, the union of human and divine through the marriage of heaven and earth."[30] As Nicholas Lossky comments in an Afterword, "This marriage of past and present in an encounter between time and eternity results in the fact that those who truly witness to their time, take their own time seriously, generally transcend their time: their witness becomes a witness for all times This is the case with the Fathers of the Church; this is the case for Grundtvig."[31]—and, we might add, also for Donald Allchin.

If Grundtvig was a major figure in Denmark, whom Donald Allchin showed as a creative theologian with significant ecumenical and contemporary resonances, the same could not be said of Bernard Walke (1874–1941), a parish-priest in Cornwall, remembered, as Donald said in a memorial lecture in 2000, for only two things—his Christmas plays produced in the remote parish of St. Hilary, and the attack on his church for its "popish," ritualist furnishings by a band of ultra-Protestant vigilantes. Donald was always discovering (and re-discovering) people and places in whom he found

28. Ibid., 309
29. Ibid., 309.
30. Ibid., 310
31. Ibid., 317–17

particular expressions of "immortal diamond" forged by God's transfiguring grace, what Charles Williams called "diagrams of God's glory." Donald had come to Cornwall as a boy on a family holiday when Walke was still alive and had noted his parents' concern when Walke's name was mentioned. Years later he received an invitation to lecture at St. Hilary (and wrote me a characteristically enthusiastic letter saying he was rediscovering things Cornish and Walke in particular). His lecture, published as *Bernard Walke: A Good Man Who Could Never Be Dull*[32] is a cameo of a man who showed, in Donald's words, "a remarkable kind of goodness, not heavy and oppressive, but light and lively, liberating and enlivening." In meeting him "you felt that he gave you the courage, the freedom to be your own true self."[33] In Walke, a pacifist during World War I, and who had authority gained through suffering, Donald saw an attractive tolerance—"not the tolerance which cares nothing about conviction, nor the optimism which can see good in everything because it has not considered the evil which corrodes our human existence, [but] the optimism of grace."[34] In this brief lecture Donald spoke of Bernard Walke's deep love of the country, of his friendship with Gerrard Collier, the founder of the Fellowship of Reconciliation, and their concern to establish a workers' co-operative for the Cornish tin miners. Walke's description of the participation of miners in prayer meetings clearly moved and impressed Donald. "Their amens and alleluias are sharp and incisive—as the ring of the pick against the naked rock . . . their prayers are often eloquent of the longing of the human hear for God, the cries of men who have spent their lives in darkness and whose souls long light and splendor . . . here was a people who unlike many industrial works, have never lost faith in God. The fire that John Wesley kindled was not altogether extinguished."[35] Donald saw in Bernard Walke, "Ber" as he was affectionately known, a priest with a sense of the transcendent, of a sacramental understanding of the world, eucharistically centred, and yet an ecumenical pioneer, with prayer for Ireland welcomed by the Roman Catholic priest in Truro and by Quakers and non-conformists. As Donald commented, for Bernard Walke, "the relation of the Eucharist to society as a whole was of fundamental importance." He quotes Walke's words:

32. Allchin, *Bernard Walke*.

33. Ibid.,7

34. Ibid., 8

35. Ibid., 16–17

At the moment of his farewell, when the Son of God was to leave his friends he had gathered round him, he had set up a common table, where men might meet, and sharing his gifts of bread and wine, find him present with them. For those who share in the gift of the *Corpus Domini*—the body of God—there must be a way, I thought, in which they could share more complete in the daily things of life.[36]

As it was for Donald, it was also important for understanding, Bernard Walke that he and his wife, Annie, herself an artist, found warm friends and supporters in the Newlyn circle of artists. "This identification with what would then have been considered a very unconventional group of people, rather than with the local squirearchy, or indeed with the neighbouring clergy, was deepened during the years of the war when the Walkes found themselves particularly isolated on account of their pacifist stance." Bernard was himself not an artist in line and colour, but in words, of which his Christmas plays, broadcast from St. Hilary, with local actors speaking in local dialect, were a unique contribution. Once again in the scandal of particularity, the uniqueness of a small very remote Cornish community, and its priest, Donald found a reflection of a larger and wider catholicity, and of a transfiguring grace that over and over again creates unique diagrams of God's glory.

"Love has a marvelous property of feeling in another." I began with these words from Traherne's *Centuries of Meditation* as capturing something of Donald Allchin's unique ability to enter into a whole range of Christian tradition and experience and to draw out from the deepest wells patterns of Christian truth, pointing to how all Christian churches and traditions need each other for the realization of that catholicity which is at their heart. And all this—Donald would be the first to say—is rooted and grounded in love, in the perichoretic communion of the love of the Divine Trinity. As Traherne goes on in the same passage from the *Centuries*: "Love can enjoy in another, as well as enjoy Him. Love is an infinite treasure to its object, and its object is so to it. God is Love, and you are His object,. You are created to be His Love, and He is yours. . . . In Him you inherit all things."[37]

In the late 1980s the Church of England was torn by tension and potential division over the question of the ordination of women to the priesthood, with implications for the creation of new barriers to Christian unity

---

36. Ibid., 15

37. Traherne, *Centuries of Meditation*, 1. sec. 52

and raising significant questions about why in the tradition the Christian ministerial priesthood and episcopate had been confined to men. Donald, together with Bishop Stephen Verney, approached Wendy Robinson (a Christian psychotherapist, who had moved from the Anglican to the Orthodox Church), and they agreed to take an initiative to gather together an inter-church group to explore the deeper issues. I was privileged to be part of that group (which met twelve times over three years,) and was grateful that in the end we were able to produce a reflective report on our meetings together, with the title (taken from William Blake) *A Fearful Symmetry? The Complentarity of Men and Women in Ministry.*[38] It sought to traverse two separate avenues of exploration—one on the mystery of masculine and feminine, and one on the mystery of priesthood. In a foreword commending our discussions, Bishop John V. Taylor, formerly Bishop of Winchester, wrote that it was "a model of what should have been taking place in every diocese . . . in place of the campaign approach to decision-making," and suggested that "it should be required reading in the Church of England."[39] I am sure we ought also to have had a third strand in all of this, on the mystery of the church, and how in a divided church decisions of such significance were rightly made. But Donald's contribution to those meetings was, as one might expect, significant, as was his initiative in bringing the group into being. The original intention was not to produce a report—but at the end of our meetings together we thought we might have something of worth to share with the church as a whole.

The character of the report does not allow individual contributions to be identified, but some of the conclusions are worth summarizing, as they are so clearly of a piece with the vision of the church which Donald had so long espoused. There is first the recognition that "the question of the ordination of women to the priesthood and episcopate is part of a larger complex of questions involving the way in which women and men relate to one another and to God within the family of the Church."[40]

> The idea of complementarity has become very important for us, not only with reference to the relationships between men and women, but also with reference to the differing ways of approach which are necessary for any at all adequate appreciation of the truth. The light which comes from the mystery of the Holy Trinity,

38. Rowell, ed., *A Fearful Symmetry?* 1

39. Ibid., vii

40. Ibid.,.52

in which total unity and complete diversity are reconciled and at one, is of endless significance for a renewed understanding and living of the mystery of unity and diversity within the family of the Church. Is it possible to envisage a form of ministry which, while giving full scope to the gifts of women, would yet retain a sense of the way in which the gifts of women and of men fulfill each other?[41]

The process in which all the Churches together are involved is, we believe, one of discovering what is the will of God for the complementarity of men and women in the ministry of the Church. It may perhaps be a long time before the Churches can come to a common mind on the issue. The gift of unanimity may come randomly and unexpectedly. We observe that different Churches have different perceptions of this. A move which to some in the West seems slow and hesitant, to others in the East seems swift and unrehearsed. But we are confident that the willingness to search together for a common mind is something which God will bless and indeed already blesses.[42]

For Christians who long to be at one in Christ, to fail to be united on an issue of this importance is both painful and humbling. No one should underestimate the pain which the controversy causes. But we believe that the pain and the humbling may themselves become a way towards growth. It is through our blindness and weakness that God's grace—which always heals what is wounded and makes up what is lacking—can be at work bringing healing, light and new life to humankind and to all creation.[43]

In his *Golden Epistle,* Abbot William of St. Thierry, writing to the Carthusians of Mont Dieu, brings his letter to an end by speaking of the time when "the understanding of the thinker shall become the contemplation of the lover, and the sharp sight of the one who thinks shall become the bliss of the one who enjoys.'[44] The vision of Donald Allchin, which suffuses all of his writing, is of this glory and love imparted by God, a love and grace which does indeed have the "marvelous property of feeling in another," and which gave him the eyes to see and know the other in the ecumenism of time, of which in this chapter we have looked at in the Tractarians, the Wesleys, Nikolai Grundtvig, and Bernard Walke-but there were many, many others.

41. Ibid., 53

42. Ibid., 54

43. Ibid.

44. McCann, ed., *The Golden Epistle,* 103 (Cap. xvi)

CHAPTER 7

"Merton was and has been terribly, terribly important for me"

The Relationship between Donald Allchin and Thomas Merton

Fiona Gardner

Co-Editor of *The Merton Journal*
UK International Advisor for The International Thomas Merton Society

The friendship between Donald Allchin and the Trappist monk and writer Thomas Merton (1915–1968) began in July 1963 when Donald wrote to Merton asking if he could visit. Merton was a Cistercian monk at the Abbey of Gethsemani, near Louisville in Kentucky. Born in France, educated for some time in England, then a student at Columbia University in New York, Merton had converted to Catholicism in the late 1930s and entered the monastery in 1941. In 1948 his autobiography *The Seven Storey Mountain* detailing his early life and conversion became an international best seller. He was a prolific writer of poetry and prose and had an extensive correspondence with a huge variety of people.

In an interview conducted by Victor A. Kramer in 1998 Donald recounted how he, "as a young Anglican," had read a couple of books by Merton. He thought one was *Seeds of Contemplation* and the other he read while on retreat was *The Sign of Jonas*. "Then I had this feeling—which I suppose lots of people have reading Merton's books—as if he was in the room talking to me. There seemed this immediate contact. . . . But I never dreamt I'd meet him."[1]

Donald was encouraged to make contact with Thomas Merton by Dale Moody a professor at the Baptist Seminary in Louisville who had met Donald while Moody was staying previously at Oxford. Donald had been attending a Faith and Order meeting in Montreal and then after a positive response from Merton, Donald visited the Abbey of Gethsemani. That visit was the start of a stimulating and mutually enriching friendship between the two men who had many shared interests. In a letter to Donald written in 1967 Merton wrote, "So many things to thank you for."[2]

This chapter will explore the relationship that developed between Donald Allchin and Thomas Merton in the 1960s based on correspondence between the two men and the accounts of three visits made by Donald to the Abbey at Gethsemani. The chapter will investigate the shared interest with Merton in Wales, Anglican writers and poets, and Russian Orthodox writers. It will also explore the ongoing influence of Merton, after his death in 1968, on Donald's thinking and interests. The important part played by Donald as honorary president of The Thomas Merton Society of Great Britain and Ireland is briefly discussed.

"There was a kind of quicksilver quality about the conversation": The Meetings and the Correspondence

This first meeting in 1963 took place as did the two subsequent meetings in 1967 and 1968 over three or four days, "On each occasion I had the possibility of long and fascinating conversations with Merton."[3] While staying with Dale Moody in Louisville, Donald had visited sites of interest in Kentucky including Shakertown, a village community at Pleasant Hill that was a thriving nineteenth-century community, but by then long uninhabited. It was mentioning this visit that sparked an immediate connection between the two men. Donald remembered saying how beautiful the buildings were and asking Merton whether he knew about the village:

1. Kramer, "A Very Disciplined Person," 235.

2. Merton, *Hidden Ground of Love*, 28.

3. Allchin, "Merton at Ninety," 2.

I shall never forget. He got up. He went over to his filing cabinet. He pulled out a drawer. He pulled out a file and there was a whole file of photographs of Shaker architecture and Shaker furniture—which in those days was not very well known. There were one or two books published in the States and available on it but not very well known. But Merton was right into it. He said, "I want to write a book about them." Well, he never did but he did write one or two very interesting essays about the Shakers and he made use of the Shaker materials to illustrate the logos doctrine of St. Maximus the Confessor in an absolutely brilliant way in his lectures on aesthetical and mystical theology which haven't ever been published. One of the most beautiful passages in that document is the way in which he uses . . . he says, "If you want to have the logos of a bed or the logos of a chair, look at a Shaker bed, look at a Shaker chair, you can see what the innermost meaning is . . . ."

So we started off on Shakers and that got us going. And from that time we never stopped.[4]

This account taken from a Thomas Merton Society conference round-table discussion held among friends of Thomas Merton reveals a shared affinity with the meaning implicit in the Shaker designs and the deeper connection across religious divides. For Merton there was an affinity between the Shaker and Cistercian spirits, similar to that found in Russian theologians—an affinity that Donald too could appreciate. In his journal Merton notes the first meeting with Donald on August 9, 1963, wishing that he had felt less tired for the visit. "I like him and he has pleasant and interesting things to say and is a nice person very interested in monasticism."[5]

Following this visit the two men corresponded and a second visit took place in 1967 and a third in 1968. Despite this personal contact Donald reminisced that during Merton's lifetime he did not tell people that he had met him and talked with the monk. He thought that most people would not have believed him, and the others would have felt so jealous and that, Donald recounted, he would have found hard to manage. This meant that each contact was experienced as a great privilege. Donald visited the hermitage in 1963. Otherwise the visits took place in the guest house.

Donald wanting to make notes of the visits and the subjects covered found this almost impossible partly because "our conversation ranged so widely and so rapidly" so many topics were covered. "We talked about so

4. Allchin, *Remembering Merton*, no pagination.

5. Merton, *Dancing in the Water of Life*, 5.

many different things." He thought that this was partly because they both had "butterfly minds" but it may be more that there were so many shared interests and a certain excitement because of this in the dialogue.

Donald Allchin and Thomas Merton. Photo courtesy of Donald Allchin.

For Merton, a comforting aspect was that Donald brought news and sometimes books or letters from people whom Merton knew or had heard about in England. Donald also provided the monk with a personal link with the Russian Orthodox circles in Paris, especially the circle round Vladimir Lossky. Lossky's work was of particular interest to Donald and he found that Merton too had read Lossky and been greatly influenced by him. Both men had been involved in studying the work of Maximus the Confessor and the early church fathers.

A further shared interest that emerged during the visits was poetry and Donald introduced Merton to some of the poets in Britain including R. S. Thomas. Edwin Muir was a favorite and both men appreciated David Jones, as Donald noted "that was a real discovery."

The visit of an Englishman, an Anglican, was of interest to the wider community and in 1967 Donald was invited to speak to the community before a service of compline. Donald remembered that overawed by the invitation he asked Merton what he should talk about, and the reply was that he should confirm the importance of monastic life, and how helpful it would be for the monks to hear this from someone outside. In his journal entry for March 31, 1967, Merton notes that Donald Allchin had arrived in the guest house a day early and they were briefly able to meet that evening where "we talked of the Epiphany Philosophers etc." The next day as it rained they sat in the Gatehouse but went for walks. Merton notes "He [Donald] does not take the 'Secular City' people seriously yet admits it is the same absurd superficiality that is after all serious in America. He said this country, religiously speaking, still seemed to be in the nineteenth century."[6] The final day of the visit Merton had to visit the doctors and returned Donald to the Baptist Seminary.

The third visit to the monastery in April 1968 was particularly memorable and it was this experience that members of the Thomas Merton Society especially enjoyed hearing about during Donald's presidential address at conferences. On April 4, 1968, the visit began with a journey out of the monastery to the Shaker village and from there lunch out in Lexington. Donald recounts an amusing incident in the restaurant where a smartly dressed fellow woman diner recognized Donald's English accent, and asked about where he was from, and a conversation took place. Donald remembered how correctly he was dressed in a clerical manner and what a contrast this was with Merton:

> Well, she talked to me for a bit and then she turned to this curious farmer who was sitting next to me and said, "And do you come from England, too?" and Merton said, "No, I come from Nelson County, lady." And she wondered what the strange old redneck was doing talking to this rather elegant young man from Oxford.[7]

However the day took a terrible and indeed potentially dangerous turn, when on the way back the news came through over the car radio of the assassination of Martin Luther King. Merton had responded by saying that they needed immediately to call in at Bardstown at Colonel Hawks' Diner. They went to this small restaurant, which was kept by an African-American, Colonel Hawks, who was himself a Catholic and a great friend of the monastery and someone whom Merton knew. As Donald describes this experience he understood that Merton knew that as a black man Colonel Hawks would be devastated, and would be anxious about his two children who were away at college,

6. Merton, "Learning to Love," 210.

7. Kramer, "A Very Disciplined Person," 246.

> ... the whole situation was at that moment in a sense very fragile. And so we went and spent the evening there. It was a very memorable occasion in many ways, particularly because it was the first time that I had really met a black American in any depth. Colonel Hawks kept coming back to us—he was busy organising his restaurant and seeing that his guests were being served—but he kept coming back to us and talking and talking and talking.[8]

Merton's account of this third visit covers the same activities and includes in his account dated April 6, 1968 his reflections of the "moving and sad experience in Hawks." The evening had been a long one before they returned back to the monastery.

> So the murder of M. L. King—it lay on the top of the travelling car like an animal, a beast of the apocalypse. And it finally confirmed all the apprehension—the feeling that 1968 is a beast of a year . . . Is the Christian message of love a pitiful delusion? Or must one just "love" in an impossible situation?[9]

Over these visits Donald remembered that he had found Merton "wonderfully ordinary" and that Merton had given undivided attention to his visitor.

The correspondence between Thomas Merton and Donald Allchin generally expresses the shared interests between them. (The letters from Merton to Allchin are part of the Allchin Archive at Gladstone's Library in North Wales.) Early in the correspondence Donald invites Merton to write an introduction to a book of translations of the sermons of Isaac of Stella which was being written by an Anglican sister from Wantage, near Oxford. Merton is hugely enthusiastic and replies, "I find the proposal to do an introduction on Isaac for Sister Penelope irresistible, though I am making firm resolutions to stop all prefaces. But no, not this one."[10] Merton also reconnects with Donald over their shared interest in the poetry of George Herbert and Henry Vaughan and says that he has been reading Dame Gertrude More. They have a mutual friend Etta Gullick and the arrangement that the two men had to send one another papers and books is established. In this letter the intellectual parameters of their correspondence over the next five years is clear.

8. Allchin, *Remembering Merton*, no pagination.

9. Merton, *The Other Side of the Mountain*, 78.

10. Merton, *Hidden Ground of Love*, 25.

One of the threads throughout their letter writing is Anglican literature. In a letter written by Merton on April 25, 1964 he offers his approval for "the remarkable little book of essays on the Blessed Virgin" (*The Blessed Virgin Mary: Essays by Anglicans*, edited by E. L. Mascall and H. S. Box). This had been sent by Donald and included an essay by him on the seventeenth-century divines. Merton comments how much he liked this essay and adds, "I liked the whole tone of the book very much."

In the same letter Merton comments that he has been tackling other Anglican reading and comments:

> It seems to me that the best of Anglicanism is unexcelled, but that there are few who have the refinement of spirit to see and embrace the best, and so many who fall off into the dreariest rationalism. For my part I will try to cling to the best and be as English a Catholic as one in my position can be. I do think it terribly important for Roman Catholics now plunging into the vernacular to have some sense of the Anglican tradition.[11]

The exchange of papers between the men, including copies of the journal *Sobernost* from Donald to Merton, and requests from Donald for articles and also Merton's offering of pieces of his writing for monastic communities in England continues throughout much of their correspondence. The focus tends to change after Donald's second visit to poetry, which for both men was of great importance. This is explored further below. One interesting aspect that emerges from the correspondence in 1967 is that Donald sought Merton's advice on whether to spend a sabbatical year living the monastic life at Crawley Down, a suggestion that Merton positively endorsed.

In the final months of their correspondence the possibility of Merton visiting Wales is raised and it is this shared connection that is now explored.

"Can we do Wales then?"

There is a fascinating paper written by Donald entitled "Can we do Wales then?" The title is taken from the final correspondence sent by Merton to Donald while Merton was travelling in Asia, and a few weeks before his untimely death on December 10, 1968.

---

11. Merton, *The Hidden Ground of Love*, 26.

In this Donald traces Merton's interest in Wales as part of his family background, especially in the person of Merton's grandmother Gertrude Grierson (1855–1956), whom he describes as "the best of the lot . . . of whom I retain the strongest impression of my childhood, she taught me the Lord's Prayer."[12] This grandmother was born in Wales and it is this ancestry that Merton claims "is the best that is in us."[13] He thinks that this is where his father's face and his own come from, "the look, the grin, the brow" and from this source he attributes the part of him that writes books and as he puts it, drives him into the woods. It is the Welsh in him, he says that counts.

In a letter to his much loved Aunt Kit in New Zealand, Merton remarks in a long and chatty letter dated May 1964, "Lately I have been reading about hermits and recluses in early Celtic Christianity and in England. Wales was a very monastic and eremitical sort of place. I think we all have some of this in our blood."[14]

Donald notes with interest Merton's fascination with the Welsh and the Anglo-Saxon/Celtic inheritance and finds this reflected in early lines of one of Merton's late poems "The Geography of Lograire":

> all my Wales a ship of green fires

It is easy to understand how fascinated Donald would have been with Merton's connection with Donald's own beloved Wales. Donald noted in 2006, "Merton's growing awareness of the Welsh element in his own inheritance."[15] And as Donald remarked somewhat poignantly at the round table conference discussion, "Well, we didn't do Wales then, but in some sense I've been doing Wales ever since."

The Shared Love of Poetry

Paul Pearson (Director of the Thomas Merton Center in Louisville, Kentucky) quotes a story that for him sums Donald up so well. When asked for his advice on what a speaker should bring to an audience Donald's immediate and simple advice was: "Give them poetry, poetry, poetry!"[16] Donald's

---

12. Allchin, "Can we do Wales then?" 2–10.

13. Merton, *Conjectures, 181.*

14. Merton, *Road to Joy, 62.*

15. Allchin, "Can we do Wales, then?" 5.

16. Pearson, "Donald Allchin and the Thomas Merton Society," 1.

love of poetry and perhaps especially Welsh poetry became something that could be shared with Merton.

Merton in essence was a poet. He wrote many poems and read other poets with an interest and an appetite that Donald undoubtedly appreciated. In commenting on Merton's interest in poets about whom they had corresponded Donald writes of Henry Vaughan, the Welsh author and metaphysical poet (1621–95), and writes that "however great his [Merton's] love for Traherne, in the end it was Henry Vaughan who most caught hold of him." In an interesting analysis of the influence of Henry Vaughan on Merton, Donald links some of the more famous lines from Merton about the dawn chorus with lines from a poem, "Rules and Lessons" by Henry Vaughan which tells us to be present with God at the moment of dawn when all creation comes to life.[17]

Donald quotes Henry Vaughan:

> Walk with thy fellow creatures: note the hush
> And whispers amongst them. There's not a spring
> Or leaf but hath his morning hymn; each bush
> And oak doth know I AM; canst thou not sing?
> Mornings are mysteries; the first world's youth,
> Man's resurrection, and the future's bud
> Shroud in their births; the crown of life, light, truth
> Is stil'd their star, the stone, and hidden food.

Merton's extract reads,

> The first chirps of the waking birds—le point vierge [the virgin point] of the dawn, a moment of awe and inexpressible innocence, when the father in silence opens their eyes and they speak to Him, wondering if it is time to "be"?[18]

Donald spoke of Merton's interest in Anglican writing, noting that Merton kept a copy of *Preces Privatae* by Lancelot Andrewes in the hermitage at Gethsemani, and how his journal entries on this book suggest that Andrewes helped Merton at times of darkness and testing and again at times of thanksgiving and fulfilment. Donald explores the inspiration that Andrewes' work gave to seventeenth-century poets, and thinks that "among the seventeenth century writers . . . perhaps the one whom Merton appreciated most was Thomas Traherne." While Merton did not write a

---

17. Allchin, "Foreword," 5–9.

18. Merton, *Turning Towards the World, 7.*

great deal about Traherne, Donald comments that "there is a page or two of luminous analysis in *Mystics and Zen Masters* when, significantly, he compares him with Julian of Norwich. He can hardly give him greater commendation than that!"[19] In the same letter to his New Zealand Aunt Kit, quoted above, Merton also adds, "Did you ever read Thomas Traherne? He is one of the very best and most delightful of Anglican writers."[20]

Their mutual interest in poetry was not limited to the seventeenth century.

> One subject we certainly began to explore was the 17th century Anglican poets. Vaughan and Traherne especially fascinated him but he was also interested in contemporary poetry from Britain. He was beginning to discover Edwin Muir—and Stevie Smith greatly attracted him. What about R. S. Thomas? He soon came over the horizon and then in the last two years, there was what for him was the great discovery of David Jones, a profoundly sacramental poet and painter, who awoke Merton's own deep sense of a Welsh family background.[21]

The Orthodox Connection

> I had not realised when I first met him how deeply he had been influenced by the eastern Orthodox tradition and in particular some of the outstanding theologians of the Russian emigration in Paris. Among them Paul Evdokimov and above all, Vladimir Lossky. Here with the Lossky family I was able to provide personal links and contacts, for while from the 1950s Merton had been much involved in their writings, I don't think he had had before any direct personal links into their circle. Through the Fellowship of St. Alban and St. Sergius, I had had a chance to know them well.[22]

In a presentation given on "Merton's Meeting with Russian Christianity" Donald writes that it became clear from certain lectures that Merton gave in the monastery in 1960, before meeting Donald, that the writings of Lossky amongst others had helped to shape Merton's basic idea of the nature of mystical theology itself. After the publication of Merton's journals

19. Allchin, "Merton and Traherne: The Two Thomases," 11.

20. Merton, *The Road to Joy*, 62.

21. Allchin, "Merton at Ninety," 3.

22. Ibid.

in the 1990s it became clearer to Donald how much Russian theology Merton was reading in the years 1957–62, and how much this was influencing him intellectually and emotionally. This discovery also reminded Donald of elements of the conversation during that first visit in 1963.

Donald notes that it could be suggested that Merton's friendship with Pasternak framed his sense of mission to the world of writers and intellectuals, but that Merton's interest in Russian Orthodoxy predated this correspondence. In a journal entry in 1957 Donald finds that Merton writes of Sergei Bulgakov and N. A. Berdyaev, "They are great men who will not admit the defeat of Christ who has conquered by his resurrection. In their pages . . . shines the light of the resurrection and theirs was a theology of triumph."[23]

Donald initially queries whether Merton has conflated these two theologians who have such manifest differences, but understands that Merton was "bearing witness to some of the thoughts which they shared, elements of their teaching which were to become more and more important to him in the development of his own thought in the years to come." It is Donald's intellectual capacity that allows him to appreciate the distillation of thought that Merton underwent in his absorption of these Russian writers. Donald is able to separate out three central aspects:

> First there is the cosmic vocation of humankind. . . . Secondly there is the vocation to a life of prayer, worship and contemplation itself. . . . Thirdly, the Holy Spirit is to be at work through our hands and through our tongues, spiritualizing the material world. All these are signs of our co-creation with the Holy Spirit the Creator of life . . . .[24]

Donald notes that Merton ranged widely over the literature available to him from the Russian community, and the writers on this subject, including Oliver Clement with whom Merton entered a correspondence. Clement's book is seen by Merton as a way through into an experience of the life and witness of Staretz Silouan, the Russian monk on Mount Athos. Merton had begun to identify with Silouan and recognised in his life a monastic experience very close to his own.

Donald writes that this discovery of Merton's

---

23. Merton, *A Search for Solitude*, 85.

24. Allchin, "Our Lives, A Powerful Pentecost: Merton's Meeting with Russian Christianity," from a talk given at Bellarmine College in 1997 and later published in *The Merton Annual* 11, 1998, 33–45.

brought us together in an unexpected way, for on my first visit to Mount Athos, in August 1955, landing at the Russian monastery . . . with a friend . . . one of the first things our guide did was to pick up a numbered skull and say "This is the skull of a monk who some of the Fathers thought was a saint," it was Staretz Silouan.[25]

Donald notes that Merton on September 11, 1960, was meditating deeply on the life and prayer of Staretz Silouan (St. Silouan of Athos), on the words spoken to him by the Lord, "keep your mind in hell and do not despair." He says, "I, for a long time thought that was the word of the Lord for the twentieth century. I now have the feeling that is the word of the Lord for our own troubled time in which Merton's voice needs to be heard more clearly than ever."[26]

Another connection for both of them was with Vladimir Lossky who wrote *The Mystical Theology of the Eastern Church*, known in French by Merton in 1950, but in December 1964, as more books became available, Merton notes in his journal that he is reading *La Vision de Dieu* a book that he greatly appreciated. Donald thinks that in some ways Lossky and Merton had much in common and that it would not have been just the contents of the book but also the spirit of it that would have appealed so much to him. He thought that reading Lossky released in Merton, "a kind of personal confession of faith which is at the same time an affirmation of the whole tradition which he received and which has become his life."[27]

It could be suggested that for both Donald and Merton the tradition and inheritance of the centuries of Eastern Orthodoxy was a life-giving experience and inspiration. In the 1996 conference round table discussion Donald adds that a year or two before Merton died he had received a prayer anthology from the Russian monastery of Valamo in Finland, *The Art of Prayer* [edited by Bishop Kallistos Ware], and that markings in the book suggested Merton was using it as a prayer book and as a meditation book.

> It is very striking, it is the passages from Simeon the New Theologian, it is the passages about the use of the Jesus Prayer which are underlined and emphasised. There are lots about how extremely

---

25. Allchin, "Our Lives, a Powerful Pentecost: Merton's Meeting with Russian Christianity," 7.

26. Allchin, *"Merton at Ninety,"* 4.

27. Allchin, "Our Lives, a Powerful Pentecost: Merton's Meeting with Russian Christianity," 9.

important in the last years of his life, that Eastern tradition of the Jesus Prayer was.

In December 1968 the earthly friendship between Merton and Donald ended. Reflecting on the news of Merton's death Donald said,

> I got a telegram at Pusey House in Oxford in December with this extraordinary thing that Merton had died. But I must say, my quite immediate reaction was, in a very mild and distant way, I suppose, what was evidently the immediate reaction of Jean Leclercq. People were really worried, when Jean Leclercq came back that afternoon, how he would respond to the news because, perhaps, he was the person there [in Bangkok] who knew Merton best. And, as you know, Jean Leclercq simply said, "Quelle joie!" "What joy!"[28]

Donald Allchin and the Thomas Merton Society

Many of us appreciated and knew Donald from his work with the Thomas Merton Society of Great Britain and Ireland. He was President of the TMS-GBI from its beginning in 1993 until his death, and yet he was so much more in being a friend and encourager to many of us associated with the Society, and others curious and interested in the works of Merton. As Pearson writes, Donald shared his enthusiasm for the life and thought of Thomas Merton, believing that Merton's message needed to be heard, shared, and celebrated and Donald took every opportunity that came his way to do this. So "Donald became the British spokesperson for all things Merton and over the years he gave freely and generously of his time and energy to speak of Merton at every opportunity."[29]

Donald was involved in an initial attempt to set up a Society in the UK in 1989 but it was not until 1993 at a conference to commemorate the twenty-fifth anniversary of Merton's death in December 1993 that the TMSGBI came into existence. In 1996 Donald became President of the Society, promoted the work and publications linked to the Society, attended the conferences and gave a presidential address at the residential conferences held every two years at Oakham School which Thomas Merton had attended.

28. Allchin, Roundtable Discussion.
29. Pearson, "Donald Allchin and the Thomas Merton Society," 2.

One of the things that Donald noted was the strongly international nature of Merton's vision and inspiration, and also the increasing relevance of some of his deepest insights to the contemporary spiritual, political, and cultural situation. Donald spoke movingly of his friendship and shared interests and brought Merton alive for those of us who only knew him through the printed word.

Reflections

At the sermon he preached at the Requiem Mass held for Donald in January 2011, Rowan Williams [then the Archbishop of Canterbury] said that,

> Perhaps one of the reasons that Donald found his pilgrimage had so much resonance with that of his friend Thomas Merton was that something of the same quality can be seen in Merton— a hospitable soul in which echoes are constantly evoked, images constantly generated again and again and again.[30]

This constant generation of images and ideas demonstrated the imaginative and productive qualities within both men. The mutuality would have meant that both were affected by their friendship in different ways. For Merton, Donald opened up further intellectual interest in Anglicanism and his personal interest Wales, and for Donald, Merton's experiential and unconventional style including psychological insights would have offered a freedom of expression, outside the usual, perhaps more English, constraints. Donald appreciated Merton's great gift for communicating and saw this as a way of expressing the particular experiences and dynamic and agonies of our contemporary world—and giving "words to experiences which people have which they find it difficult to name."[31]

Merton's pushing out towards other faiths helped Donald towards ecumenism, and expanded Donald's thinking on what this shared experience might mean in this country.

In 1969, the year after Merton's death, in a paper celebrating the life of his friend Thomas Merton, Donald wrote of Merton as a liberator, and it is hard not to see that as Donald's personal experience of the relationship,

> How much he was himself; how totally impossible to describe or define. He knew that each human person is unique and

30. Williams, "The Sermon Preached by the Archbishop of Canterbury," 4–6.
31. Kramer, "A Very Disciplined Person," 253.

incomparable. He knew too that each one mysteriously contains the whole universe. . . . He not only knew this, but he lived it, and for this reason to meet him, whether in person or in his writing, was liberating[;] . . . he set out at the beginning to liberate us from the illusions of the world.

In the same paper he returned to the theme of the Shakers, that subject of immediate connection in their first meeting and wrote about Merton's contemplation of the natural order,

. . . something of its original meaning of a loving regard for the mystery of things which discerns and liberates in them, the hidden flame of the divine word. It was thus that he saw the Shakers both in their life and in their work as authentic exponents of the contemplative way, "the Shaker cabinet maker enabling wood to respond to the 'call' to become a chest, a table, a chair, a desk." It was thus that he himself through the honesty and humility of his work was able to liberate something in those who came in touch with him, through his writings or in person, so that they too might respond to the call to become what God had meant them to be . . . .[32]

The suggestion in this chapter has been that for both men their friendship liberated aspects of their intellectual and emotional life. The obvious shared interests were at the surface level but underneath these interests there was a deeper spiritual connection, and an understanding of how the portal of the intellect leads in the context of the religious life to inner transformation. The joyful bond with the land of Wales, the sparse truths found in poetry, and, the spiritual insights from the Russian mystics all took both men beyond the time-bound encounters of meeting and correspondence. Both, energized by their friendship, were opened further to the creative energy of God.

32. Allchin, "A Liberator, a Reconciler," 2.

PART FOUR

Donald Allchin as Interpreter of Anglican Tradition and Theology

"Many of our current controversies in Christology seem to stem from an inadequate understanding of the doctrine of God, an understanding which does justice neither to his total transcendence nor to his total immanence. Corresponding to this inadequate vision of God there stands an equally inadequate vision of our human nature. We no longer see our humanity as created for union with God, capable of being made one with God, called to be the place of God's indwelling. Without the doctrine of our deification by grace the doctrine of the incarnation in the end loses its meaning and finality. For how can God enter into man unless man is made from the beginning to enter into God?"[33]

"It is furthermore Christian spirituality which is here under discussion, the Christian faith as it is actually lived and prayed, the life of God in the life of man, the life of man's spirit transformed and renewed in the coming of the Spirit of God."[34]

33. Allchin, *Participation in God: A Forgotten Strand in Anglican Tradition,* 5–6.
34. Allchin, *The World Is a Wedding,* 13.

CHAPTER 8

The Dialogue of the Spirit
Interpreting the Anglican Tradition

The Rev. Dr. Charles Miller
Team Rector of Abingdon-on-Thames in the Diocese of Oxford

Writing in the Introduction to his second book, *The Spirit and the Word*, Donald Allchin explained the purpose of his study as, in part, a response to reactions to late nineteenth- and early twentieth-century theologies which were "too ready to sacrifice the mysterious, living quality of Christian truth for the sake of clarity and definition."[1] A chief aspect of that reaction was what he described as "an impatience with the past." "Among Anglicans at the present time," he judged,

> there is a reluctance to look to tradition, the tradition of the Church, as providing an essential element in the answer to the problem. For the drily historical nature of a good deal of Anglican theological writing, which has tended to substitute the historical examination of the course of Christian teaching in the first four centuries, for a living reflection on the mystery of God's acts in creation and redemption, has itself led to a further reaction, an impatience with the past, which will write off the Church's history as something which no longer vitally concerns us.[2]

1. Allchin, *The Spirit and the Word*, 12.
2. Ibid.

In the studies which that slender volume contains Donald was working out what we might loosely call a theological epistemology, that is, an
understanding of how authentic theology—knowledge of God—is possible. Basic to his position is the view that "in Christ, past and present are
not divided."[3] We must remind ourselves of that epistemic benchmark if we
are to grasp the motivations behind his commitment to Christian Tradition generally, and to his own Anglican tradition. Donald's varied, life-long
explorations of the "Anglican" and broader English religious tradition were
motivated by the belief that aspects of that tradition "vitally concern" each
new generation as it seeks to live the life of its Lord.

In his treatment of the Anglican tradition Donald eschewed a survey
approach; he had no interest in broad descriptive presentations. Most of
his essays on the subject, spanning the sixteenth to the twentieth centuries,
focused on individual representatives of . . . of what? Donald's description
of them as *dramatis personae* offers an important clue.[4] Those whom he
presents to his readers are actors in a theo-drama, and the drama which
Donald decodes for the reader is the Spirit's taking the tradition's spokes-
men and women beyond "the orthodox expression" and fashioning their
minds in the "orthodox consciousness, which is deeper and larger than the
expression."[5]

That, in turn, helps us understand Donald's hermeneutical approach *viz-à-viz* "the Anglican tradition." This particular culturo-national
tradition of the Christian tradition—"a respectable suburb of the city of
God"[6]—finds validation in so far as it carries within it both an "orthodox
consciousness" and a properly proportioned orthodox content. The former
Donald would identify—and here he reveals strong Tractarian influence—
as "a primitive consciousness of organic participation in the risen life of
Christ."[7] The latter is an inter-connected "central knot of doctrines"[8] which
together form the bed-rock of the entire Christian experience, faith, and
hope: Trinity, Incarnation, and deification. Donald does not, therefore, ap-

---

3. Ibid.

4. He uses that phrase in Allchin, *The Joy of All Creation*, 212.

5. Allchin, *The Spirit and the Word*, 27. The expression is that of Fr. R. M. Benson, one
of the two subjects in Allchin, *The Spirit and the Word*.

6. He quotes Evelyn Underhill in Allchin, *The Kingdom of Love & Knowledge*, 188.

7. Allchin, *The Spirit and the Word*, "The Fathers, Our Contemporaries," 26, quoting
C. C. J. Webb in *The Religious Thought of the Oxford Movement*.

8. Allchin, "From Ken to Heber," in *The Joy of All Creation*, 135.

proach the Anglican tradition from a disinterested or neutral point of view. The validity of the tradition is under scrutiny from a doctrinal perspective which is not particular to the Church of England or Anglicanism, and to which, by its own founding vision, that tradition is accountable. This interpretive project, extending throughout his life, was a search for the orthodox consciousness and orthodox content in "true proportion"[9] within a tradition notoriously diverse historically, and tragically unaware of its own theological inheritance.

We should ask, then, how Donald was led to this posture and "method" in interpreting his tradition. Two key influences seem to me to have been at work in forming him in this way. The first was Russian Orthodox theologian George Florovsky, from whom Donald adopted the idea of *ecumenicity in space and time*. Such a two-dimensional ecumenicity lay at the foundation of Donald's entire theological programme from *The Spirit and the Word* onward. But Donald felt free, even obliged, to apply that bi-focal ecumenicity to his own tradition under the complementary inspiration of Florovsky's slightly younger English contemporary and acquaintance, Michael Ramsey.[10] In his ground-breaking book, *The Gospel and the Catholic Church*, Ramsey had neatly put aside any and all Anglican triumphalism, and argued that the vindication of "*Ecclesia Anglicana*" lay precisely in its "credentials" of "tension," "travail," and, most importantly, "*incompleteness*."[11] There lay the permission, we might say, for Donald's exploration and interpretation of the Anglican tradition: a tradition that, because of its incompleteness, stood in need of a fuller awareness and embrace of the "orthodox consciousness" and the orthodox content to which its title documents and its irreducible ecclesial ministries and structures pointed.

Such a project could have been pursued with an interest only in the "drily historical" origins and evolution of ideas. But Donald's deep and searching theological and spiritual sensibilities did not permit that. However much his works betray hesitation and criticism of many contemporary trends—remember that *The Spirit and the Word* appeared the same year as John Robinson's *Honest to God*[12]—Donald always brought the witnesses

---

9. He employs that phrase in his treatment of Frank and Thorndike in Allchin, *The Joy of All Creation*, 89.

10. On the link see Chadwick, *Michael Ramsey: A Life*, 64–67.

11. Ramsey, *The Gospel and the Catholic Church*, 220; italics mine.

12. Donald dated the "Foreword" to *The Spirit and the Word* March, 1963, the very

of the past into direct dialogue with the circumstances of the present and the opportunities of the future, in-as-much as the past, present, and future are the Spirit's sphere. This chapter's title phrase "dialogue of the Spirit" is meant to underline just that, an ecumenicity in time enriching ecumenicity in space, since, as Donald so firmly believed, "in Christ, past and present are not divided."[13] So, as an interpreter of the Anglican tradition Donald was, of course, dealing with the past; but he and his readers shall always be concerned with the past, he insists, as that past "makes itself known to us in the present, and always as it makes it possible for us to live creatively toward the future."[14]

The Possibility of "Orthodoxy": From Allchin's *The Spirit and the Word*

In our days, as then, it is often asked whether there can be such a thing as orthodoxy, a true belief in, a true worship of, God, if we set aside the infallibilisms of Pope or Bible. As I shall have occasion to use the term more than once, I must explain a little what I mean by this word "infallibilism." I do not imply by it a necessary criticism of those who centre Christian authority either in the Bible or the Papacy, still less of those who take the authority of the Church and Bible seriously. I have in mind rather an attitude unfortunately too common in this country, which in the case of the Bible will tend to think in terms of the verbal inspiration of every sentence, in the case of Rome of extending the concept of infallibility to cover every encyclical. In both cases, the means by which we hear God's authoritative voice comes to be thought of as itself the authority. It is an attitude which refuses to recognize the many uncertainties which surround the great foundation certainties of the faith, and is too ready to sacrifice the mysteriously, living quality of Christian truth for the sake of clarity and definition . . . .

During the nineteenth and the earlier part of the present century, this attitude was particularly in evidence in the victorious ultra-montane party among English Roman Catholics. In fact it has come to be an integral part of the impression made by Roman Catholicism in this country, a feature attracting some and

month SCM Press published *Honest to God.*

13. Allchin, *The Spirit and the Word,* 12.

14. In the chapter "The Presence of the Past" in Allchin, *The Living Presence of the Past,* 18.

repelling others. How far it is from representing the main tradition of theology within the Roman Catholic Church can be seen, in the whole movement of theological self-criticism and renewal at work in the present Council, and also by the fact that it was never altogether typical of the greatest English Roman Catholic theologian of the nineteenth century, John Henry Newman, a man as widely appreciated abroad as he is ignored in his own country. In more recent years its most striking manifestation has been in the powerful revival of Conservative Evangelicalism within the Church of England, and to a lesser extent in the Free Churches. In both cases a true and proper respect for the givenness of revelation and the authority which rightly belongs to Bible and Tradition becomes distorted by a failure to pass beyond all manifestations of the divine will, to God himself, alone the seat of absolute and infallible authority. For it is one of the characteristics of orthodoxy that, while paying attention to the forms of the Divine revelation, its manifestation in thought and act, it always sees the forms and vehicles of grace, in relation to that ineffable glory from which alone they draw their meaning . . . .

This orthodoxy is not an intellectual system invented by men. It is the self-revelation of the Father in his Son Jesus Christ through the work of the Holy Spirit, present amidst the sons of men, and it calls forth in response the amazed adoration and assent not only of the human heart and will, but also of the human mind. And here is the work of the theologian, to be drawn into this revealed glory, to reflect upon the mystery of the Spirit and the Word living and at work in the one Catholic Church.[15]

The Anglican Position: From Allchin, *The Spirit and the Word*

But for the present our main concern is with the Anglican position. How far, if at all, is it significantly different from that of the other Reformation confessions? Article VI clearly states "the sufficiency of the Holy Scriptures for salvation," though it is worth noticing the negative terms in which it is couched, "Holy Scripture containeth all things necessary to salvation: so that whatsoever is not read therein, nor may be proved thereby, is not to be required of any man, that it should be believed as an article of Faith," which is far from saying that all that is contained in them is to be believed as an article of Faith, and which does not deny that there may be

15. Allchin, *The Spirit and the Word,* 10–13

things in the Church's life and faith, which though not derived directly from Scripture, and therefore not *de fide*, are yet proper parts of its organic development. It was on this point that much of the controversy between Anglican and Puritan turned in the hundred years after the Reformation. Indeed, Article XX speaks of the authority of the Church "in matters of Faith," so it be not contrary "to God's Word written," and Article VIII declares that the three Creeds "ought thoroughly to be received and believed." These declarations ought surely to be read in conjunction with the clause in the act of Uniformity which speaks of the authority of the first four General Councils, and with the article agreed upon in the Convocation of 1571 where it is decided that preachers "shall take heed that they teach nothing in their preaching, which they would have the people religiously observe and believe, but that which is agreeable to the doctrine of the Old Testament and the New, and that which the Catholic Fathers and ancient Bishops have gathered out of that same doctrine. . . ."

Dean Church, in a remarkable passage of his study of Lancelot Andrewes, says of the Anglican writers of this time that in turning from the bitter polemics of their own period, ". . . they found what they wanted in the language, the ideas, the tone and tempo of the best early Christian literature. That turned their thoughts from words to a Person. It raised them from the disputes of local cliques to the ideas which have made the Universal Church. It recalled them from arguments that revolved around a certain number of traditional formulae about justification, free-will and faith, to a truer and worthier idea both of man and of God, to the overwhelming revelation of the Word Incarnate, and the result of it on the moral standard and behaviour of real living men. It led them from a theology which ended in cross-grained and perverse conscientiousness, to a theology which ended in adoration, self-surrender and blessing."[16]

We should give particular attention to the statement that their thoughts turned "from words to a Person."[17]

16. Church, *Pascal and Other Sermons*, 72–73.

17. Allchin, *The Spirit and the Word*, 20–22.

The Gradual Emergence of the Anglican Theological Point of View: From Allchin, *The Kingdom of Love and Knowledge*

If we are looking for the key concepts in Hooker's theological thought, we shall find them in terms such as mutual participation and conjunction, co-inherence and perichoresis. God is in Christ; Christ is in us; we are in him.

"Life, as all other gifts and benefits, groweth originally from the Father and cometh not to us but by the Son, nor by the Son to any of us in particular but through the Spirit. For this cause the Apostle writeth to the church of Corinth, 'The grace of our Lord Jesus Christ, and the love of God, and the fellowship of the Holy Ghost.' Which three Saint Peter comprehendeth in one, 'The participation of the divine Nature' . . . ."

It is true that Hooker here avoids the explicit language of *theosis*, (or deification) but it does not escape our attention that when he speaks of Christ "making us such as he himself is" he affirms the underlying mystery which the word expresses . . . .

The balance and proportion which mark the work of Richard Hooker are to be found in a different form in the writings of his younger contemporary, Bishop Lancelot Andrewes. In his case the heart of his theology is to be found not in his controversial writings, the argument with Bellarmine for instance, but in the great series of sermons preached at Christmas, Easter and Whitsun before the royal court in London, where year by year he expounded the mysteries of Christ's birth, death and resurrection and the coming of the Spirit, with amazing erudition and skill. Here we find the depth and power of his exposition of the Church's faith in Father, Son and Holy Spirit, a faith enriched and enlivened by the wealth of his biblical and patristic knowledge. I intend to examine simply one strand of this fabric, his exposition of the doctrine of *theosis* as the consequence and completion of the doctrine of the Incarnation. I quote from a sermon for Pentecost in which he compares the work of Christ with the work of the Holy Spirit:

"These, if we should compare them, it would not be easy to determine, whether is greater of these two: (1) That of the Prophet, *Filius datus est nobis*; or (2) that of the Apostle, *Spiritus datus est nobis*; the ascending of our flesh, or the descending of His Spirit; *incarnatio Dei*, or *inspiratio hominis*; the mystery of his incarnation, or the mystery of our inspiration. For mysteries they are both, and 'great mysteries of godliness' both; and in both of them 'God is manifested in the flesh.' In the former by the union of His

Son; in the latter by the communion of his blessed Spirit. But we will not compare them, they are both above all comparison. Yet this we may safely say of them: without either of them we are not complete, we have not our accomplishment; but by both of them we have, and that fully, even by this day's royal exchange. Whereby, as before he of ours, so now we of his are made partakers. He clothed with our flesh, and we invested with his Spirit. The great promise of the Old Testament accomplished, that he partake our human nature; and the great and precious promise of the New, that we should be *consortes divinae naturae,* 'partake his divine nature,' both are this day accomplished . . ."[18]

There is in Lancelot Andrewes none of that reticence towards the doctrine of *theosis* which is to be found in many Western theologians.[19]

Mary: Where God Is To Be Found: From Allchin, *The Joy of All Creation*

But if Mary is never to be confused with God, always to be seen as one who draws all her grace and glory from God, she is nevertheless one who is highly, uniquely favoured, one who is, in a certain sense, the place where God is to be found, one whose child-bearing stands at the very centre of the Church's life. This point is brought out very vividly in a passage from one of the sermons for Epiphany, where Frank is commenting on the coming of the Magi, who enter the house and see the young child with Mary his mother and fall down and worship him.

"I do not wonder interpreters make this house the church of God. It is the gate and court of heaven, now Christ is here; angels sing round about it; all holiness is in it, now Christ is in it; here all creatures, reasonable and unreasonable, come to pay their homage to their Creator; hither they come even from the ends of the earth, to their devotions; a 'house of prayer' it is 'for all people,' Gentiles and all; hither they come to worship, hither they come to pay their offerings and their vows; here is the shrine and altar, the glorious Virgin's lap, where the Saviour of the world is laid to be adored and worshipped; here stands the star for tapers to give light; and

---

18. Andrewes, *Complete Works*, 1841–54, Vol. III, 108–9.

19. "Trinity and Incarnation in Anglican Tradition" in Allchin, *The Kingdom of Love & Knowledge*, 96–99.

here the wise men this day become the priests—worship and offer, present prayers and praises, for themselves and the whole world besides, all people of the world, high and low, learned and ignorant, represented by them."[20]

It is a remarkable passage. In the first place it shows his strong sense of the liturgical year. In the worship of the Church the mystery commemorated becomes a present reality. God is with us, in our midst. The Church's liturgy involves much more than a simple remembering of the past. Then, further, we see that his presence and manifestation in the world acts as a power for reintegration, drawing together all people, all creation around this centre of light. But Mary's part is not less striking for she also is at its centre; not herself the object of worship and adoration, but the altar, the shrine, the holy place where God is to be found.[21]

Theology as Life and Ascent in Love and Knowledge: From Allchin, *The Joy of All Creation*

Towards the end of the 1650s when he was living in Northern Ireland, he could write to a friend of "the experimental secret way" of progress and religion.

"My retirement in this solitary place hath been, I hope, of some advantage to me as to this state of religion, in which I am yet but a novice. . . . I beg of you to assist me with your prayers, and to obtain of God for me that I may arrive at that height of love and union with God which is given to all those souls who are very dear to God."[22]

We sense something of the same quality in the notable sermon which Taylor preached at Trinity College Dublin in the following decade on the relation between life and doctrine. The whole sermon is an urgent plea for the putting aside of angry polemic and controversy, for a willingness to listen and understand, for a recognition that doctrine is to issue in life and to issue from life.

"The way to judge of religion is by doing of our duty; and theology is rather a divine life than a divine knowledge. In heaven indeed we shall first see and then love; but here on earth we must

20. Frank, *Sermons*, Library of Anglo-Catholic Theology, vol. ii, 48–49.

21. "'The Virgin Mother, the Eternal Son,' Mark Frank and Herbert Thorndike," in Allchin, *The Joy of All Creation*, 84–85.

22. Quoted in Cropper, *Flame Touches Flame*, 143.

first love, and love will open our eyes as well as our hearts and we shall then see and then shall perceive and understand"[23]. . .

Behind and through such hints and affirmations we can perceive something of great significance, a sense of the human calling to union with God; a profound conviction about the meaning of a life wholly given to the inner work of prayer; some intuition, some glimpse of the meaning of the contemplative life, still vividly present in the seventeenth century, despite the absence of monastic communities. It gives us an insight into the quality of seventeenth-century religion and the depth of prayer which lies behind Taylor's liturgical interests and projects. Human life can expand and unfold, can grow and mature towards God inwardly as well as outwardly. There is an inner journey, as well as an outer one, with its own dangers and temptations. "Those graces which walk in a veil and silence"—the phrase is one which justifies Taylor's older reputation as a stylist—"make great ascents to God."[24]

How a Tradition Expands: From Allchin, *The Joy of All Creation*

None of the leaders of the Oxford Movement was more consistently faithful to the post-Reformation tradition of the Church of England than John Keble. "What my father taught me" was his constant point of reference. For him the seventeenth-century tradition was not something to be laboriously unearthed from the past, it was something, which at least in principle, he knew as a living reality which he had received in his childhood, in observing the faith and practice of the older John Keble. . . . Keble refers to having learnt from his earliest years, through daily recitation of the Magnificat at Evensong, to pray with Mary and to be aware that she and all the saints were near . . . .

Keble was well aware that, almost without exception, the seventeenth-century theologians had discountenanced any direct address to the Blessed Virgin or to the saints as liable to lead to dangerous consequences and especially to an equation of the creature with the Creator. To ask God to hear the prayers of the saints on our behalf, as is done in the Canon of the Roman Mass, is one thing, and some of the early Anglicans maintained—Richard Field and Herbert Thorndike, for instance—that it is not only

23. Jeremy Taylor, *Selected Works*, 361.

24. "'The Virgin Mother, the Eternal Son': Mark Frank and Herbert Thorndike," in Allchin, *The Joy of All Creation*, 60–61.

permissible but admirable to do so. To ask the saints directly for their intercession is something else. George Herbert had written a poem explicitly on this question, in which he says that he would have gladly turned to Mary for assistance, had he had any written warrant from the Lord for doing so. But not having such authority, he dare not go beyond what Scripture seems to prescribe. And here is Keble [in his poem "Mother out of sight"] asserting that this practice, which nearly all Anglicans since the Reformation had abandoned, is one which has the support of "all saints in all lands." He is being, in fact, almost as provocative as W. G. Ward, or those of Newman's younger and more enthusiastic disciples, who were asserting clearly that the norms of catholicity were not to be found in the Church of England at all, but elsewhere in Catholic Christendom.

What had happened to bring about this firm conviction in a man who did not commit himself to changes without careful thought? The factors involved become clear in the third of the stanzas quoted. There may be dangers in an exaggerated cult of Mary and the saints, but they are not very menacing for nineteenth-century Englishmen. On the other hand, there are dangers which had already been seen in embryo in the seventeenth century—we recall Mark Frank speaking of "our Lord being wounded through our Lady's side"—dangers which have now grown to monstrous proportions. There is the possibility of a complete rejection of the religion of the incarnation, a rejection which will sometimes be explicit and total, sometimes more gradual and insidious, beginning with a rejection of those doctrines and practices which, as we have seen, the Tractarians believed to be bound up inseparably with a right faith in God the Word's taking our human nature. In face of these dangers, it is only through an outspoken and explicit acknowledgement of Mary's part in the work of redemption, that we can hope to maintain the true proportions and the fullness of the faith. In face of a wholly changed situation, the reserve of the seventeenth-century Anglicanism no longer has the meaning it once had. It should be abandoned.[25]

25. "John Keble and B. F. Westcott," in Allchin, *The Joy of All Creation,* 156–57.

A Tradition of Fullness and Joy: From Allchin, *Participation in God*

From this reappropriation of the patristic understanding of the indwelling of God in man there flow many consequences, practical and theoretical, for our understanding of our human nature and of our calling towards both God and our fellow-man. There is in man an openness towards self-transcendence both in love and in knowledge which takes many forms. There is, for instance, a new awareness of the fact that while God's love for each one is personal and unique, a thing on which the Evangelicals had greatly insisted, it is never merely individual as opposed to personal.

. . . One of the last letters he wrote, less than a month before his death in 1882, is addressed to her [Sister Clara (Clarissa Powell)]. Its words reveal something of the human content of this theological vision of our capacity for love, human and divine, a vision which had been worked out in long years of prayer and devotion, of silence and spiritual friendship.

Pusey speaks in this letter of love as "a wonderful thing," nothing less than "a spark out of the boundless, shoreless ocean of His Fire of Love," and he goes on:

"You, I hope, are ripening continually. God ripen you more and more. Each day is a day of growth. God says to you 'Open thy mouth and I will fill it.' 'Only long. He does not want our words. The parched soil by its cracks, opens itself for the rain from heaven, and invites it. The parched soul cries out to the living God. Oh then long and long and long, and God will fill thee. More love, more love, more love."[26]

The last words of the letter—its writer was eighty-two—speak eloquently of the sense of *epektasis*, that eager looking forward, that constant growth of the human person into the fullness of God, that continual journey further on into the boundless, shoreless ocean of God's love. They open up the way ahead. The teaching about deification shows itself to be anything but theoretical. It is lived and experienced through the self-surrender and the aspiration of a life-time.[27]

---

26. The letter in [sic] in Liddon, *Life of E. B. Pusey*, vol. IV (1898), 376, though with no indication of who it was sent to. See also Cobb, "Dr Pusey and Sister Clara" and also Williams, *Lydia Priscilla Sellon*, 2nd ed., 1965.

27. "A Life which is Both His and Theirs: E. B. Pusey and the Oxford Movement," in Allchin, *Participation in God*, 58–60.

Tradition: Past, Present, and Future: From Allchin *The Living Presence of the Past*

Running throughout this book there have been references to the work of T. S. Eliot, in particular to two of his critical essays and to some of the outstanding passages of *Four Quartets*. In this chapter we shall listen once more to Eliot's words . . . .

From the opening lines of *Burnt Norton* to the concluding section of *Little Gidding*, the theme of time present and time past, their relationship and meaning, is never far from the surface in the *Four Quartets*. As we have already seen, *Burnt Norton* begins with the words,

"Time present and time past
Are both present in time future . . ." (I, 1–2)[28]

It is a tentative statement, a statement which captures the mood of this whole poem, elusive, shining, hinting at meanings not yet articulated. But some things are already clear. Life when it is confined to the dimensions of past and present, to a totally linear view of time becomes futility, "a twittering world." And this is very much the condition of our civilization, as we hear in *The Dry Salvages*.

"When there is distress of nations and perplexity
Whether on the shores of Asia, or on the Edgware Road.
Men's curiosity searches past and future
And clings to that dimension . . ." (V, 197–200)

This condition is linked inescapably with the failure of our society to confront the fact of death, the moment when for the individual time comes to an end. Our inability to prepare for death, our failure to realize the importance of this moment in the life of man, our unwillingness even to look at the body after death, an object of sometimes startling beauty, are all signs and symptoms of a disquieting failure on the part of our civilization. Earlier societies, whatever their own weaknesses and limitations may have been, had their rituals for meeting this moment of crisis. We seem helpless before it. The threat of death and meaninglessness, so powerfully felt in Eliot's earlier poetry, is still strongly present in the work of his maturity. It is part of its greatness that it confronts the matter so directly. How is death to be overcome? Where is meaning to be found? Meaning is found, or better, given at moments which seem to be outside time, and which we may at

---

28. For the quotations from the *Four Quartets*, owing to the variety of editions, I have simply given references to the sections and line numbers in the various poems.

first be tempted to think are without relation to time. But, in fact, it is at such moments, "At the still point of the turning world," that we find that "past and future are gathered." And in the course of time as the timeless moments are recalled, we find that it is "only through time that time is conquered." Time and eternity are more closely inter-related than we thought. They can lead us in a move-ment toward meaning . . . .[29]

Conclusion from Charles Miller

"The Dialogue of the Spirit: Interpreting the Anglican Tradition"

This selection of excerpts from the writings of A. M. Allchin, beginning with his early published works and continuing through those of the 1980s, seeks to illustrate two formative influences on the development and content of Allchin's theology. On the one hand, Allchin's understanding of the An-glican tradition was shaped by the pioneering study of A. M. Ramsey's *The Gospel and the Catholic Church* and his application of the kenotic principle to the future of Anglicanism. As a complement, and as a tool in opening up the fabric of Anglicanism to the full potentials of its inheritance, Orthodox theologian George Florovsky's two-dimensional concept of ecumenic-ity—in space and through time—is paradigmatic for Allchin. The selection from Allchin's writings on selected English theologians illustrates his un-derstanding of those two perspectives as ways by which the Spirit enlivens latent aspects of the Anglican tradition in the service of a fuller catholicity, a "dialogue of the Spirit."

---

29. "The Decent into Hell" in Allchin, *The Living Presence of the Past,* 108–9.

CHAPTER 9

Participation in God

Donald Allchin's Understanding of the Mystery of the Life of God in Humankind

David G. R. Keller

I met Donald Allchin for the first time through his writing. *Participation in God: A Forgotten Strand in Anglican Tradition*[1] transformed my understanding of the fundamental core of Christian life. Following a tradition that begins in the New Testament, Donald asserts that human beings are called to participate in the very nature of God. He demonstrates that *theosis* (deification), as audacious as it seems, is nothing new. It was the passionate desire of Jesus of Nazareth for every person. It was a center of early Christian preaching, has been the heart of the spiritual life of Eastern Orthodox Christians, and was a major influence in the formation of my own Anglican spiritual tradition. "The central affirmation of the Christian faith declares that God himself has entered into our human situation and in doing so has totally transformed it."[2] Simple as it may seem, this gave me a new way of seeing the life, teaching, death, and resurrection of Jesus. In Donald's words, "Such a statement necessarily implies that the Christian gospel cannot be simply fitted into the world as it now is. It

1. Allchin, *Participation in God*.
2. Ibid., 1.

involves its radical transformation. It means a revolution not only in our idea of God but also in our idea of humankind and of the world in which we live."[3] Donald's insights placed the priorities of my Christian path beyond "right belief" and "right behavior," although both are important. He declared that human transformation, the kind that took place in Jesus through his relationship with his Abba, is the simple and profound center of Christian life. This great truth lies at the heart of Donald Allchin's wisdom and witness. It flows through his personal life, his scholarship, his pastoral concerns, and his witness to life in Jesus Christ.

My second introduction to Donald was through essays in an earlier book, *The World is a Wedding: Essays in Christian Spirituality*.[4] I could not resist the title. It seemed so whimsical and full of delight. But once into the essays I realized that this was no simplistic or superficial treatment of spirituality. It began with an aspect of life most modern people do not want to experience: mystery. We prefer things we can define and control. Life seems easier or more predictable that way. But Donald's introduction makes it clear that if we want to experience God and authentic human life we must "do justice to the unfathomable mystery of human life, particularly when it is lived in a growing realization of the presence and power of God."[5] Human life is lived in a dialog between the "initiative of God and the response of human beings."[6] The Christian form of this dialog rests on the Scriptures and traditions of the Christian community; it cannot be understood from the outside. One must be part of the dialog to discern what is taking place. The "wedding" cannot be experienced by sitting on a wall and watching the festivities! Each person must help with preparations, contribute to the feast, join in the dance, celebrate the love of the bride and groom, and become part of the wedding. Donald's essays explore the unique and powerful aspects of the Christian understanding of the world, human life, God's presence in life, and the disciplines and sacraments that sustain the Christian community and our individual and corporate relationships with God and each other. Tradition provides identity and roots but it is not an end in itself because "the attitude which is asked of us is not one of blind and slavish submission; it is one of respect and diffidence before the accumulated experience of the centuries, a willingness to let our eyes be opened to

3. Ibid., 1.

4. Allchin, *The World is a Wedding*.

5. Ibid., 13.

6. Ibid., 15.

new and disturbing realities."[7] Donald declares that the significance of the "wedding" is not perceived simply through our present experience, for we will not discern the wedding's integrity and richness without the roots and identity of tradition. When we are firmly rooted in whom we are and called to become, we can risk the boldness of venturing into our unknown future. The essays in *The World is a Wedding* give a description of the process of human transformation within the Christian tradition. They do not give a "how-to" approach, but provide a description of the life of a two-thousand year old community and how it has learned to remain in dialog with God, each other, and the world.

My third introduction to Donald Allchin took place a year after reading *Participation in God*. I was on sabbatical at St. Deiniol's Residential Library (now Gladstone's Library) in Hawarden, North Wales. I mentioned how much Donald's book meant to me to the Librarian, Patricia Williams, and she said, "Why don't you go and see him. He lives just an hour away in Bangor." I called Donald and he immediately agreed to see me and gave directions from the Bangor train station to his home. The next day I took the train to Bangor and arrived in so much rain and wind that I got lost walking to his home and in the process soaked to the skin. When I finally found his house I knocked and when he opened the door and looked at me he said, "Oh, you must be one of the hermit Seiriol's ancient monks just come from Ynys Seiriol in a coracle! I've been expecting you." He led me in, gave me dry clothes, some hot tea, and a sandwich. Soon we were in animated conversation about *theosis*, Celtic spirituality, Welsh poetry, and the integrity of ancient holy sites. Three hours were gone in a flash and a twenty-two year friendship had begun.

7. Ibid., 14–15.

David Keller and Donald Allchin in Donald's study in Bangor.
Photo courtesy of Emily Wilmer."

In twenty-two years I learned that to spend time with Donald Allchin is to catch a glimpse of the boundless grandeur of life proclaimed in the one-hundred-fiftieth psalm. Although he is a scholar, respected teacher, storyteller, literary critic, and prolific author he makes no effort to define the glory and mystery of God whose essence is unknowable and yet is the source and sustenance of all creation and each human life. Donald places you in the midst of the "wedding" and lets you discover God's presence for yourself. He lures you in with a taste of poetry, a commentary on an ancient document, a theological conversation during a good meal, a visit to a holy well, a tale about a Welsh saint, an opportunity to meet and listen to the personal agony of a friend who is isolated and mistreated by his peers because he is gay, or by listening to the unsentimental images in the mystical hymns of an eighteenth-century rural Welsh woman whose unremarkable, yet deeply prayerful life bore witness to the world's wedding. Donald's attitude and enthusiasm about life is his threshold into the wedding and there he becomes aware of both the immanent presence and untamable mystery of God's relationship with human beings. This is the source of his delight in life and the energy with which he writes about Christian spiritual theology in such a variety of traditions and experience. Although thoroughly Anglican, he has pioneered substantive dialogue and shared experience with Eastern Orthodox theologians through his friendships with Vladimir Lossky, Nicholas Lossky, Dumitru Staniloae, and Kallistos Ware.

Donald Allchin commenting on the life of St. Seiriol at St. Seiriol's Well and hermitage at Penmon, Angelsey, North Wales. Photo courtesy of David Keller.

At the same time, Donald's abilities as a theologian, professor, and writer are blended with his genuine compassion for and enjoyment of friends and strangers alike.

**Donald Allchin and Emily Wilmer during a visit in Donald's flat in Bangor.
Photo courtesy of David Keller.**

Above all Donald was a pastor whose pastoral charism was empowered by his life of prayer and experience of God. He was guide and mentor to students (some of whom are now professors, bishops, and archbishops), a canon at Canterbury Cathedral, and a visitor, pastor, and confessor to communities of female contemplative religious communities. To say all this is not to infer that Donald was followed everywhere by a "romantic halo." He was a hard working, disciplined scholar yet acquainted with life's unresolved pains and uncertainties. He was an ordinary man who appreciated the little things in life. Donald did not stand out in a crowd, yet he was accessible to anyone, whether Oxford scholar or neighbor just down the street in Bangor. More than once I saw him take the same personal investment in the needs of a neighbor as he relished the latest tome of a fellow theologian.

When I read *Praise Above All: Discovering the Poetic Welsh Tradition*[8] I realized that Donald was aware of what we know about God from God's presence in life. Donald experienced and celebrated life's blessings. At the

---

8. Allchin, *Praise Above All.*

same time he acknowledged and did not turn from the unknowable aspects of God and the darker side of life. Speaking of experience of God he says,

> There is a way of negation of images which is a necessary complement and corrective to the way of affirmation, a way of negation which in the end goes even further. Unless we remember that the God to whom all names apply is also the god who is utterly beyond all names, *innominabile* as well as *omninonimabile,* the words which we use about him will tend to become too definitive and literally understood. There is a danger that we shall become too comfortable in our affirmation of God's glory seen in the face of his creation, that we shall take ourselves and our words too seriously, too literally, and lose sight of the immeasurable inadequacy of every part of the created universe to represent fully the infinity of the Creator. Then our words and concepts will become solid objects in themselves, idols which imprison us, rather than windows or doorways which open out a way for us beyond all words and images into the silence, the mystery, the infinity, the nothing of the divine being. For God is indeed *no thing* that we could comprehend or say in any final or definitive way.[9]

Reflecting on the poems of the Welsh poets Saunders Lewis and Morgan Llywd that demonstrate this "unknowing" about God and life, Donald recognizes that "We have to go to God through the discipline of silence and the discipleship of prayer."[10] And this experience

> . . . of silence and darkness in prayer is itself a kind of death, a dying to our own light, our own life, our own understanding. . . . The glory which the Christian poet seeks to embody and declare is the paradoxical glory revealed in its fullness in the self-giving of the cross. The life and love which he celebrates is a mystery which is wholly gift, and never wholly our possession. As the ninth century [Welsh] master declares of God's glories, "no words can contain them, no letters can express them."[11]

9. Ibid., 158–59.

10. Ibid., 160–61.

11. Ibid., 161.

Theosis (Deification)

The following excerpts from *Participation in God* describe Donald Allchin's understanding of the New Testament's witness to the presence of God in humankind mirrored and summarized in a bold statement in the second letter of Peter.

> His divine power has given us everything needed for life and god-liness, through the knowledge of him who called us by his own glory and goodness. Thus he has given us, through these things, his precious and very great promises, so that through them you may escape from the corruption that is in the world because of lust, and may become participants of the divine nature.[12]

Theosis is a Fundamental Part of Christian Experience: From *Participation in God*[13]

> It is the contention of this book that the doctrine of our deifica-tion, our becoming partakers of the divine nature by God's grace, is inseparably and necessarily bound up with the other two doc-trines which stand at the heart of classical Christian faith and life, the doctrine of God as Trinity, and the doctrine of the incarna-tion of God the Word. All three doctrines belong together, and it may be our neglect of the one which has made us uncertain about the others. It is very striking that when the fathers of the Church, Athanasius, Gregory of Nazianzen or Cyril of Alexandria, for instance, wish to prove the divinity of the Holy Spirit, they turn at once to the fact that the Spirit makes us truly sharers in God's nature, makes us sons in the Son, temples of God. We know that the Spirit is God because he makes us participant in God. There is an immediate appeal to experience. The doctrine of God as Trinity is intended to safeguard both the transcendence of God and his immanence. God who is utterly beyond his creation yet comes to be present at the heart of his creation comes to identify himself with his creation in order to lift it up into union with himself. Thus union, established once for all in the person of Christ, is constantly renewed in varying ways in the coming of the Spirit.

12. 2 Pet 1:3–4.

13. Allchin, *Participation in God,* 5–6.

Many of our current controversies in Christology seem to stem from an inadequate understanding of the doctrine of God, an understanding which does justice neither to his total transcendence nor to his total immanence. Corresponding to this inadequate vision of God there stands an equally inadequate vision of our human nature. We no longer see our humanity as created for union with God, capable of being made one with God, called to be the place of God's indwelling. Without the doctrine of our deification by grace the doctrine of the incarnation in the end loses its meaning and finality. For how can God enter into man unless man is made from the beginning to enter into God?

It is true that the explicit affirmation that we are partakers of the divine nature occurs only once in the New Testament (2 Pet. 1:4). But the Pauline teaching about our incorporation into Christ through the work of the Holy Spirit, and the Johannine teaching about God's dwelling in us and we in him, both affirm that the Christian "is taken into a relation of unlimited intimacy with God."[14] Throughout the New Testament a co-inherence of human and divine is implied, a relationship of union and communion which overthrows our customary ways of thinking both of God and humankind, and opens the way towards the wonder of our adoption into the circulation of the divine life. This faith and experience is not something peripheral to the New Testament writings. It is at their heart.

It is similarly at the heart of the faith of the Church both in East and West for at least the first millennium of the Christian era. In the West we might think of a simple expression in the prayer which accompanies the mingling of the water and the wine at the Eucharist, in which we pray that as God became partaker of our human nature so we may become partakers of his divine nature. In the East this doctrine has remained more clearly at the centre of the Church's teaching. Indeed many would regard it as one of the distinguishing marks of Eastern Orthodoxy. As John Meyendorff points out in his classic study of Byzantine theology, it has many consequences for our understanding both of human and divine nature: "Man, while certainly a creature and, as such, external to God, is defined in his very *nature* as being fully himself only when he is in *communion* with God." To become fully human, to realize our human potential, we need to enter into communion with our Creator. We can become ourselves only by transcending ourselves. He that will find his life must lose it. There is nothing static about

14. See the article by R. D. Williams, "Deification," in *A Dictionary of Christian Spirituality*, edited by G. S. Wakefield. London, 1983.

this communion. It is the beginning of the process which will lead us through death into life, life in this world and life in the world beyond this one, "an eternal progress into the inexhaustible riches of the divine life."[15]

The Outward Manifestations of Theosis in Daily Life: From *Participation in God*

The Word of God is at work in all things. It is the clear affirmation of the New Testament writers. [The Church Father] Maximos [the Confessor 580–662 CE] takes it and articulates it in his own particular fashion. He sees the whole creation as full of the *words* of God, God's creative and dynamic intentions and will for his creation. These *words* in their almost infinite diversity are gathered together and find their fulfillment in the one Word who is God, thus allowing God to manifest his glory and his love throughout creation. But in this process we have a crucial part to play. We are placed in the midst of this material world, ourselves part of it, yet with the capacity to go beyond it. We are part of the world; Maximos insists much of the importance of the body which links us with that world and with all our fellow human beings, and on the part which it plays in our journey towards God. Humankind is placed in this focal position in creation with the task of bringing this work to completion, of being the place in which this noble exchange of human and divine can take place. "In his way to union with God, may in no way leaves creatures aside, but gathers together in his love the whole cosmos disordered by sin, that it may at last be transfigured by love."[16]

What more precisely does Maximos have in mind when he speaks of God being humanized, made man? He speaks of *the* incarnation of course; "the Word was made flesh and dwelt among us." But that is not an isolated incident. It is a focal point of all creation. So when he speaks of incarnation Maximos speaks of much more. We share in the nature of God, become partakers of the divine nature, and God shares in our nature, expresses himself in our humanity, as little by little we learn to live a life of active and suffering love, thus sharing in God's own love. By the action of

15. Meyendorff, *Byzantine Theology*, 225–26.

16. Words of Vladimir Lossky summing up the teaching of Maximos in Lossky, *The Mystical Theology of the Eastern Church*, 111.

God's grace, which is no created affect of God's action but is God himself at work in us, we become sharers in his nature and he in ours. The most authoritative interpreter of Maximos in our time, the Romanian theologian Fr. Dumitru Staniloae, puts it like this:

"The most shining demonstration of the action of grace within us is in our sympathetic awareness of our neighbor. By grace we long to make those who are in need at home with us, as we wish to make God at home with us. Nothing contributes so much to our growth in righteousness, to our drawing close to God, to our deification, as compassion showed to those in need."[17]

God suffers in those who suffer, taking their pain into himself, but God heals in those who heal, in those who show by their actions that they share God's own perception and understanding of things. "Maximos uses the doctrine of the uncreated energies of God to underline the fact that God holds us all together with himself, by reason of his active suffering with all. . . . For the energies of God are not shut in on themselves, but come out into the world, and are active throughout creation."[18] By our action in service of others we make these energies our own, and thus the whole of the human family is bound together by the action of God energizing in the action of man, the suffering of God at work in the suffering of man, the love of God in the love of man.

In this way the deifying grace of God enters into the simplest of human actions, a cup of cold water given to a child, a visit made to someone in sickness. Of course the Godward dimensions of such actions need not be conscious . . . but the divine transcendence and the divine immanence are brought very close together in them, and things which are called mysticism and spirituality are directly related to things which we call social and political concern. The incarnation of the Word of God at Bethlehem, in Galilee, in Jerusalem, is not an isolated wonder, but a central focal point in a network of divine initiatives which spreads out into the whole of human history, indeed into the whole universe. The story of Jesus is the story of the meeting of God with man and of man with God. It is a story which is not yet completed. It begins with the initiative of God, which has its origins solely in him. But for its proper telling it will always need to be told in two ways, both from the Godward and from the manward side. It needs from the human point of view to be seen in relation to the whole previous history of man, not only to the history of the people of Israel, which lay

17. Staniloae, *Prayer and Holiness: The Icon of Man Renewed in God.* 14–15.

18. Maximus the Confessor, *Philosophical and Theological Questions*, vol. I, Introduction and Commentary by D. Staniloae, 248–49

directly behind it, and also in relation to the subsequent history of humankind, of which your history and mine is a part. It is a story which will lead us to reflect on the ec-static nature of God and man, on the mystery that God is a God who can come out of himself and dwell in man; that we human beings are creatures who can come out of ourselves and dwell in God, indeed creatures who can only truly become ourselves by going beyond ourselves, can only become fully human by finding ourselves in God. There is within our nature an infinite and unbounded capacity for God. God can joy in man and man in God.

And man participates in God, and God participates in man, not only through deeds of active compassion, through the deepening of our human solidarity with one another. There is also a more hidden, intimate relation between God and man, which forms the heart of that activity we call prayer, and without which no true growth in inter-human solidarity is ultimately possible. Here again there is a reciprocity and co inherence deeper than we think. Prayer is not our shouting to a distant indifferent God. As a contemporary poet, R. S. Thomas, puts it,

"It begins to appear
this is not what prayer is about.
It is the annihilation of difference,
the consciousness of myself in you,
of you in me . . . ."[19]

We have to realize, in the words of an outstanding American spiritual father:

". . . that we *are* the glory of God . . . We live because we share God's breath, God's life, God's glory. Take this as your *koan*; 'I am the glory of God.' . . . You are the place where God chooses to dwell, you are the *topos tou theou* (God's place) and the spiritual life is nothing more or less than to allow that space to exist where God can dwell, to create the space where his glory can manifest itself."[20]

Such affirmations have almost unlimited implications for our understanding of the nature of man and of the nature of God who is pleased to dwell in him.[21]

It is tempting for readers of *Participation in God* to assume that Donald Allchin is writing for scholars. While it is true that Donald's writing is rarely

19. R. S. Thomas, "Emerging," in *Laboratories of the Spirit*, 1.

20. Bamberger, qu. In H. J. M. Nouwen, *The Genesee Diary*, 53.

21. Allchin, *Participation in God*, 70–73.

used in parish education programs and that most clergy and lay persons do not have Maximus the Confessor, Gregory Palamas, Richard Hooker, Launcelot Andrewes, Vladimir Lossky, N. F. S. Grundtvig, or Dumitru Staniloae on their "must read" lists, Donald was intent on demonstrating to the whole church how these and other writers boldly remind us of what is most fundamental in the Christian path. His words from the beginning of this chapter are worth repeating: "The central affirmation of the Christian faith declares that God himself has entered into our human situation and in doing so has totally transformed it." Donald's message is for every baptized person and gives a vision of the life baptism makes possible.

It is important, as well, to understand that when Donald says, "You are the place where God chooses to dwell . . . ," he is not describing an interior form of human transformation that is focused solely on the individual. Donald is clear that the awareness of God's presence in a person's life is an invitation for that person to accept the responsibility and challenge of collaborating with God in healing and redeeming a chaotic and broken world. In doing so Donald mirrors the life of Jesus and the wisdom and lives of the writers mentioned in the previous paragraph, especially his colleague and friend Dumitru Staniloae. Donald makes this very clear toward the end of *Participation in God*:

> At a moment of such intense conflict in human history, how is the light of God to be perceived? How is the joy of God, the delight of God in humankind and in creation to be made known? How can that joy become at this moment in history, [after] the century of Auschwitz and Hiroshima, the reality which dwells not only in the heart of each one of us but also at the heart of the whole of humankind, how can it inhabit the central place of the whole of the human family? Very evidently it cannot happen through any abdication of our responsibility for the things of this world, a pietistic withdrawal into some imagined sphere of religious invulnerability. Rather we need to face together the issues which God himself sets before us in our time.
>
> . . . Only in the rediscovery of the co-inherence of God with man and man with God can we respond to the extremity of this situation. Linked with this is the need for a new discovery of the mystery of human co-inherence which lies at the heart of the gospel: that we are all one in Christ Jesus; that each one of us is everyman; that the whole history of the human race is, in a hidden way, recapitulated in the life of each one of us. The inclusive uniqueness

of the person of the Christ reveals to us the unfathomable mystery and uniqueness of each human person.

This is why, while there can be no place among Christians for an abandonment of our share in responsibility for the public issues of our day, there is also an urgent need for a rediscovery of the inner depth in each one, that inner depth in which we find the presence of God within us, and finding that, find our fellow women and men in it. Again what we call mysticism cannot be separated from what we call politics. The churches of the West, which have terribly neglected this inner experiential element of our heritage, have a particular and urgent responsibility to rediscover its fullness. It is this which will enable us to make a true response to the religions of the East, to Buddhism and Hinduism. This is a rediscovery which will also involve a new appreciation of the fragility and beauty of the things of this earth, a new realization of our unity with our fellow human beings, and a new sense of God's utter transcendence made known in his complete immanence. There is a promise of a new heart, a new mind, a new birth in the Spirit now in this moment of crisis and judgment, which like all movements in our human history, whether personal or universal, is also a moment when God's creative energy longs to be revealed, when the divine energies are already powerfully at work bringing to birth the reality of a new creation.

For the things which belong to the story of Jesus are not yet completed.[22]

22. Allchin, *Participation in God*, 75–76.

CHAPTER 10

Solitude and Communion

Donald Allchin as Interpreter of the Monastic Vocation and the Mystery of Personhood

Martin L. Smith

Episcopal priest, retreat leader, and author in contemporary spirituality

I have never forgotten a simple science experiment from my schooldays. Our physics teacher had placed a large sheet of paper on the lab table. We gathered around as he sprinkled iron filings over it from a sugar caster. "Now pound your fists on the table," he said, and as we obeyed the filings jumped around chaotically. The instant we stopped at his signal they fell into an exquisite radiating pattern like the leaves of a fern. The secret of this transformation? A large bar magnet hidden beneath the paper. It comes back to me as a simple image for the influence of spiritual mentors: those who help put us within range of the attractive forces of grace so that our lives, our emotions, our actions, our perceptions become aligned with the divine energies. And since what awed me most was the beauty of the patterns the experiment exposed, it is no wonder that this scene reminds me of the life-long influence of Donald Allchin on me, and on so many. What struck us was the compelling attraction he was experiencing, radiating from the gospel and welling up from the collective experience of the Triune God that we call orthodoxy, the tradition he found so inexhaustibly fascinating.

Part Four: Allchin as Interpreter of Anglican Tradition and Theology

When Donald gave a talk at St. Swithin's, Worcester, in 1964 on "The Mass and the Mission" he unwittingly assumed the role of mentor to a teenager in the audience who eagerly introduced himself afterwards! A few months later my schooldays at the Kings's School were complete, and to fill the time before I took up my place at Oxford I volunteered to join an international team of construction workers at Taizé. With the celebration of the twenty-fifth anniversary of the founding of the community fast approaching, our task was to complete the Orthodox chapel, new guest lodgings, and camp sites for the youth groups from all over Europe and beyond that were making Taizé a goal of pilgrimage. Among the thousands streaming to Taizé were bishops and experts taking part in the Second Vatican Council, young men and women sensing a new springtime in the Catholic Church, and hundreds of members of religious communities opening their eyes to the exciting possibilities of renewing the monastic way. The ecumenical movement was intensifying, and those of us gathered at Taizé in the spring of 1965 knew we were at the epicenter of a grand seismic shift.

Within a few days of arriving at Oxford that fall to begin my theological studies, I went to Pusey House to bring Donald greetings from dozens of people from all over the world whom I had met at Taizé. I had had my first inkling of the extraordinary richness of the web that connected him personally with men and women of amazingly varied traditions. In no time at all I became part of this community, regularly meeting with him, hearing him preach, serving at liturgies he celebrated, and joining the intriguing ecumenical group formed around the house of St. Gregory and Macrina, and the Fellowship of St. Alban and St. Sergius.

It didn't take long to realize that the living community into which he was drawing us included a myriad men and women of the past whom most members of the academic circles in which we spent much of our time regarded as purely historical personages, objects of theological connoisseurship. But it was impossible in Donald's company not to sense that those who formed the great cloud of witnesses were actually more alive than we were, figures of the present and, even more, of the future, spurring us on while the testimony of their deeds and writings inspired us. No one I had ever met seemed so deeply engaged in a living conversation with the spiritual witnesses of the past, or who could draw us into a round dance with so many partners at once. We came to expect a uniquely eclectic spectrum of references whenever he spoke. Within an hour, in addition to living souls such as Thomas Merton, we would be connected with N. Grundtvig, who seemed to be holding hands with Ann Griffiths, Fr. Benson of Cowley with Thomas Traherne, St. Seraphim of Sarov with Julian of Norwich, St. Isaac of Nineveh with Lancelot Andrewes, St. Peter Damian with the Staretz Silouan, Newman with some anonymous Welsh poet of the middle ages. It was a kaleidoscopic eclecticism we could affectionately parody sometimes, but Anglicans like myself particularly delighted in the freedom he enjoyed to claim as our own the saints of all traditions and cultures.

He showed us that appropriating the tradition demands deep inner work and prayer: it is a way of conversion. It is one thing to trick oneself out with an array of insights culled from extensive reading. It is another to be accomplishing within oneself the unity of the church. And more than any one I had ever met Donald seemed engaged in the enterprise that Thomas Merton expressed so succinctly in his *Conjectures of a Guilty Bystander:*

> If I can unite *in myself* the thought and the devotion of Eastern and Western Christendom, the Greek and the Latin Fathers, the Russians with the Spanish mystics, I can prepare in myself the reunion of divided Christians. From that secret and unspoken unity in myself can eventually come a visible and manifest unity of all Christians. If we want to bring together what is divided, we can not do so by imposing one division upon the other or absorbing one division into the other. But if we do this, the union is not Christian. It is political, and doomed to further conflict. We must contain divided worlds in ourselves and transcend them in Christ.[1]

What intrigued us was Donald's assumption that this vocation wasn't a rare task for a few exceptional spiritual virtuosi. Rather it was a potential that all could participate in, insofar as they were growing into the renewed personhood that was the gift of union with Christ. The gift of personhood in Christ brought out of latency the human capacity to be a microcosm of creation, to realize our interconnectedness with all human beings, all living thing. The appropriation of this gift didn't proceed from some gnostic illumination, but from being "crucified with Christ," from the inner death of our broken selfhood that had been malformed by an environment mired in competition and a hundred forms of defensive mutual antagonism. This new capacity for communion grew with the active practice of our baptismal death and resurrection and the actualization over time of our reception of the Spirit. With our capacity for communion rooted in an inner appropriation of union with Christ came our call to share in Christ's ministry of

---

1. Merton, *Conjectures of a Guilty Bystander,* 21

reconciliation, the exercise of a particular spiritual gift that contributed to the divine movement to "unite all things in him."

I have chosen to present an extract from a talk that Donald gave to the annual conference of the Fellowship of St. Andrew in the summer of 1965, published in *Sobornost* the following year: "The Holy Spirit in Christian Life." It is from talks like this that we learned in Donald's company to take great words like "microcosm" and "mediator" and recognize that they were not mere grandiose concepts but powerful lenses for discerning and clarifying our own spiritual calling.

It is through the exploration of these themes that Donald was outstanding as an interpreter of the monastic vocation. It was not in the institutional or practical aspects of religious life that he could make his most lasting contribution, though he was a true friend and guide to the Sisters of the Love of God at a time when the community was especially dynamic, and to other communities as they sought to renew themselves in the aftermath of Vatican II. Rather he invited everyone to look to the deepest core of the monastic identity: a call to undergo an inner unification—to become *monos*, single in heart—that stretched and deepened our capacity for solidarity with a broken world, and a costly, empathic participation in its reconciliation at the deepest level of prayer. He took Evagrius' definition of the monk, "separated from all and united to all" and made it not a slogan for an exotic elite, but a mirror in which each Christian could see that she or he was called to be, again in Evagrius' words, "one who thinks of himself as one with all, because he unceasingly thinks he sees himself in everyone."[2]

So Donald's reflections returned again and again to the paradigm of the solitary vocation. By reflecting on the life of the hermit, rather than a member of one of the structured monastic institutions we were familiar with, he brought us to consider the gospel call to disentangle ourselves from the collective mentality that rivets us to a culture of rivalry and imitation in order to discover the mystery of our real communion with one another in the living God. At first glance this eremitical theme might appear an absurd preoccupation indicating a perverse indifference to the real mission of the church to engage critically with contemporary culture and the politics of a world in turmoil. But Thomas Merton was giving us a powerful example of one drawn deeper into the practice of solitude even as his ability to read the signs of our own times was becoming more penetrating.

2. Evagrius, *On Prayer*, 124–25

The influential philosopher of culture Jean Girard writes of the way in which the literary eroticism of the present day exposes in this latest generation a poignant and disturbing "double inaptitude to solitude and communion"[3]—a phrase that exposes in a flash the aching deficits that belie the hyper-connectedness of the new culture created by the internet. It struck me because it also echoes the title of book that was the fruit of a conference on the solitary life in St. David's in 1975; *Solitude and Communion*.[4] I had the pleasure of playing a role in organizing this extraordinary gathering at which Donald gave one of the major presentations. Surely this was the first conference for men and women living the solitary vocation and those who guided and supported them! We enjoyed the seeming contradiction of a conference for hermits, and relished the fact that would have seemed implausible only to outsiders; our liturgies, in spite of the barriers that separated different church allegiances and nationalities, were deeply intimate and connected. The Eucharist we celebrated in the cathedral was an experience of communion that I shall never forget.

Donald was a gifted historian and theologian of the religious life, and spent a great deal of his ministry supporting religious communities. But many factors have been bringing about marked decline to many of them. Thriving monasteries are the exception and the future of traditional communities is difficult to predict. Yet during this very time the fascination with monastic traditions has steadily grown. Donald realized that we were living in an epoch where the monastic spirit seems to have burst institutional bounds, to be claimed by thousands of people as the inspiration for their lives of discipleship lived in normal circumstances of marriage and work and public life; he often wondered how much the authenticity of this diffusion of monasticism would depend on the continued flourishing of a core of vowed monks and nuns, and solitaries, who could provide focal points for the widening circles. Today new models of residential and diffused communities are being claimed as harbingers of a "new monasticism." In some instances the grasping at monastic identity seems to be associated with a deficient sense of lay spirituality, and a tendency to automatically identify any disciplined practice of spiritual life, any form of common life, or any manifestation of the contemplative orientation as "monastic." Nevertheless the Spirit is clearly attracting many people to explore for themselves

---

3. Girard, *Deceit, Desire, and the Novel: Self and Other in Literary Structure*, 161

4. *Solitude and Communion: Papers on the Hermit Life given at St. David's, Wales in the Autumn of 1975*

the radical spiritual commitment that the monastic call and the solitary vocation represent. It is a safe guess that Donald's teaching will be prized in years to come as a spiritual compass for those engaged in the movement for which we can fittingly borrow St. Tikhon of Zadonsk's telling expression, "interiorized monasticism."[5]

The Holy Spirit in Christian Life: From an Article by Donald Allchin in *Sobornost*

I want in this lecture to consider our subject of Christian life in relation to our faith in the Holy Spirit and in the activity of the Holy Spirit in the Church and in each individual. We would all agree that in principle being a Christian and being a Church member ought not to be two separate and different things, but that it should be through and in our loyalty to the fellowship of the Church that our life in Christ deepens and grows. But we all know that in practice it is not quite like this, and that for the majority of our fellow human beings in this country, there is all the difference in the world between being Churchy and being Christian. As for ourselves we know that too often the life of the Church as an institution seems opposed to, and cramping of, the life of ourselves as individuals. Why should this be? I shall suggest two groups of reasons: one connected with our view of man, with our Christian anthropology; and one group connected with our view of the Church, our Christian ecclesiology. In both cases I shall suggest that the clue to our present dilemma is to be found in God the Holy Spirit, and in the way in which our life in Christ is built up and grows through our participation in the fellowship of the Holy Spirit. For in the words of a great nineteenth century Danish theologian, N. F. S. Grundtvig, it is the Holy Spirit who binds together 'outward and inward, bodily and spiritual, time and eternity, human and divine, the individual and the universal. And again,

"The Gospel of Christ would not only be a laughable fancy but a shameful fraud if there were not always a living relationship between Christ and his believing disciples. Such a living relationship can only come into being when his Spirit as a divine, self-authenticating power of life ensouls and works through the Church. It is therefore no wonder that the traces of such a relationship in real signs of life are nowadays both few and weak. For faith in the Holy Spirit as a divine person, as Christ's representative upon earth,

5. Tikhon of Zadonsk quoted in N. Gorodetzky, *St. Tikhon of Zadonsk*, 48

his Church's power of life, its pastor, teacher and guide, evidently belongs to the realm of Christian archaeology. . . . From this lack of understanding of the Holy Spirit comes our time's abstract concept of spirit and spiritual reality, and its material concept and freedom and personality, which where they are dominant make any living relationship between heaven and earth, God and man, and thus between Christ and us, evidently impossible."[6] "Abstract concept of spirit and spiritual reality and material concept of freedom and personality." It is here that I should like to begin by challenging the common view of the division between the spiritual and the material. Rather I should like to explore the biblical and patristic view of the unity of body and soul in man. Our biblical scholars and theologians constantly speak of man as a psychosomatic unity. They point out that, for instance, in S. Paul, spirit stands for the whole man, including his body, turned towards God and open towards his neighbor, while flesh stands for the whole man, including his soul, closed from God and closed against his neighbor. And this biblical view in which the wholeness of man is stressed, and in which the unity of body and soul is underlined rather than their dichotomy, is taken up and carried on in the theology of the Fathers. In this view man is not isolated from the rest of creation but is bound up with it by his very nature, so that, as S. Paul says, the whole creation awaits the future glory of the sons of God. The stories of the friendships between saints and animals are not only food for sentimental reflection; they describe in a vivid and naïve way the restoration of the harmony between man and the created world. Through man the praise of the whole creation is to find expression. This is why S. Isaac the Syrian says that "a loving heart burns with love for the whole creation, for men, for beasts, for the demons, for all creatures." Whatever we may feel about the work of Père Teilhard de Chardin there can be no doubt that this vision of the unity of mankind with the created order is brilliantly expressed in his writings, in terms which bring it to life for our generation. In particular we find in him a restatement of the view that the material world is not dead and irrelevant to the realm of God and to spiritual reality but that it is itself potentially transparent to God's Being and shot through with the divine glory. Man is a microcosm and he is so precisely because he has a body which contains the elements of the material universe within itself. S. Gregory Palamas indeed argues that it is just this mixed nature of man which gives him a higher vocation than the angels, who are pure spirits. It is this which gives him his calling to unite all things

6. N. F. S. Grundtvig, *Vaerker i Udvalg*, Vol III, 430–31.

in love, to work out the task which is set before him in Christ Jesus. It is as microcosm he is called to be mediator, to gather together in love the whole cosmos disordered by sin that it may be transfigured by grace, by the power and presence of God.[7] When we speak of the Holy Spirit in the life of the Church and of each Christian we must always keep this cosmic dimension in mind. If we do not, we shall cease to speak of the restoration of man in all the variety of his thoughts and activities, and instead begin to speak of what is called religion. Thus to stress again the importance of man's body in his relationship to God not only reasserts his kinship with the stones of the field, the elements of the universe, but it also brings into view all man's ordinary this-worldly relationships, those of eating and sleeping and working and social life, the whole fabric of civil society through which man can come to union with God, finding the divine light and life in and through the service of his fellow men,, precisely in their ordinary needs. False religion is a work of the flesh, mending drains is a work of the spirit. For the Spirit, God present in man, is made known and is at work not only in man's thoughts and prayers but in his hands and in his actions.

But if it is important to reassert this view of the range of man's horizontal relationships with his fellow men and with his fellow men and with the created order, so the vertical dimension of his life, its height and depth needs to be reasserted. And here it is necessary to make a distinction between the words, person and individual, awkward though this distinction may be. Individual here means in his separateness and transitoriness, in his self-assertiveness, man as over against others, living by competition, by conquering others, by asserting his own will. In this context love means to possess and to dominate. Self-expression in this sense means the death of the true self because for the true self to grow, man has to become not an individual but a person. And a person is one who recognizes the unity of his nature with that of all men. We can only grow into the uniqueness of our own personal being by recognizing this common nature which we share. "When thou seest the naked, cover him and hide not from thine own flesh" (Isaiah). "Whoever debases another debases himself" (James Baldwin). "Thou shalt love thy neighbor as thy self." To love in this context means not to dominate and to possess but to be willing to give ourselves to the utmost. These are all statements about the nature of man. As the Staretz Silouan says, "Our brother is our life." This unity of mankind is discovered in the depth of our being when we cease to think of ourselves as individuals who live by

7. For a full exposition of this view see Thunberg, *Microcosm and Mediator*.

separating ourselves from others and tyrannizing over them, and begin to see ourselves as persons who live by relationship.

This view of man derives, of course, from a reflection on the mystery of God's self-revelation in Christ. The distinction of nature and persons, which is not an abstract idea but a necessary concept for Christian living, comes from the reflection on God's nature as Trinity. The idea of a union which does not destroy the unique qualities of things united but brings them to perfection in uniting them derives from a reflection on the union of human and divine in Christ. The Gospel of Jesus Christ not only reveals to us the nature of God, but also the true nature of man who finds his fulfilment in the free unity of many persons in a common principle of life. And this is essential for our view of the relation of each member of the Church to the Church as a whole. The dilemma of individual and institution already begins to be seen in a new light. The Church is not an agglomeration of individuals—"a sandheap of individual perfections" in Father Congreve's words—but a unity of persons, the fellowship of the Holy Spirit. In the Church, as in the divine nature itself, the opposition of the one and the many is overcome, for the Church is to be within creation the image of the Trinity, mankind restored in his true nature in God's image and likeness. There are many persons but one body, different gifts but one Spirit. And the gifts are not divided out separately to each, but what belongs to all belongs to each one, and what belongs to all belongs to each one, and what belongs to each is common to all.

The vision of the Church as a union of persons is the theme of a whole section of S. Peter Damian's *Book on the Lord be With You*. Certain hermits had enquired whether when saying the Offices alone they could use the words "the Lord be with you" or not. Damian replies that they may:

"Indeed the Church of Christ is united in all her parts by such a bond of love that her several members form a single body and each in one the whole Church is mystically present, so that the whole Church universal may rightly be called the one Bride of Christ, and on the other hand every single soul can, because of the mystical effect of the Sacrament, be regarded as the whole Church"[8]

Peter Damian had noticed something in his reading of the Bible that has attracted a good deal of attention among modern scholars and commentators; the identification of the whole people with one is so strong, that the one may stand for the whole people.

"If we look carefully through the fields of the Holy Scripture we will find that one man or one woman often represents the whole

8. Peter Damian, *Selected Writings on the Spiritual Life*, 57

Church, for though because of the multitude of her peoples the Church seems to be of many parts, yet she is nevertheless one and simply in the mystical unity of one faith and one divine baptism. For indeed although holy Church is divided in the multiplicity of her members, yet she is fused into unity by the fire of the Holy Spirit, and so even if she seems, as far as her situation in the world is concerned, to be scattered yet the mystery of her inward unity can never be marred in its integrity. 'The love of God is shed abroad in our hearts by the Holy Ghost which is given unto us.' This Spirit is without a doubt both one and manifold, one in the essence of his greatness and manifold in the diverse gifts of his grace, and he gives to holy Church which he fills, this power that all the parts shall form a single whole, that each part shall contain the whole. The mystery of undivided unity was asked for by the Truth himself when he said to his Father concerning his disciples, 'I do not pray for these alone but for them also who shall believe in me through their word, that they may all be one as thou Father art in me and I in thee, that they also may be one in us that the world may believe that thou has sent me.'"[9] (10)

Again, further he writes:

"By the mystery of her inward unity the whole Church is spiritually present in the person of each human being who has a share in her faith and her brotherly love. . . . Indeed we who are many are one in Christ, each of us possesses the whole, and so in our bodily solitude we seem to be far from the Church, yet we are most immediately present through the inviolable mystery of unity. And so it is that that which belongs to all belongs to each, and conversely that which is particular to some is common to all in the unity of faith and love. . . . Now just as the Greeks call man a microcosm, that is to say, a little world, because his body is composed of the same four elements as the universe itself, so each of the faithful is a little Church since without any violation of the mystery of her inward unity, each man received all the sacraments of human redemption which are divinely given to the Church"[10] Here we have an expression of what Charles Williams meant by coinherence and exchange, and what the Russian writers of the last century mean when they use the word sobornost in its particular sense.

It is not by accident that this teaching about the unity of the Church should come in a treatise which speaks of the solitary life, a form of life whose significance, whose very existence indeed has

9. Ibid., 58–59

10. Ibid., 63–64 The last words are particularly interesting if, as seems probable, some of the hermits to whom S. Peter writes were laymen.

for a long time been almost forgotten in the West and not only among Protestants. The life of the hermit, the solitary, i.e. of the monk in the original sense of the word, the one who is alone, has been for centuries almost unknown in our Western Christendom. Among Roman Catholics it has been totally overshadowed by the emphasis on active congregations and institutions and on the idea of community as the one goal of the Religious Life. In Protestantism it has appeared meaningless and selfish. But by a life-giving paradox he who dwells alone with God is, by reason of his realization of his life in Christ, most at one with his fellow Christians. To quote Father Congreve again:

"Perhaps none have realized as intensely the saving mystery of fellowship, the love of the brethren, as those whom God has called to live by prayer in the greatest solitude, even in the continual contemplation of the hermit."

In such a life we see the primacy of the person over the Church as an institution, and the unity of human nature in Christ in the Spirit. It is no accident that both in the Roman Catholic Church and in our own at the present time this form of life should be being rediscovered. A very striking example of this rediscovery and of its meaning can be seen in the lives of two of the most significant saints of our time, Charles de Foucauld and Staretz Silouan. If you want to understand the question of the Holy Spirit in Christian life, turn rather to these living examples than to books. It is they who can teach us In Charles de Foucauld we see the power of a life of withdrawal and apparent defeat, its power to give new life to all who come into contact with it. In the life of the Staretz, we see an identification with the life of the whole Church and a profound understanding of the spiritual dilemma and agony of our century in a man who is apparently completely out of contact with both of these things. It is not those who live in the midst of the smoke and dust of this world who always see the true outline of the conflict, but those who are withdrawn from what we mistakenly call reality and by that withdrawal have entered into the true reality of God. The life of the hermit reproduces in our own time the supreme paradox that it is in the moment of utmost isolation and complete apparent uselessness, in the desolation of the Cross, that the Lord is able to bring about the atonement and reconciliation of man with God. We see here that the Cross is life-giving, and we see here something of the "mounting of the Cross" which is at the heart of the monastic life.

The solitary gives us, therefore, a vivid parable of something which is true of all Christians. By our rebellion against the "world" and our withdrawal from it as a structure of social relationships centred in itself and turned against God, God is able to give back to us not only true social relationships, thus making reconciliation possible, but also the one unfallen world, the "world" in the other sense of the word, the world as good and created by God. Only those who have renounced the holding of the world as their own possession can receive it as a gift. Here is the source at which all our seeing may be cleansed and a clue for our Christian understanding of the nature of art and science. For whether it is in social relationship whereby through justice, love and forbearance in our actions, man seeks to draw together into one those who are estranged and at enmity; or whether it is in investigation of the natural world, or in the work of artistic creativity, whereby man tries to uncover the inner principles of things, those principles which give the world coherence, dignity and meaning; in all these ways man is fulfilling a task of reuniting and bringing together what has been divided so that all things may find their unity in Christ.[11]

11. *Sobornost*, Series 5: No. 3 (1966), 170. Used with permission.

PART FIVE

Donald Allchin and the Welsh Spiritual Tradition

What thoughts above understanding,
Shall I find there within myself,
When I see the Godhead
Perfect and pure, and I are one?
There is a bond
Which there is no language able to express.[12]

Commenting on the last verse of a hymn by the Welsh poet Williams Pantycelyn, Donald writes, "These verses speak of a union and fusion of God with humankind. On the way to that union they pre-suppose a union of human capacities which brings about a wholeness of love and knowledge, an integration of the capacities to love and know which are to be found within the human person. To apprehend the divine glory is not a matter of thought alone. It demands a fusion of the two."[13]

12. A verse from a hymn by the eighteenth-century Welsh poet Williams Pantycelyn quoted in Allchin, *Resurrection's Children*, 10.

13. Ibid.

CHAPTER 11

A Poet's Perspective on Donald Allchin's Prayerful Approach to Poetry

Ruth Bidgood

Donald Allchin was a good and dear friend, and an inspiring one, whom I shall always miss.

He was a tremendous enthusiast, an Englishman who fell in love with Wales and eventually moved to spend many rewarding years there, in Bangor, where he became an honorary professor of the University of Wales. In fact, Wales was one of the two great loves we shared, the other being poetry.

It was in the 1970s that we met first, at the hospitable vicarage of Llanwrtyd Wells, where lived at that time our mutual friends James and Stevie (Stephanie) Coutts. We quickly struck up a friendship which was to last, and which I am very grateful to have enjoyed. Donald's much-valued appreciation of my poetry was expressed practically in his advocacy of my books, and in arranging poetry readings for me. I read twice in Canterbury during his time there as a residentiary canon and Cathedral librarian, and near there too on a family occasion, the eightieth birthday of his cousin Avice. With Donald too I read in another cathedral close, Salisbury, during a Liturgical Festival.

After his Canterbury years, Donald returned to his university, Oxford, as director of the St. Theosevia spiritual center. It was there that he gave a party to launch one of my selections, in 1992. In Bangor, too, later, he gave several parties at which I read my poems, one of them shared with his brother Bill, who came to live next door to him, and himself wrote some sensitive poetry.

Donald's generous support of my work included writing about it, in reviews and articles in a number of journals, mentioning it to friends, giving books as presents—in short promoting it kindly and tirelessly. It was all part of that love of poetry, and sense of its importance, which he expressed so well in his books, especially in *Praise Above All*, and *God's Presence makes the World*. *Praise Above All* is subtitled "Discovering the Welsh Tradition." With his great love of poetry, Donald combined insight into the poetic process, particularly in his favourite Welsh poets. Commenting on the Welsh language—with its abundance of words for beauty, excellence, and splendour—Donald says "The practice of praise stands at the heart of the Welsh poetic tradition, and the purpose of praise, as Waldo Williams (1904–71) put it, is 'to create an unblemished world.'"[1] A propos of Dafydd ap Gwilym's poetry (1320–70), Donald comments on Dafydd's poem "The Skylark." "The Welsh language is rich in synonyms for beauty, clarity, shining, radiance. The whole world is full of that light, that brightness. Here above all is the thought of prayer which is dominant. The bird rises towards God, penetrates into the divine world, held up by no earthly support. It is God himself whose grace sustains him in his song."[2]

For Donald, as well for the Welsh writers he loved, poetry was, above all, a practice of "praise of God's glory, God's beauty, seen shining out in all the things of earth." A man of great and very joyful faith, Donald always saw this beauty as "a glory which calls men and women on through its celebration to a knowledge and a love which go beyond this world and touch on the world of eternity."[3] He quotes Dylan Thomas's famous prefatory words: "These poems . . . were written for the love of Man and in praise of God."[4] Donald also cites the Australian poet Les Murray on the "simultaneity of stillness and racing excitement" of a poem. . . . It is, as St. Thomas said, '*radiant.*' . . . *It is complete, finite, yet inexhaustible.*"[5]

Donald always saw what so often links poetry to things greater than its ostensible subject. In the preface to *God's Presence Makes the World* Donald

1. Allchin, *Praise Above All,* 3.

2. Ibid., 23.

3. Ibid., 3–11.

4. Ibid., 4.

5. Ibid., 7.

writes "In Wales . . . vision [of God's presence in the world] . . . is carried forward and expressed through a particular understanding and practice of the art of poetry, seen as sacred art to be offered in God's service and expressed in God's praise."[6] One might surmise that in our contemporary Wales there are many writers for whom this would not be an obvious vision. Yet how true is Donald's picture of what cannot be denied—"the excitement . . . in penetrating further into [the] terra incognita,"[7] as he found it to be in 1997, of the Welsh tradition, and the excitement, too, inherent in all creativity, the link with profundities that lie at the root of being.

I remember affectionately the exuberant phone calls telling me of Donald's discoveries in the realm of centuries-old Welsh poetry, or of his thrilled appreciation of later Welsh writers (in Welsh and English)—Ann Griffiths was a particular enthusiasm, and poets he loved also included Waldo Williams, Gwenallt, Euros Bowen, R. S. Thomas (whom he knew), Menna Elfyn, and Gwyneth Lewis. Of this last-named poet's bilingual achievement he wrote "The gift is here, and we need to rejoice in it." "Need"—how typical of Donald Allchin is that emphasis! One should mention too the part he played in helping to build the reputation of Hereford's seventeenth-century poet and prose-writer, Thomas Traherne, and the thrill he felt at one discovery after another of previously unknown and extraordinarily strange and beautiful prose by this for-some-time half-forgotten writer.

Sensuous Glory was published in 2000, a book on the Welsh poet D. Gwenallt Jones, written by Donald in collaboration with D. Densil Morgan and with translations of Gwenallt's poetry by Patrick Thomas. Donald felt that Gwenallt had helped him discover Wales more fully, with all that it meant. He wrote of Gwenallt's celebration (in the poem "Credaf") of "the ancient traditions of devotion and Christian culture which are the peculiar possessions of his land."[8] The Welsh people's "life, their work, their prayer, their sorrow, their joy, their thanksgiving, all are touched by the transfiguring light of God."[9] In Gwenallt's work Donald found, sometimes unexpectedly, "a deep, hidden joy,"[10] coming from "his faith in God's incarnation

---

6. Allchin, *God's Presence Makes the World,* xii.

7. Ibid., xiv.

8. Allchin, Morgan, and Thomas, *Sensuous Glory,* 33.

9. Ibid., 41.

10. Ibid.

in our world"[11]—a joy I always felt that Donald himself knew keenly and deeply.

For myself, I owe a great debt to his advocacy of my work. One piece of writing he himself felt to be of significance was the modestly entitled "Afterword" he added to my Canterbury Press book, *Symbols of Plenty*, a selection of longer poems, among which Donald was particularly fond of an early commissioned radio poem, "Hymn to Sant Ffraid" (Saint Brigid). He and I took part sometimes in readings of this (for me) unusually long poem (for three voices).

In the Bangor days I was taken on a number of explorations of Donald's favourite Anglesey churches. This little poem from a sequence "Encounters with Angels" was written after our visit to Penmynydd church.

Faceless Angel
Stone sword at his side, dog at his feet,
he has a small angel each side
of the stone pillow, to prop his head.
This one sits huddled up to him,
wings folded, robe in changeless folds,
but the faithful have scrabbled for centuries
at her pretty face, to steal
some powdery take-away holiness.
The sculptor's image of a higher being
enduring lowly service is stronger now
by accident, faith itself having humbled
the little angel by revering her . . . .

There were, too, fascinating drives along the Llyn peninsula. These sometimes included a visit to his old friend, the scholar Mary Chitty. Occasionally these drives, too, resulted for me in new poems. I wrote a sequence of three poems on "Llyn," about Clynnog Fawr church, lunch on a stormy day at Aberdaron, and the misty view of Bardsey Island from the headland.

Memories such as these sustained Donald's friends through the twilight of his latest years, and still live on. I count myself fortunate to have had his friendship, and to have felt the influence of someone so imbued with joy—"praise above all." As Bardsey was one of his favourite places, I will end with my poem "Enlli" (its Welsh name).

11. Ibid.

Enlli

Faint and grey, Bardsey came out of the mist.
We could just catch, out there, what a poet saw
seven centuries back: the white waves leaping
around the holy island of Enlli.
No sound from them; the wind was too loud,
and the sea too loud, against the headland,
beating, tearing.
That's how the island
has stayed with me, a far silence
within storm, a shadow hardly seen,
beyond the clarity of gorse on the hill,
and the blurred surging of the autumn sea.
I have never landed there; the place
remains more visitant than friend.
Why it should be so loved, though,
I can sense, unclearly, as I still see
that shape far out in spume and rain,
beyond the silent waves that leap and leap
around the holy island of Enlli.

CHAPTER 12

Donald Allchin and the Welsh tradition

Professor D. Densil Morgan
University of Wales Trinity St. Davids at Lampeter

I first heard Donald Allchin as an undergraduate student in the Department of Welsh in the University of Bangor in 1974 or 1975. He had been invited to share his thoughts on the Welsh literary tradition, or those parts which had resonated most forcefully with his own specific interests, by his friend Bedwyr Lewis Jones, professor of Welsh and head of department. The name and title "Canon Allchin" had already become known in Welsh language circles as referring to an English ecclesiastic—as it happened a *very* English ecclesiastic—who was building bridges between his own community and those of us who were involved in the renaissance of all things Welsh which characterized those decades. I have no recollection of the detail of his address, but I do remember a clerically dressed gentleman in the company of two religious sisters speaking most enthusiastically about some of those subjects into which we, as undergraduates, were being initiated at the time.

It was not for nearly two decades that I would come to know Donald, and begin to count him not as a "name" or an acquaintance but as a friend. Following my student years at Bangor and graduate work between 1979 and 1982 at Regent's Park College, Oxford, next door, as it happened, to Pusey House where Donald had served as librarian a decade earlier, I was ordained into the Baptist ministry. Six years in the pastorate led to my return to Bangor in 1988 as a lecturer in Contemporary Christianity in the Department of Religious Studies with responsibility also to teach church history and doctrine in the Faculty of Theology to which the North Wales Baptist College was affiliated. One of my fellow members in the local Baptist church was James Nicholas, poet, lay theologian, former Archdruid of the Gorsedd of Bards and, by 1993, president-elect of the Baptist Union of Wales. That year's annual assembly meetings were held in Crymych, Pembrokeshire, not far from James Nicholas's home locality and the area most associated with the poet and visionary Waldo Williams. It was typical of Donald's expansive ecumenism to have accepted James Nicholas's invitation to spend three days as a guest of the Baptist Union's assembly though I suspect that the prospect of spending time following the footsteps of Waldo possessed an appeal of its own. (As it happened, Rowan Williams, soon to be appointed Bishop of Monmouth, but at the time Lady Margaret Professor of Divinity in Oxford, visited Bangor to deliver a series of lectures and on hearing of Donald's Baptist jaunt, quipped: "Donald's a one-man ecumenical movement!") It fell to me to act as his chaperone, guide and interpreter during that assembly; he hardly needed a translator though the arcane mysteries of the Baptist faith in its Welsh language guise did require some interpretation for a man who was more used to the Anglican-Orthodox dialogue. I had by that time read Donald's great trilogy *The World is a Wedding, The Kingdom of Love and Knowledge,* and *The Dynamic of Tradition,* so there was much to discuss. It was there that we became firm friends, a friendship that was deepened considerably following his move from Canterbury to Bangor in the mid-1990s when, as honorary professor in the university's Departments of Theology and Welsh, he became a valued colleague as well as a neighbour. Our joint venture in catholic evangelicalism *Sensuous Glory: The Poetic Vision of D. Gwenallt Jones* appeared in 2000, a collaboration that was for me a rich experience indeed. It is on that background that I venture to contribute this brief assessment of Donald Allchin and the Welsh tradition.

Donald's first extended interaction with the historic legacy of Welsh Christianity was his 1976 contribution to the University of Wales Press's "Writers of Wales" series on Ann Griffiths. He had first been made aware of the existence of this late eighteenth-century Calvinistic Methodist hymn writer through the translations of her work by H. A. Hodges, Professor of Philosophy at Reading, a fellow member in the Fellowship of St. Alban and St. Sergius. Before converting to Catholic Anglicanism, Hodges had been a Methodist and retained a huge appreciation for the hymns of Charles

Wesley. What Donald found in Ann was a rounded incarnational theology which served as the context for the atoning sacrifice of Christ expressed through a poetry of rapture and mystical devotion: "It is the image of the Old Testament, the mountain and the cloud, the journey through the wilderness, the river of life and the tree of life, which predominate her work, and which come to life again and again within its narrow compass with incomparable power."[1] Subsequently there was hardly a book of his in which Ann is not mentioned, while the volume was reissued a decade later as *Ann Griffiths: The Furnace and the Fountain* (1987).

Donald would remain under Ann's spell for the rest of his life. He found in her so many of the themes that were dear to his heart: a devotion of rapture, a mystical appreciation of the person of Christ, the Pauline doctrine of union with Christ which he believed to be so close to the *theosis* of the Eastern church, a piety, though Methodist, that had been bred in the Anglicanism of Ann's youth, and a catholic sense of wholeness. She was also a poet, or at least her hymns were crafted within a centuries-old bardic tradition which had expressed the genius of the Welsh people for over a thousand years. It was through this that the *traditio* or *paradosis*, the handing down of the faith from generation to generation, had occurred. Above all Donald was a synthesizer. Sometimes this led him into difficulties as he saw similarities and parallels that the evidence could not support. Nevertheless Ann, in concert with the nineteenth-century French Carmelite Elizabeth of Dijon, was appropriated as part of Donald's zeal for a shared spirituality which was faithful to the core convictions of orthodox Christianity and spoke powerfully to a generation which had little to say to the institutional church. His essay *The Gift of Theology: The Trinitarian Vision of Ann Griffiths and Elizabeth of Dijon* was republished as recently as 2005.[2]

In the trilogy which was published in the late 1970s and early 1980s, sufficiently far away from the 1960s not to be intimidated by secular theology and close enough to charismatic renewal to be comfortable with an experiential emphasis on the Holy Spirit, the Welsh theme is intertwined with topics that his readers would have found more familiar. As spirituality is the undergirding subject of *The World is a Wedding*, the Welsh poets Gwenallt, Waldo and David Jones feature side by side with T. S. Eliot and Edwin Muir and, among the prose writers, including Thomas Merton. Donald is at his most comfortable with Golden Age Anglicans such as

1. Allchin, *Ann Griffiths*, 3.
2. Allchin, *Gift of Theology*.

Hooker, Andrewes, Nicholas Ferrar, and Jeremy Taylor and, among the poets, Thomas Traherne and another seventeenth-century Welshman of the same ilk, Henry Vaughan "the Silurist." In the versatile discussion of Orthodoxy which dominates *The Kingdom of God and Knowledge*, Ann Griffiths appears among such luminaries as St. Symeon "The New Theologian," the nineteenth-century Dane Nikolai Grundtvig, the Anglicans F. D. Maurice and Evelyn Underhill, and, of course, the prime figure in the twentieth-century Orthodox renaissance Vladimir Lossky. A key chapter entitled "The Liberating Power of Praise," specifically on Welsh religion and theology in the truly excellent *The Dynamic of Tradition*, foreshadowed his book-length analysis *Praise Above All: Discovering the Welsh Tradition* which would be his most rounded appreciation up till then of a subject that he was finding increasingly absorbing. "Like most English people," he would write later, "I grew up in almost total ignorance of the existence of Wales. Only in my thirties did I begin to discover that there was another people in the south of Britain with a language, a culture, a history of their own."[3] *Praise Above All: God's Presence Makes the World, Resurrection's Children,* and *Sensuous Glory* constitutes a body of work in which he relates to what Gerard Manley Hopkins once referred to as "this world of Wales."[4] In so doing not only did Donald interpret this world to Christians from beyond its borders, but he provided rich insights for those for whom it had been their birthright as well.

The two sections of *Praise Above All*, "The Tradition Surveyed" and "The Tradition Considered," showed how Donald's knowledge and understanding of this material had deepened and matured since his earliest work on Ann Griffiths. For one thing, he had gone back in time, to the Middle Ages to consider the greatest Welsh poet ever, namely the fourteenth-century Dafydd ap Gwilym, and even farther back than that, to the period between the sixth to the ninth centuries, the so called "Age of Saints" including David in south Wales and his north Wales counterparts, Deiniol, Seiriol and Cybi, and the nature poetry of the eighth century. He had also gone forward, to his own generation and the poets of the twentieth-century renaissance: Saunders Lewis, Gwenallt, Waldo Williams, and Euros Bowen. One of the things that Donald found remarkable about modern Welsh poetry was its unabashed and sophisticated Christian content. Apart from the highly a-typical Eliot (sneered at by Virginia Woolf: "He has become an

---

3. Allchin, Morgan, and Thomas, *Sensuous Glory*, 3.
4. Hopkins, "In the Valley of the Elwy," in *Poems and Prose*, 32.

Anglo-Catholic believer in God and immortality. I was shocked. A corpse would seem to be more credible than he is"[5]), to be a Christian believer and a poet in England was an oddity if not grotesque. This was not the case in Wales. "Even more remarkable is the fact that in the last fifty years, to be precise since about 1936, a large part of this poetic production has been the work of poets of deeply Christian convictions. At a time when all the churches at the public and institutional level have been declining in influence and numbers . . . there has been a reaffirmation of Christian vision which is admirable and wholly unexpected."[6] What bound these poets together—one was Catholic, the other a Calvinist, the third a Quaker and the fourth an Anglican—was a deep sacramentality, a refusal to divide creation from redemption, a wholehearted commitment to social and political action as well as exceptional creative ability.

In assessing the tradition in Part Two of the volume, he returns to Ann Griffiths now considering her work on the basis of a more intimate acquaintance with Welsh literature as a whole, moving on to a more prolific hymn writer and one whose impact on Welsh life was considerably greater than Ann's, namely William Williams of Pantycelyn. The prism through which he sees Pantycelyn is von Balthasar's theological aesthetics, a reading which is as rewarding as it is unexpected, thereafter he roams freely and eclectically linking Solzhenitsyn with the Methodist revivalists, Grundtvig with the short story writer D. J. Williams, author of the outstanding autobiography *Yr Hen Dŷ Ffarm* ('The Old Farmhouse'), John of Damascus with Donald's Baptist friend, James Nicholas, making a host of other allusions and references as well. The theme that underpins the whole is that of glory: "The glory which the Christian poet seeks to embody and declare is the paradoxical glory revealed in its fullness in the self-giving of the cross. . . . In creation and redemption alike, God's glory goes beyond all that we can think or say."[7]

By the 1990s the vogue for "Celtic spirituality" was strong, and Donald tried to connect his knowledge of and zeal for the Welsh tradition with this late-twentieth-century emphasis on the divine immanence, ecological integrity, and a spirituality of egalitarianism and gender parity. He was sensitive to the dangers of faddishness and, as a scholar, knew the difference between a "Celtic spirituality" which pandered to quackery and the

5. Quoted in Hastings, *A History of English Christianity*, 236.

6. Allchin, *Praise Above All*, 34.

7. Ibid., 161.

valid historical discipline of "Celtic Christianity." If defensive, his inaugural lecture as honorary professor in Bangor University in 1993 was an eloquent plea to merge that which was academically persuasive with the needs of the time: "I have become almost painfully aware in the last four or five years that we are living at a moment when, for whatever reason, the subject of Celtic Christianity, or Celtic spirituality is arousing intense interest not only in Britain and Ireland but in North America and to some extent across the English-speaking world."[8] The strength of the analysis was that Donald, who could by now access the vernacular material with ease, analyzed poems from the medieval sources, "The Loves of Taliesin" from the fourteenth-century Book of Taliesin though the poem was composed much earlier, and the stanzas on God the Trinity from the Black Book of Carmarthen written around 1250. He also, in good Celtic style, refers to place and to pilgrimage. The place was Pennant Melangell, not far from Ann Griffith's Llanfihangel-yng-Ngwynfa in mid-Wales, but the context is medieval, the shrine to the fifth century saint Monacella, in Welsh Melangell: "In that remote upland valley the Irish princess had come to stay seeking silence and solitude. There she was joined by others who sought to share the secret of her life. The whole content of her legend is . . . centred on the one episode in which the local chief out hunting comes into the valley to chase his prey. The animals . . . flee to Melangell for protection. Her prayer, by a miracle, brings their safety. She becomes their patron ever after."[9] The story, linked to such a beautiful location, is in itself compelling. As it was also within walking distance of the home of the (very Protestant) Ann, the allusion was irresistible.

The works of the late 1990s blend this Celtic emphasis with Donald's earlier interests in medieval verse and prose, Methodist hymns and modern poetry. In *God's Presence Makes the World: The Celtic Vision through the Centuries in Wales* he attempts a panoramic view of the legacy. In seven rich chapters he treats a now familiar story: the earliest literary witness from the sixth century, the praise theme from the early medieval poetry, the piety of the High Middle Ages, the progression of religion between the Reformation and the Evangelical Revival, leading to three closing chapters on a range of twentieth-century poets including, this time, Bobi Jones and Gwyneth Lewis. In *Resurrection's Children: Exploring the Way towards God* he returns to his favourite subjects, including the medievals, Guto'r Glyn and Meilir

8. Allchin, *Celtic Christianity: Fact or Fantasy?* 1.

9. Ibid., 15.

Brydydd, and the moderns, Gwenallt and Waldo, and (of course) Williams Pantycelyn and Ann. Knowing of my own admiration for the craggy, masculine and pugnacious verse of D. Gwenallt Jones, it was at around this time that he suggested: "We ought to write a book together about Gwenallt!" He had come to refer to Saunders, Gwenallt, Waldo, and Euros as "the four doctors of the church," and his final project, had he been granted health, was to have written a detailed assessment of their contribution. Be that as it may, in *Sensuous Glory: The Poetic Vision of D. Gwenallt Jones*, the contrasts between our shared appreciation of the poet's witness and verse are as pointed as the comparisons, but the book is, I hope, no worse for that: "This book proceeds from a shared conviction of the importance of Gwenallt's verse for the twenty-first century. . . . The catholic evangelicalism to which he had slowly won his way, far from being a piece of ecclesiastical joinery proved to be the source of a renewal of faith and experience which enabled him to see that deeper than the depths of human tragedy and loss are the depths of the redeeming love of God."[10]

In our leisurely theological discussion, usually over lunch every few months in "The Fat Cat" restaurant in Bangor, I would often rib Donald about his ingrained Catholic Anglicanism and he would do the same with me over my inveterate Barthian Nonconformity. When he would wax eloquent over the role of the Blessed Virgin as *Theotokos*, I would remind him that she too was a sinner saved by grace and her place was in the congregation looking towards Christ and not with her back to the altar looking towards the people. When I would insist gently that he should have written more about justification by faith than participation in God, he would smile indulgently and shake his head at my obtuse intransigence. If I was a sceptic about the phenomenon of "Celtic spirituality," he was an enthusiast, though always scholarly and never uncritical. Where I would talk about sin and redemption, he would remind me of God's good creation and the doctrine of the *imago Dei*. If I played the part of the preacher of the cross, he was undoubtedly one of "resurrection's children." "You know what we are, you and I," he would say; "We are just two old-fashioned Christian believers." It was Waldo Williams who wrote about the knowledge that is awareness, friendship, and wisdom: "*Cael un gwraidd/Dan y canghennau*" ("To have one root/beneath the branches").[11] The reference, though oblique, is to the

---

10. Allchin, Morgan, and Thomas, *Sensuous Glory*, ix, xi.

11. Williams, *Dail Pren*, 67.

Good Vine of John 15. If there was anyone who was rooted in the Good Vine it was Donald Allchin. It was a huge privilege to have him as a friend.

SELECTED EXCERPTS THE WORKS OF DONALD ALLCHIN

Ann Griffiths: Mystic and Theologian

There are few points at which we come closer to Ann than in the stories which tell something of that hidden prayer of the heart which was hers. We hear of her retiring to the outhouse, sometimes many times in one day, in order to have solitude and silence to pursue this inward converse with the Lord. We hear of her sitting at the spinning wheel, the Bible open on a little table beside her, the tears streaming down her cheeks. We hear of moments of exaltation when she could not contain the audible expression of joy, we hear of nights of testing when she would wake up Ruth [Evans, her companion] to share her overwhelming sense of eternity and judgment. If Isaac of Stella, with all the resources of the monastic tradition around him, in common life and prayer, in spiritual discernment and advice, frequently found himself at a loss to understand his inner turmoil, how much greater must her need have been. We need not be surprised if there is sometimes a sense of strain in her. She tells us little about this secret prayer, but what she tells us is all important, and it is constantly pointing to . . . "the anointing, the touch of God's spirit on man's spirit, there in the inmost place of the heart." . . . For her, the doctrine of the Trinity was particularly associated with her conviction that the love which God has for us is a love which has existed from all eternity within the life of God himself. "Sweet it is to remember the Covenant that was made yonder in the Three-in-One, to gaze eternally upon the Person who took the nature of man . . . ." And again, ". . . Here are the foundations of the second covenant, here is the counsel of the three-in-One. Here is the wine which is able to cheer, to cheer the heart of God and man." In this assurance that the salvation of man is rooted in the eternal counsel of the Three in One, Ann is not alone among the hymn writers of her time. We may remember the striking lines from Pedr Fardd (Peter Jones, 1775–1845): "Before earth was made, or the bright heavens stretched out, before the sun or the moon or the stars were placed above, a way was set forth in the counsel of the Three-in-One, for the salvation of poor, lost, guilty man." In these hymns of Welsh Methodism we have a verbal equivalent of the greatest of Russian icons, the Old Testament Trinity of Andrei Rublev, in which the three persons are seated around a table on which stands the cup of sacrifice, the symbol of self-giving love.[12]

The Stabilizing of a Tradition: From *Praise Above All*

We may think of the picture of another rural neighbourhood, another parish, painted more than a century later [than Ann Griffiths], when the first fore had passed from the form of religion as it had become part of a whole way of life. I refer to D. J. Williams's portrait of the district in which he was brought up as we find it in *Hen Dŷ Ffarm*, in English, *The Old Farmhouse*.

This is indeed a portrait which rediscovers and re-expands for us that beloved district in such a way as to enrich and enlarge a vision of all other places. Yet it is certainly there. Consider for a moment the care with which the writer tells us about the practice of family prayers, *y ddyletswydd*, in his childhood home:

"Between my grandfather and my father after him the family devotion was observed in Penrhiw and Abernant for over sixty years without a break. Moreover if I may suggest it in all humility, it is probable that this tradition if it could be traced, reached back to the old home in Llywele, and had come down from father to son from the conversion of Wiliam Siôn, my grandfather's grandfather, in the beginning of Methodism in the vicinity, a hundred years before the sixty I have spoken of."

Here there is indeed the tracing of an apostolic succession. Think again of what we are told about the writer's father.

"His nature had no trace of deceit or jealousy. His great gift was the gift of prayer. It was a joy to listen to him when he knelt. . . . I think he was always on good terms with his Creator. I know that he was on the best terms possible with his neighbours, every hour of the day and every day of the year. That was a part of the secret of the life of the Old Neighbourhood."

If what D. J. tells us of his father reveals part of the secret of the life of that place, what he says of his mother lets us still further into the secret. Here the prayer in question is not public but hidden.

12. Allchin, "Ann Griffiths: Mystic and Theologian," in *The Kingdom of Love and Knowledge*, 62, 63–64.

"Very often when she was busy at her work without dreaming that anyone was listening, I would hear her chanting her prayers and meditations in a gentle, adoring monologue, weaving through them in a beautiful way, psalms and verses of hymns. . . . [M]y mother did not speak much of her religion beyond praising the goodness she saw in others and being tender-hearted towards their weaknesses. It is my belief that her life, every minute of it as it came, was all one secret prayer."[13]

There is a hidden link between Penrhiw [home of D. J. Williams] at the end of the [nineteenth] century and Dolwar Fach [home of Ann] a hundred hears earlier."[14]

Spirituality in Modern Welsh Poetry[15]

To join together the names of Saunders [Lewis (1893–1985)], Gwenallt [Jones (1899–1968)], Waldo [Williams (1904–71)] and Euros [Bowen (1904–88)] in the way that I have done might suggest that they were members of a single group or school. This was not at all the case. As we shall see, they were very varied in their poetic style and approach. They were also varied in the history of their religious convictions. But of course they all had certain things in common. All came out of the world of Welsh Nonconformity. Within the smaller world of Welsh-speaking Wales the influence of eighteenth-century Methodism was all-pervasive in a way it could not be in England. The social and literary culture of twentieth-century Wales has been overwhelmingly indebted to that eighteenth-century movement. But all our writers felt the need to explore further. Saunders Lewis became a Roman Catholic in the 1930s, greatly influenced by the French Catholicism of his time. Gwenallt, after a Marxist period in his youth, in the 1940s became an Anglican of a distinctly Catholic type. But in his later years, appalled by the Englishness of the Church in Wales at that time, he returned to Calvinistic Methodism. Waldo grew up as a Baptist, but in mature life became a Quaker. He was much influenced by the writing of Berdyaev and . . . had strong Catholic sympathies. Euros came from a family of Congregational ministers.

13. Waldo Williams, *The Old Farmhouse*, 224–26.

14. Allchin, "Diversity of Tongues," in *Praise Above All*, 133–34.

15. Allchin, "Spirituality and Welsh Poetry, 1930–80," in "Spirituality, Imagination and Contemporary Literature," Supplement to *The Way* (1994) 70–78 [quotation on pp. 71–73].

He alone of the four entered the ordained ministry; Saunders and Gwenallt were both university lecturers. Waldo was for most of his life a primary-school teacher.

All four were consciously and specifically Christian in their affirmation. All were consciously and explicitly nationalist. But just as their religious convictions made them explore beyond the confines of the specific tradition in which they grew up, so their passionate assertion of Welsh national and linguistic identity involved them in a deeply committed statement of European and international solidarity. The foundation documents of Plaid Cymru in the early 1930s, largely the work of Saunders Lewis, express a resolutely international nationalism. Over against the largely unconscious and often self-centred nationalism of an ill-defined imperial "Britain," the Welsh placed a vision of a Europe made up of nations living together in mutual interdependence and respect. In the poem on St. David, Gwenallt sees the saint as our contemporary.

"He spoke to us of God's natural order,
The person, the family, the nation and the society of nations
And the cross which prevents us from making any of them into a god.
He said that God had made our nation for his own purposes
And that its death would be a breach of that order.
Anger darkened his forehead as he castigated us
For licking the arse of the Saxon Leviathan
And allowing ourselves in his own country to be turned into Pavlov's dogs."[16]

Thus, if all were internationalist, all found themselves constantly at odds with a "British" government which failed to respect the specific identity of their people. Their spirituality was in this sense a spirituality of subversion and revolt. Gwenallt was imprisoned during the 1914–18 war as a conscientious objector, more on political than religious grounds. Waldo Williams was imprisoned during the 1950s for refusing to pay taxes which would go to support the Korean war, a war being fought with the use of napalm. Saunders Lewis was imprisoned for nine months in 1936–7 for his leading part in the act of civil disobedience, the burning of the bombing range in the Llŷn peninsula, which more than any other event signalled the beginning of a new and heightened phase of Welsh national consciousness.

16. For Patrick Thomas's translation see Allchin, Morgan, and Thomas, *Sensuous Glory*, 100–101.

I have insisted on this nationalist element in their whole religious attitude because it is something which English people often find hard to acknowledge, and because it is an attitude which can throw light on the problems of national identity and national rootedness at present confronting the whole of Europe in the formerly Communist world. The answer to blind destructive nationalism is not bland and superficial internationalism, but a sane and balanced awareness of national differences and the necessary interaction of nations with one another. This involves a particular recognition of the rights of small and threatened linguistic communities. If, as I should maintain, the four writers we are considering were all basically catholic in their attitude toward Christian faith, all were convinced that catholicity is best expressed and rooted in particular places and people. The principle of the incarnation, like the gift of Pentecost, unites and diversifies at one and the same time.[17]

Celtic Christianity: From *Celtic Christianity, Fact or Fantasy?*

Celtic Christianity, fact or fantasy? Fact indeed, the texts are there, hidden in the old manuscripts, hidden in the scholarly editions. The places are there too, easily overlooked, waiting for our love and care to waken them into new life. What is given in this enterprise is not the creation of our fantasy, not the imaginary land which Tolkien conjured up out of the creativity of his mind and width of his studies. It corresponds to the given realities of flesh and blood, a history which was worked out in the lives of men and women, who wrestled with God in darkness and despair as well as in glory and delight. But the facts are in themselves inert and unproductive until we come to meet them. The texts may be ignored, the places forgotten, built over and exploited for all kinds of ends which are unworthy of their splendour. The language itself we know is always under threat. It reminds [us] of the mortality of all human languages without exception. To facts we must bring fancy, not in the sense of mere whim, mere unsubstantiated longing, but in the sense of that work of the trained and disciplined imagination which in different ways is characteristic of both poet and historian. "It is not merely the mind nor yet the senses which bring reality before us, but some other faculty which is both higher and older than these." It is the offering of this faculty which we can bring to the gifts which are hidden in the past, uniting our love

17. Allchin, "Spirituality and Welsh Poetry, 1930–80," 71–73.

with our knowledge in our acknowledgment of an inheritance which can be ours, if only we will work to accept it.[18]

18. Allchin, *Celtic Christianity, Fact or Fantasy?* 20.

CHAPTER 13

Donald Allchin, Welsh Holy Places, and The Saint from Dolwar Fach

The Rev. Dr. Patrick Thomas
Vicar of Christ Church, Carmarthen
and Canon Chancellor St. Davids Cathedral, St. Davids, Pembrokeshire

One the main reasons for Donald Allchin's attraction to Wales was his sensitivity to "thin places" (a description borrowed from Iona) where the witness of past holiness had left an indelible influence. These were places where, as T. S. Eliot wrote of Little Gidding, "prayer has been valid," and so can still have an impact on those who come there either as conscious pilgrims or simply as visitors. Catherine Daniel wrote about Enlli (Bardsey), the island at the end of the Llŷn peninsula which became one of Donald's best loved "thin places":

> To those who sense the atmosphere of old places, and are con-
> scious of the enchantment of old churches where the shadow of
> the past remains profound, there is an inexhaustible enchantment
> in the earth of Enlli. Almost no-one sees it without becoming
> aware of the "serious silence" that surrounds it.[1]

The English name Bardsey is derived from the name of a Viking chieftain. Enlli, however, according to Dr. Enid Roberts, an authority on medieval Welsh etymology, means "great current." The waters around the island

---

1 Catherine Daniel, *Enlli: Porth y Nef*, 31 (translation by Patrick Thomas: "serious silence" is an attempt to convey the meaning of "*dwys distawrwydd*"—a quotation from the eighteenth-century hymn-writer William Williams, Pantycelyn).

can be extremely dangerous, as some of the early Welsh poets who visited Enlli vividly testified.[2] That is presumably why, in pre-Reformation times, three pilgrimages to Enlli were regarded as the equivalent of one to Rome.

As he reflected on Enlli's long connection with the monastic tradition, both in the pre-Norman "Age of Saints" and in the medieval period, Donald saw these centuries of prayer as having had a transforming influence on the island. To his mind, it had become a place where there was neither past nor future—only the present moment as a moment of eternity. He commented that on Enlli "phrases like 'the communion of saints' and 'the cloud of witnesses' take on a new significance for us. We are 'with angels and archangels, and with the whole company of heaven.'" It is perhaps not surprising that Donald devoted an entire chapter in one of his later books to the famous *marwysgafn* (death-bed poem) of the early medieval poet Meilyr Brydydd, in which the bard expressed his passionate desire to be buried on Enlli, the island of saints, where he would find salvation and ultimately resurrection through Christ.[3]

If Donald regarded Enlli as having an especially numinous quality, the same was true of his view of Pennant Melangell, which he described as "a liminal place, a threshold place."[4] This rural church in a secluded Montgomeryshire valley is linked to one of the most attractive stories in Welsh hagiography, which survives in versions from the sixteenth and seventeenth centuries. Melangell (whose Latin name is Monacella) was an Irish princess, who fled across the sea to Wales in order to avoid being married off by her father to a wealthy nobleman. She took refuge in the remote valley, living a life of quiet prayer. One day her solitude was interrupted by Brochwel Ysgithrog, prince of Powys, who was hunting in this far-flung corner of his domains. His dogs pursued a hare, which disappeared into a bramble bush where Melangell was praying, and took refuge under her cloak. Although the prince tried to urge his hounds on, they ran away howling with fear. Brochwel then questioned Melangell, listened to her story, and was so impressed by her that he turned the valley into a place of perpetual sanctuary and asylum.[5]

It was not only Melangell's legend which drew Donald to her valley. It was also the fact that sufficient fragments of her twelfth century shrine had

2. Enid Roberts, *A'u Bryd ar Ynys Enlli*, 12, 78–80.

3. Allchin, *Enlli*, 3 and Allchin, *Resurrection's Children*, 90–107.

4. Allchin, *Celtic Christianity, Fact or Fantasy?* 17.

5. See H. Pryce, "A New Edition of the *Historiae Divae Monacellae*."

been carefully preserved in such a way that in 1991 it was possible to reconstruct it in the chancel of Pennant Melangell Church. In addition, he was fascinated by the underlying tradition of devotion to the saint which seems to have persisted in the area during the eighteenth century. Ezekiel Hamer, vicar of the parish from 1788 to 1812, wrote a short poem in which he saw his valley as being only a footstep away from heaven—an idea with which Donald concurred.[6] However, despite his love for Melangell, her church and her shrine, and his enthusiasm at its rediscovery as a place of pilgrimage, another Montgomeryshire parish and another female saint inspired Donald's most important contribution to the history and understanding of Welsh spirituality.

Fifteen miles from Pennant Melangell is the rural community of Llanfihangel-yng-Ngwynfa. In August 2005 Donald and I took part in an unforgettable Eucharist in the parish church there, to commemorate the bicentenary of the death of one of the most remarkable figures in Welsh religious history: the mystic and hymn-writer Ann Griffiths, Dolwar Fach. The congregation was drawn from a wonderful cross-section of Welsh Christianity. As they came forward to receive the sacrament Donald's face shone with joy. Several years before, he had written:

> *Gwynfa* surely means blessed place or paradise, and the name of the church to which Ann Griffiths went Sunday by Sunday in her youth is surely suggestive enough. A hilltop church of St. Michael the Archangel is a suitable site for the baptism and burial of one who longed so ardently to share in the vision and the song of the angelic hosts.[7]

Donald had described Llanfihangel-yng-Ngwynfa as one of those "places touched forever by the mystery of Ann's life and song . . . where Christian people of all traditions may be united in common acts of praise and thanksgiving, places whose holiness demands to be recognized more widely than it has been up to now."[8] As we gave thanks for the young Montgomeryshire farmer's wife whose spiritual, poetic and theological insights had been such an inspiration to him, his vision became a reality.

Ann Griffiths was born Ann Thomas in 1776, the daughter of a tenant farmer, who was a church warden and a folk poet. He was a devout

---

6. Allchin, *Pennant Melangell*, 17–19.

7. Allchin, *Praise Above All*, 89.

8. Ibid.

Anglican. In his biography of Ann, published in 1865, Morris Davies wrote of her father:

> In his religion, John Thomas was a conscientious Churchman, and brought up his family in that religion. He was more religious than most of his neighbours; and it is said that he would hold family worship regularly, evening and morning, through reading parts of the Book of Common Prayer, and perhaps some other forms of prayer; which was good, as far as it went . . . .[9]

Although her Nonconformist biographer was somewhat patronising about this element in Ann's religious upbringing, Donald was fascinated by the way in which her early grounding in the Prayer Book may have given her the vocabulary and the conceptual framework that enabled her to communicate complex theological ideas with concision and directness.

Another element in Ann's Anglican upbringing which attracted his attention was the influence of *Plygain* carols. *Plygain* is a Welsh Christmas service, traditionally held before dawn. Morris Davies describes the form it took in the parish church in Llanfihangel-yng-Ngwynfa in Ann's day: "there would be, besides the set morning service, singing of carols and songs on the birth of the Saviour."[10] The carols and songs were composed by local poets (*clochyddion*—sextons—seem to have had a special gift for this in many parishes).

In a chapter on "The Plygain Carols and the Work of Ann Griffiths" Donald noted the five characteristics of *Plygain* carols, which had been identified by Dr. Enid Pierce Roberts. They are "resolutely biblical in their contents"; they "express corporate rather than individual devotion;" "while they dwell on the story of Christmas and the mystery of the incarnation . . . they look on to the whole story of Christ, not least to his suffering and death, to his resurrection and to his coming in glory;" "they often contain a strong element of moral exhortation" and "they are above all songs of joyful celebration."[11]

Donald looked for themes, methods and interests in *Plygain* carols to see if they reflected any influence on the content of her hymns (which he stressed were *not* carols, because of their highly personal devotional nature.) The carols which he used for this analysis dated from the nineteenth century, after Ann's death. However, had he had the opportunity to

9. Morris Davies, *Cofiant Ann Griffiths*, 19 (translation by Patrick Thomas).

10. Ibid., 30 (translation by Patrick Thomas).

11 Allchin, *Praise Above All*, 96.

examine the earlier Welsh carol tradition, he would have discovered that Ann Griffiths belonged within a poetic lineage of reflection on the paradox of the Incarnation which goes back through the *Plygain* verses of the seventeenth-century Anglican vicar Rhys Prichard to the thirteenth-century Franciscan friar, Brother Madog ap Gwallter.[12]

Ann's Anglican upbringing may have provided her with a religious foundation and a theological vocabulary. However, along with the other members of her family, she was soon drawn to the powerful spiritual movement which transformed the life of eighteenth- and nineteenth-century Wales. Welsh Methodism had begun in the 1740s inspired by three hugely influential figures: Daniel Rowland, Curate of Llangeitho in Cardiganshire, Howel Harris, a lay evangelist from Breconshire, and William Williams, a prolific and gifted hymn-writer and spiritual counsellor from Carmarthenshire. Williams was an Anglican deacon, but the Bishop of St. Davids would not ordain him priest, writing in his register "A Methodist refused." He was also unwilling to ordain Harris. Rowland's father, brother, and son were successively Rectors of Llangeitho, but Daniel himself was eventually driven out of the church by the diocesan authorities, and had to establish a place of worship of his own.

Welsh Methodism was Calvinist in its theology. Despite the hostility shown towards it by the Anglicized episcopate, until 1811 the movement remained within what was then the Church of England in Wales. During Ann's lifetime, Welsh Methodists relied on sympathetic Anglican clergy for the sacraments. Ann would walk across the hills to Bala to receive Communion from Thomas Charles, an ordained Anglican who had become one of the leaders of Welsh Methodism. Religious experience was at the heart of the movement in Ann's time. Groups of Methodists would meet together in *seiadau* ("experience societies") to support one another's spiritual development.

It was actually a minister from another strand of Welsh religion who was responsible for the turning-point in Ann's life, which seems to have taken place in 1797. She had gone to the nearby market town of Llanfyllin, apparently, according to her biographer, intending to take part in the dancing and merry-making associated with the local *Gŵylmabsant* (Patronal Festival). However, she met a former maidservant of the family who persuaded her to go to listen to a visiting preacher in an Independent

---

12. See "Brother Madog's Song; The First Welsh Christmas Carol," in Patrick Thomas, *Brechfa and Beyond*, 20–24.

(Congregational) chapel. His words made such an impact on her that she began to reconsider her whole way of life. She became disillusioned with the parish church after hearing some inept and inappropriate remarks by the local parson, and joined the Methodist *seiat* in the village of Pontrobert.

In 1804, after her father's death, Ann married Thomas Griffiths, a local farmer who was also a staunch Calvinistic Methodist. After ten months their only child, Elizabeth, was born. She only survived for two weeks. Ann herself died shortly afterwards. She left a small but priceless legacy: the volume of her writings edited by E. Wyn James, with an introduction by Donald, contains eight letters and thirty hymns (twelve of which only contain a single verse).[13] Tony Conran, one of the finest translators of Welsh verse into English, has said of Ann's hymns that they "represent the culmination of fifteen hundred years of Welsh poetry, the ultimate mystical apotheosis of where it's at," yet one of the most remarkable things about Ann is that any of her writings have survived at all.[14]

Ann had been taught to read and write Welsh by a Mrs. Owen from a neighbouring village. She could also speak a certain amount of English, but was not fluent enough to be able to read an English book. Only one of her letters, written to her friend Elizabeth Evans, survives in her own hand. She added to it a verse from one of her hymns, the only surviving autograph manuscript of her poetry. Everything else has come down through others. Ruth Evans, the maidservant at Dolwar Fach, played a key role. As she milked the cows in the cowshed and did other chores, she would listen to Ann singing her verses, and would learn them off by heart. Ruth was able to read Welsh, but could not write it. Ann would write some of her hymns on scraps of paper, and hide them under a cushion on a chair in the kitchen. Ruth would secretly take a peep at them and try to learn them.

Before Ann's death, Ruth tried to persuade her to collect her hymns together so that they could be preserved. Ann, however, regarded them as something private and personal, written for her own spiritual comfort, and did not feel that they were worth preserving. Ruth disagreed. After her mistress had died, Ruth recited Ann's verses to Thomas Charles of Bala, the prominent Methodist. He was impressed, and asked the newly-wed Ruth to get her husband to write them down. That husband was John Hughes, a

---

13. E. Wyn James and A. M. Allchin, *Rhyfeddaf Fyth . . . Emynau a llythyrau Ann Griffiths ynghyd â'r byrgofiant iddi gan John Hughes, Pontrobert, a rhai llythyrau gan gyfeillion.*

14. Conran is quoted in Allchin, *God's Presence Makes the World*, 87.

member of the *seiat* in Pontrobert, and someone to whom Ann had often turned for spiritual counsel. John was a weaver who became a schoolteacher and then a Methodist preacher. As well as preserving Ann's hymns, John Hughes also copied seven of her letters into his notebook.

Donald was introduced to Ann Griffiths' work by his friend H. A. Hodges, Professor of Philosophy at Reading University. The two had already collaborated in producing an anthology of the hymns of John and Charles Wesley.[15] In 1976, the bicentenary of Ann's birth they each produced a volume about the hymn-writer from Dolwar Fach. Hodges' volume, produced by Church in Wales Publications, included an introduction to Ann's life and work, and his translation ("Ann Griffiths: A Literary Survey") of a lecture given by Saunders Lewis, perhaps the most prominent Welsh writer and literary critic of the twentieth century. It also had the text of Ann's hymns, with Hodges' English translations. Herbert Hodges died in the summer of 1976, and the material in the book was assembled by the Reverend James Coutts.[16] Donald's contribution was a monograph about Ann in the "Writers of Wales" series published by the University of Wales Press on behalf of the Welsh Books Council. A revised edition was published in 1987, and this also appeared in the same year under a different title in America, with an introduction by Fredrica Harris Thompsett of the Episcopal Divinity School.[17]

Donald began his study of Ann Griffiths by comparing her with another of his great enthusiasms, the great Danish hymn-writer Nikolai Grundtvig. It enabled him to assert the central place of hymnody within the European cultural tradition. He noted that "in Welsh there can be no question about the place of hymns within the literary heritage of the nation."[18] He referred to their role as public and popular poetry, and to the fact that their explicitly religious nature did not seem to embarrass the irreligious. It's certainly true that, almost forty years after Donald first published his monograph, the crowds continue to belt out "Bread of Heaven" at the top of their voices during rugby matches in Cardiff's Millennium Stadium.

---

15. Allchin and Hodges, *A Rapture of Praise: Hymns of John and Charles Wesley*. London, 1966.

16. *Homage to Ann Griffiths: A Special Bicentenary Publication*.

17. Allchin, *Writers of Wales: Ann Griffiths*, (Cardiff, 1976); Allchin, *Ann Griffiths: The Furnace and the Fountain* (Cardiff, 1987); Allchin, *Songs To Her God: Spirituality of Ann Griffiths* (Cambridge, MA, 1987). The American edition includes Professor Hodges' translations of Ann's letters and poems.

18. Allchin, *Writers of Wales: Ann Griffiths*, 3.

Whether many, or indeed any, of those singers have much awareness of the religious meaning or literary value of the verses of William Williams Pantycelyn's great hymn, is rather more questionable.

In his monograph Donald compared Williams Pantycelyn and Ann, suggesting that their view of themselves as hymn-writers differed. Unlike Pantycelyn, he remarked, Ann had "no sense of what we should call literary proprietorship."[19] It is certainly true that William Williams reached his Methodist audience in a very deliberate way. His hymns were printed in easily affordable booklets. He would fill his saddle-bags with copies of the latest collection, and distribute them as he travelled around the Methodist societies scattered throughout Wales. Their impact was sometimes quite astonishing. It was claimed that the arrival of Pantycelyn's new booklet of hymns, Y Môr o Wydr ("The Sea of Glass"), was largely responsible for the dramatic religious revival which broke out at Llangeitho in 1762.[20]

Donald suggested that, in contrast to those of Pantycelyn, Ann's hymns were transmitted "rather in the way that the knowledge of folk songs spreads." He saw it as a process beginning with Ann immediately sharing her new verses with Ruth, through whom they would pass into use in the local Methodist societies.[21] It's an attractive idea, but it doesn't seem to square with Ann's early biographer's account of her hymn-writing as an essentially personal and private activity: something that flowed from the deepest level of her relationship with God in Christ. Morris Davies remarks that Ann had originally intended to keep a spiritual diary, but that she then found that composing verses came more naturally to her. That she hid those verses that she wrote down, as well as her remark to Ruth Evans that she only wrote her hymns, "er cysur i mi fy hun" ("for my own comfort"), would seem to imply that the verses were intended to help her analyse and express her spiritual condition, and were not intended for a wider circle. As a devout Calvinist (like Ann herself), Morris Davies saw their survival as an act of Divine Providence.[22]

In Ann's time Welsh Bibles and Books of Common Prayer were normally bound together in a single volume (the exception being a Welsh Bible with a commentary included, which the Reverend Peter Williams produced to avoid copyright restrictions). Given her father's use of the Prayer Book in

19. Allchin, *Writers of Wales: Ann Griffiths*, 14.
20. Gomer Morgan Roberts, *Hanes Methodistiaeth Galfinaidd Cymru: Cyfrol 1*, 299.
21. Allchin, *Writers of Wales: Ann Griffiths*, 14–15.
22. Davies, *Cofiant Ann Griffiths*, 70, 80–81.

family devotions, it is likely that such a composite volume would be among the most treasured possessions in Dolwar Fach. Donald emphasized the influence of both Bible and Prayer Book on Ann. He stressed the way in which she used a very traditional form of biblical interpretation, based on the unity of Old and New Testaments: "in her hymns, which are woven out of a tissue of biblical quotation and allusion, Old Testament types are constantly seen in reference to Christ."[23]

The absorption of passages from the Prayer Book from her childhood onwards, may well account for Ann's ability to (apparently quite effortlessly) express complex elements of Christian teaching in a clear and accessible way. Donald noted that Ann's "grasp of both Trinitarian and Christological doctrine is remarkably sound," and that "equally remarkable is her capacity to sum up in a few lines, a whole history of teaching and experience." As someone who preaches in Welsh almost every Sunday, I have lost count of the times I have quoted in my addresses the verse about Christ which Donald chose to illustrate that second assertion—the literal word-for-word translation in his monograph loses some of the power of the Welsh original:

> Y mae ddyn i gydymdeimlo
> A'th holl wendidau i gyd,
> Mae'n Dduw i gario'r orsedd
> Ar ddiafol, cnawd a byd.
> (He is man to sympathise with all thy weaknesses together, he is
> God to win the throne over the devil, the flesh and the world.)[24]

Donald looked in detail at the hymn of Ann's that is most frequently sung in modern Wales. Perhaps the main reason for the contemporary popularity of "*Wele'n sefyll rhwng y myrtwydd . . .*" ("Behold, standing among the myrtles . . .") is the tune to which it is now set. "Cwm Rhondda" is probably the best known of all Welsh hymn-tunes. Whereas in English it accompanies a translation of one of Williams Pantycelyn's hymns, in Welsh the words are those of Ann Griffiths. Donald was troubled by the hostility expressed towards the created world in the final verse of her hymn, where Ann speaks of rejecting "*eilunod gwael y llawr*" ("the wretched idols of the earth"). In fact her preference for the love of "*Iesu mawr*" ("great Jesus") to such distractions is characteristic of the great Welsh Methodist hymn-writers. Pantycelyn can sing quite cheerfully of being in heaven and gazing on the loveliness of Christ's face while the earth goes up in flames.

23. Allchin, *Writers of Wales: Ann Griffiths*, 17.
24. Quoted in Allchin, *Writers of Wales: Ann Griffiths*, 23.

Looking for a positive element in this attitude, Donald wrote of Ann:

> She finds all created things of little value, not because she despises them in themselves, but because she has seen something else, a vision of eternal splendour with which they cannot compare. We may not share her experience, but we can hardly doubt its reality for her, or fail to acknowledge that many bear witness to it through the centuries.[25]

The world-denying aspect of Ann's thought was clearly something which Donald, given his sacramental approach to creation, and his delight in a God who is both immanent and transcendent, found very difficult to accept. Yet there is no doubt that it played a central part in Ann's most profound spiritual battles.

Morris Davies, drawing on the memories of those who had known Ann, gives a picture of her during these times of inner conflict:

> There would be times when she was at her spinning-wheel spinning, with her tears running down her clothes, and her appearance a clear proof that she was then in great affliction of mind; and she would frequently go aside to her secret room, and liked to have complete silence when she was in this state. It is said that she often used to go to pray in an old peat shed at the side of the house—sometimes three times a day, or more, and would usually come out soaked with tears.[26]

This anguish, and the only escape from it, is reflected in two of Ann's most powerful verses:

> Rhyw hiraeth sy am ymadael
> Bob dydd â'r gwaedlyd faes,
> Nid â'r arch, nac Israel,
> Ond hunanymchwydd cas;
> Cael dod at fwrdd y Brenin,
> A'm gwadd i eiste'n uwch,
> A minnau, wan ac eiddil,
> Am garu yn y llwch.
>
> Er cryfed ydyw'r stormydd
> Ac ymchwydd tonnau'r môr,
> Doethineb ydyw'r peilat,

---

25. Allchin, *Writers of Wales: Ann Griffiths,* 30.

26. Davies, *Cofiant Ann Griffiths,* 62 (translation by Patrick Thomas).

A'i enw'n gadarn Iôr,
Er gwaethaf dilyw pechod
A llygredd o bob rhyw,
Dihangol yn y diwedd
Am fod yr arch yn Dduw.

(Every day there's a longing to escape from the bloody battlefield—
not from the ark, or Israel, but from loathsome self-importance; to
come to the King's table, who invites me to sit higher up, and I,
weak and helpless, wanting to love in the dust.

Although the storms and the swell of the sea's waves are so strong,
Wisdom is the pilot, and his name is powerful Lord. In spite of sin's
deluge and corruption of every kind, [I shall] escape in the end,
because the ark is God.)[27]

Despite a certain antipathy to the world-denying side of Ann's Calvinistic Methodism, Donald sympathetically analyzed her inner struggle,
reflected in her surviving letters as well as her hymns. He saw her "constant
disappointment with herself" as springing "from her acute sense that if
God can occupy the first place in man's heart and man's mind, then it is a
betrayal of his love, a denial of the very source of life and meaning, to allow
anything else to take that first place."[28] This view of Ann's spirituality, and
his own profound interest in the nature of the religious life, led Donald to
ponder the question of what might have happened had Ann come from a
different setting. Had she lived in medieval Wales, or nineteenth-century
France or Russia, he speculated that "she would very possibly have found
her place within a monastic community."

Such a flight of the imagination, combined with his own breadth of
learning, led Donald to some interesting parallels and contrasts between the
hymn-writer from Dolwar Fach and the nineteenth-century French Catholic mystical theologian Elizabeth of Dijon (Sister Elizabeth of the Trinity).[29]
There is certainly an ecumenism of the Spirit, which Ann Griffiths shares
with many other mystical writers, particularly poets. When I first stum-
bled across *Speaking to God from the Depths of the Heart*, Thomas Samu-

27. Quoted in James and Allchin, *Rhyfeddaf Fyth,* 27 (translation by Patrick
Thomas).

28. Allchin, *Writers of Wales: Ann Griffiths,* 47.

29. Ibid., 55; Allchin, *The Gift of Theology: The Trinitarian Vision of Ann Griffiths and
Elizabeth of Dijon* (2005)—a revised edition of Allchin, *Women of Prayer* (1992).

elian's translation of the masterpiece of the tenth-century Armenian poet and mystic St. Grigor Narekatsi, I was startled by the similarity between passages written by the ascetic monk on the shores of Lake Van and verses by the farmer's wife from the hills of Montgomeryshire. However, on reflection, it became clear that the source of such parallels were a profound knowledge of Scripture and an intense life of prayer rooted in an awareness of the human capacity for sin and self-deception, and Christ's love which alone can overcome it.

Paradoxes do not present a problem for poets, indeed they are often at the heart of their creativity. Donald shared with the Welsh Roman Catholic (and former Calvinistic Methodist) critic Saunders Lewis a particular admiration for a hymn of Ann's which Lewis considered "sums up all her themes and paradoxes." He remarked that "in my judgment it is one of the majestic songs in the religious poetry of Europe."[30] The hymn begins with the wonder of the Incarnation, something which was central to the *Plygain* carol tradition in which Ann had been brought up. Donald noted that for Ann "the basic problem is that of man's finitude and God's infinity, and so for her the starting point is the belief that he who is *the giver of being, the generous sustainer and ruler of everything that is,* has entered into his creation, has accepted the limitations of our human state, vividly symbolised by the swaddling clothes in which the infant Jesus is wrapped."[31]

As has been mentioned above, a similar fascination with the paradox of the Incarnation has a long history in Welsh religious poetry. In his poem on the birth of Jesus, the *"Cawr mawr bychan"* ("great little Giant"), the thirteenth century Franciscan friar Brother Madog ap Gwallter wrote:

Ych ac asen, Arglwydd presen, preseb piau,
A sopen wair yn lle cadair i'n Llyw cadau;
Pali ny myn, nid uriael ei ginhynnau,
Yn lle syndal ynghylch ei wâl gwelid carpau.

(The Lord of the world in a manger belonging to an ox and an ass,
and a heap of straw instead of a cradle for the Lord of hosts; he
does not want embroidered silk, his nappies are not of fair linen,
Instead of delicate cloth, rags are seen around his resting place.)[32]

---

30. *Homage to Ann Griffiths*, 27. For Alan Gaunt's excellent metrical translation of the hymn, see Ann Griffiths, *Hymns and Letters*.

31. Allchin, *Writers of Wales: Ann Griffiths*, 34–35.

32. Quoted in Rhiain M. Andrews and others, *Gwaith Bleddyn Fardd a Beirdd Eraill y Drydedd Ganrif ar Ddeg*, 359.

While Ann would not have known Brother Madog's poem, there is a distinct possibility that she might have come across the verses of Rhys Prichard, the seventeenth-century Vicar of Llandovery, whose didactic doggerel rhymes were widely circulated (and often committed to memory) among both Anglicans and Nonconformists for two-and-a-half centuries. His Carmarthenshire dialect words and Anglicisms were glossed by editors, to make them comprehensible in other parts of Wales. Prichard's best-known carol calls on its hearers to go to Bethlehem. It contains the verse:

Awn i weld concwerwr ange
Gwedi' rwymo mewn cadache;
A'r Mab a rwyga deyrnas Satan
Yn y craits, heb allu cripian.

(Let's go to see death's conqueror wrapped up in nappies; and the Son who tears apart Satan's kingdom, in the manger, unable to crawl.)[33]

The paradox of the Incarnation leads Ann to another paradox: through Christ the Word she can venture in safety across a boundary that would otherwise inevitably lead to destruction. Even through the smoke is billowing from Mount Sinai, she will remain safe as she crosses the boundary between the profane and the sacred because of the reconciliation between God and humanity won by Christ's self-sacrifice for her. The reference to Sinai inevitably made Donald think of Gregory of Nyssa's "image of the way in which the believing heart and mind must approach the presence of the inaccessible God." He regarded the second verse of the hymn as "one of the most remarkable examples of the way in which Ann restates a basic theme of Christian spirituality which she can hardly have known directly through her reading."[34]

In the verses which follow, Ann reflects on the mysteries of the crucifixion and Holy Saturday. The executioners who nail Jesus to the cross are only able to do because of the strength which he has given them. Later, when Christ's body lies in the grave, the whole of creation is still moving in him. These paradoxical ideas particularly caught Donald's theological imagination. He found parallels in Byzantine hymnody, Eastern Orthodox iconography, and the writing of the twentieth century Roman Catholic theologian Hans Urs von Balthasar. They illustrated once again the way in

33. Quoted in Nesta Lloyd, *Cerddi'r Ficer: Detholiad o gerddi Rhys Prichard*, 5 (translation by Patrick Thomas).

34. Allchin, *Writers of Wales: Ann Griffiths*, 35.

which Ann's particular religious experience tapped unconsciously into the deepest streams of Christian tradition and spirituality.

The final section of the hymn is profoundly personal. Ann expresses her thanksgiving to the object of her worship: the true immortal and living God who had been willing to become the weakest and most wretched of humankind. Shedding her corrupt body she will finally see the Invisible, once dead and now alive, and live in inseparable and eternal unity and communion with her God. Her soul will be completely in his likeness, and she will "kiss the Son to eternity, and never turn away from him again." Donald commented:

> It is a communion without intermediary, made possible in the full restoration of the image of God in man, that capacity for God that is latent in every man. It is a union which, at the supreme moment of her song, Ann can only express in terms of the kiss exchanged between the beloved and the beloved, the bridegroom and the bride.[35]

Herbert Hodges, Donald's friend and collaborator, drew attention to another aspect of Ann's mysticism: the use of water imagery in her poetry. He noted that she drew on three biblical images: the pool of Bethesda, Ezekiel's vision of the life-giving river and the Book of Revelation's river of the water of life. He said of Ann: "her own contribution is to make these waters broaden out into a sea which has no shore and no bottom, but in which the redeemed can freely swim." He went on to speak of "her picture of the glorified soul perpetually exploring the breadth and depth of the sea of divine wonders, and never finding a limit."[36]

One of the passages which drew these comments from Hodges was said by Morris Davies to have been composed by Ann when she was travelling home across the mountains after attending a Communion service in Bala. He wrote that on that occasion:

> [S]he had such exalted insights into the mystery of the Trinity, and the mystery and the glory of the person of Christ and the joy o being able to go to see him as he is, and be like him, and be eternally with him, that her thoughts were so completely caught up, that she knew nothing of herself until she came across the Berwyn hills, to the top of the parish of Llanwddyn; which was about five

---

35. Allchin, *Writers of Wales: Ann Griffiths*, 40–41.

36. *Homage to Ann Griffiths*, 13.

miles away, and that while riding an animal which used to be fairly unmanageable.[37]

The verse which Davies links to this experience is:

O! ddedwydd awr tragwyddol orffwys
Oddi wrth fy llafur yn fy rhan,
Ynghanol môr o ryfeddodau
Heb weled terfyn byth, na glan;
Mynediad helaeth byth i bara
fewn trigfannau Tri yn Un;
Dŵr i nofio heb fynd trwyddo,
Dyn yn Dduw, a Duw yn ddyn.

(O joyful hour of eternal rest for me from all my labour, amidst a sea of wonders without seeing an end or a shore; a wide everlasting entrance into the dwellings of the Three in One; water to swim in without going through it, man as God, and God as man.)[38]

What makes the imagery particularly astonishing is that, during her short life, Ann never actually saw the sea. The largest stretch of water that she would ever have come across was Llyn Tegid (Bala Lake). Her physical horizons were distinctly limited, and yet, as Donald undoubtedly believed, "her stature is to be measured against the great and unquestioned figures of the Church's history, a St. Theresa of Avila or a Julian of Norwich, a St. Symeon the New Theologian, or a St. Seraphim of Sarov." However, he was wise enough to add that this "in no way cuts her off from her own people, from the nation that gave her birth."[39]

Writing of the communion of saints, Donald made a comment that seems especially appropriate when thinking of the Montgomeryshire farmer's wife whom he had no hesitation in numbering among the greatest spiritual figures of Christian history:

[T]he communion of saints is never an abstract or ethereal thing, a piece of superfluous doctrine. It is rooted in this earth, in places where people have lived and loved, and seen the glory of God shining out in the common light of every day. But those who have been constantly with God in prayer have even in this life become somewhat freer of time and space than most of us are. In prayer we

37. Davies, *Cofiant Ann Griffiths*, 73 (translation by Patrick Thomas).
38. Quoted in James and Allchin, *Rhyfeddaf Fyth*, 23 (translation by Patrick Thomas).
39. Allchin, *Writers of Wales: Ann Griffiths*, 64.

come more intimately into touch with those unconscious levels of our being which seem to be less tied to the time sequence than our consciousness is. Beyond them, we begin to enter into the deep places of the Spirit.[40]

Ann Griffiths certainly entered into such places, and a part of Donald's remarkable contribution was to enable people both in Wales and far beyond its borders to follow her there. For that he is owed an enormous debt of thanks and gratitude.

40. Allchin, *The Communion of Saints,* 9–10.

All Things Shout "Glory"

An Interview with Donald Allchin:
Part One of Three, July 11, 2007

David Keller, editor of *Boundless Grandeur,* interviewed Donald Allchin on the Feast of Saint Benedict, July 11, 2007. This was the first of three hour-long interviews over a three-day period. The edited transcripts that follow represent the only known example of Donald speaking about his life, his spiritual formation, the personal relationships that influenced his Christian vision and theology, and his understanding of the Trinity as the template for the unity of all creation and human life. The interviews also demonstrate Donald's focus on the resurrection of Christ that, in his understanding, makes transformed human life possible and is the source of human responsibility and efforts to mend and transform broken human lives and institutions.

The transcripts present an extemporaneous summary of Donald's Christian vision in his own words. As always, Donald sees and articulates connections between a variety of people and things. This explains his sometimes "rambling" and repetitive style. Yet, the redundancy and eclectic content of Donald's responses to questions often reinforces and articulates insights and wisdom that might otherwise be lost in concise and measured writing. Donald's verbal style also reflects his delight in people and human life, his sense of humor, and his realization that praise is at the heart of our life with God.

After the final interview Donald gave permission for the transcripts to be published in both print and audio formats. This was his final comment: "I am very grateful to you for asking me these things, and making me think about various things I don't usually think about. I perhaps should put some more of this down on paper. What I am very conscious of is that as you get older, it is very important to remember to put down more memories. I think perhaps I ought to."

KELLER: Your book, *Participation in God* (1988) describes the ancient Christian understanding of, in your words, "the life of God in the life of man" and the mystery of human transformation. You trace this fundamental truth called "theosis" and "deification" from the patristic period to our modern period, showing how it influenced both Anglican spirituality and the Methodist tradition. What prompted you to write *Participation in God?*

(Interviewer's Note: Donald's response to this question begins with a description of his early life and the people and experiences that influenced his own spiritual formation. Donald's writing and teaching came from the crucible of his experience of life and God's presence in life, as well as his interests in the history, writings, and personalities that form the Christian tradition. He shows that *Participation in God* came from his life experiences, persons who influenced him, and his study and reflection. It was not simply an academic exercise summarizing Christian theology.)

ALLCHIN: I was born on Easter day. Then I realized, as a child, that Easter was not going to come on my birthday again until I was seventy-five, which was a little bit of a damper. Nevertheless, the fact that I had been born on Easter day and my elder brother had also been born on Easter day, nine years before me, was something of which my mother was very happy about. She didn't talk about it much but you knew that she was very pleased, and I was very pleased.

One of things that influenced me at that time, thinking of the fact of having been born on the day of the resurrection, is that as soon as I came across Christianity where the resurrection was emphasized, I felt immediately attracted. As a child I was fascinated by history and thought I wanted to be an historian. When we went as a family almost every year to Cornwall, I didn't want to sit on the beach; I wanted to go up the river through the woods and visit old churches and castles. But that isn't how we spent the holidays. I was fascinated by the past. I had no idea what Celtic meant in those days but Cornwall entered deep into me and it was only about twenty years ago [around 1987] that I began to realize that perhaps that was the origin of this whole Celtic exploration which has been an important part of my life since I was about thirty or forty. It has been a part, never the whole.

I think that in school I was fascinated by medieval English writing and Langdon. I read little bits of *Sir Gawain and the Green Knight*. I suppose that fairly on, somebody must have given me a modern translation of Julian of Norwich—an absolute revolution in terms of understanding Christianity. I didn't understand it very much but I could see it was saying all kinds of things. It said extraordinary things about the presence of Christ in the middle of human life and about Christ being our mother. When I was at Westminster school, during the war, I met for the first time the Cowley Fathers. They had (and still have) a house very near Westminster School, and that is where I first made a retreat, and first made my confession, and first came across the whole thing of monastic life, which enormously impressed me. I didn't feel a particular calling to be a monk, but I was fascinated that there *were* monks. I talked Father Manson who had given his life to God being a monk. This meant an enormous amount to me. I said to Father Manson: "Wouldn't it be more consistent for me to be a Roman Catholic?" All this about being an Anglican and a Catholic at the same time. He said "You haven't really looked for the Eastern churches have you?" I said no. He said "Before you start to think more about Rome discover more about *them.*" I found a book called *The Russians and Their Church* by Nicholas Zernov, and six months later I discovered I could meet Zernov; he was a most attractive, lovely person, and very welcoming to this school boy.

I got into this thing called The Fellowship of St. Alban and St. Sergius in my late teens. There I met Antony Bloom, who afterwards became famous. He was a very powerful person who impressed you with his absolute authenticity—given this Orthodox Christianity. There I met a man called Vladimir Lossky who was undoubtedly the best theologian I had every heard. I was in my twenties and thirties. I became great friends with his sons and his two daughters. I was the eldest in that Lossky family, and I was very much the youngest in my own, so it became a kind of second family for me. I was very close to them and often stayed with them when I was in Paris. I was devoted to the whole family and I am still devoted to the one brother and the one sister who are still alive, and some of their children. Lossky himself was a brilliant man.

In 1951 or 1952 when I was twenty-one or twenty-two I went on my first real pilgrimage with them, because the Lossky family went on a pilgrimage. They did not go to Lourdes; they went to La Salette, this other Mary appearance, where Mary appeared to two peasant children in 1846. This was up in the mountains near Grenoble. We walked for two or three days before arriving there. It was an extraordinary experience walking with a Russian immigrant family. Father and mother—intensely intelligent people and the children also all pretty intelligent, and all of them taking Orthodox Christianity absolutely for granted—some a bit more critical than others, but it was just how they lived. I was fascinated, but a bit puzzled. When we got up to La Salette, at the end of the first evening we were there, I was standing at the back (during the service) with the younger of the two Lossky sons, and we were suddenly snatched by a French someone in a cassock and pulled up the steps into the tower. There were three bells and then three bells being rung: one by a young Russian orthodox, one by a young Anglican, and one by a Celtic Christian. Sounding out the graces of Mary across the mountains. That's where my book *The Joy of All Creation* came from. It was then I began to think to myself: "Look at the Losskys. They are so much more deeply Christian people than many people I've ever known before. Mary and devotion *to her* is so much just a natural part of Christianity with them—it can't be wrong." I wondered: "There must be something in my tradition. Is there anything in my tradition that corresponds?" So I wrote the book *The Joy of All Creation*.

In this context, I got caught into this kind of Christian unity thing. The Christian unity thing is still very much part of my whole understanding of transformation. If Christianity is true, then the church must be one. In my lifetime, yes, I have lived through a lot of things. On the whole, the churches *have* come together. Not as much as we thought or hoped they would, but thinking back to how it was in the 1940s and 1950s, especially between Roman Catholics and all other Christians. That is gone; something has changed radically. Christian unity is central to my being a person of faith. In the last twenty years I have been thinking gradually that Christian unity is only the beginning. From there, we have to go on to interfaith unity—that all of the major religions should listen, understand and love one another, and understand what the Almighty is saying to all of them, together. All of that has developed very rapidly in the last ten years (1997–2007).

To me it has developed primarily because first of all, I met Thomas Merton three or four times in the 1960s when I was in Gethsemane (Merton's abbey, in Kentucky). It would be interesting to talk about how I got to Gethsemane. It began in the United States in Louisville, KY. The first person I met and knew in the U.S., was a man who taught at the Baptist seminary, Dale Moody, who took me around Kentucky showed me what the United

States really was. He introduced me to Merton because he already had very good contacts with him. This was in 1962. The Roman Catholic Second Vatican Council was only just beginning. As I met Merton and reflected on my experience with my Russian friends, I was puzzled—what do I have to say to Merton, a world famous writer? In Kentucky, he was getting very few visitors from England, so I could bring news from there. I had not realized how *deeply* influenced Merton was by the Russian theologians in Paris. I knew some of them personally. One was Paul Evdokimov, a layman. He got married a second time—which was very irregular in the Orthodox world. His first wife died. He married a charming Japanese lady who works as an interpreter. We (Merton and Allchin) talked a lot about Russian Orthodoxy. Ever since Merton died, I have been most deeply moved by what I call his "non-disintegrating explosion" which takes place during the last five years of his life (about 1963 to 1968), where he seems to be studying all the major monastic traditions. All while he is living his hermit life, his monastic life, and writing all kinds of things. He is studying the more mystical elements in Judaism. He's been interested in Jain since he was a student. Interested in other forms of Buddhism. Then interested in the Hindu world, and finally, in the last year or two he is deeply into Sufism. Never writes about it, but there are endless tapes of him talking in his most light hearted, irresponsible way about Sufism. He is fascinated by Sufism. Then you discover that on his way to the Far East in October 1968—going to an international conference—he stops in Alaska, because it might be a good place to have a hermitage. He is reading the latest of Lossky's posthumously published book *In the Image and Likeness of God*. So Merton is obviously trying to study something about Tibetan Buddhism, because he is going to meet the Dali Lama, and will speak to him for three full days. [At the same time] Merton also has a traditional Christian book with him in French by a Russian Orthodox theologian. Merton has been an immense influence in my life, giving me a much greater liberty in terms of studying religions. I was open to learn and wanted to learn.

I was very influenced in the last [few] years by my friendship with David Ford—professor in Cambridge—who has been a very active member of a group in New England (but it has now spread and has a branch in Europe) which began with Jewish and Christian people studying very much traditional scriptural exegesis together. Trying to see if in the Christian tradition and the Jewish tradition they actually *could* speak to each other, *how* they could speak to each other, and the *difficulties* of speaking to each other.

After they had been doing this for five or six years, every time he came back [to the UK] David would say "This is the best thing I have done this summer." About two years before 9/11 for the first time [David] began to have Islamic scholars as well talk about the traditional ways of scriptural exegesis of the Koran. How these [separate traditions] seem to have rather strange and fascinating things to say to each other. All of the problems of course are not resolved, but people involved say something very creative in relation to the awful relationship between them. As you know, Osama bin Laden's second in command has made a great attack on the British, and on the Queen in particular because she is giving this Knighthood to Salman Rushdie. The [British] people don't understand the anger of the Islamic people because they know so little about Islam. Just as [Muslims] know very little about the Queen—as though the Queen is going to bang them over the head with a sword. They know absolutely nothing about English people, and certainly nothing about the Queen. Out of this terrible ignorance, the whole of this conflict between the Middle Eastern world and our Western world goes on, and it centers itself in Palestine.

KELLER: One of the things I am hearing as I listen to you talk about your own early experiences is how people around you formed you and led you to others and that this relates to the critical situation in the world today. You frame it by saying that no one really knows enough about each other to begin to look towards reconciliation in a substantive way. To me, this points to the importance of human transformation. It leads to questions like: "How can we change our consciousness?" "How can we want to take the risk of understanding the enemy, or people we don't agree with, or other religious traditions?"

(Interviewer's note: Donald's response to this question is to describe a dialog between Thomas Merton and a civil servant in the Pakistani government rather than giving how-to advice or a theological narrative on how to bring about a change in human consciousness. At the same time, at the end of his response, he points out that the dialog between persons flows from an inner dialog between each person and God.)

ALLCHIN: I think Thomas Merton is wonderful here, because our politicians have no idea [about changing our consciousness in relation to each other]. On the other hand, this wonderful correspondence in the first big volume of Merton's correspondence—between Merton and Abdul Aziz, who was a civil servant in the Pakistani government, and who was a deeply thoughtful and prayerful Islamic scholar [and] a Sufi. He is put in touch with Merton and they began by writing and recommending books to one another. The Pakistani man asks about St. John of the Cross and what he ought to read about him. Merton asks about Rumi. Out of this comes an extraordinary personal exchange. We've only got printed Merton's side of the correspondence. We've been told there is plenty of Abdul Aziz's correspondence that still exists. (The last time Bonnie Thurston and I met she said that she hopes we can publish a selection of the correspondence because it is about two men living on different sides of the world, thirty years ago.) But Merton, at the end of his letters often says "The great powers are not behaving well." It is the 1960s, and he is obviously worried about the threat of nuclear war. He says "We are living in very dark times." The letters from Merton might have been written *five years ago*, not thirty-five years ago. [These two men] are really listening to one another, and [Abdul Aziz] is very inquisitive. You can tell from Merton's replies he is asking Merton to tell him more about what his timetable for prayer is, and how he lives in the Hermitage. Eventually, Merton writes and says "Now you've asked me about these things." And he will tell Abdul under the condition that he doesn't tell others because he doesn't want it to be published. It is private—between him and God. In a beautiful letter of about two to three sides, he tells him about the times [for prayer] he keeps when he gets up in the morning and when he is silent, living in the Hermitage. We've got these beautiful letters. I believe that this [dialogue] is happening in lots of places—with Jewish, Christian, and Islamic people.

Christians are not so close historically and doctrinally [with Islamic people] as we are with Jews, [with whom] we are intensely close because we have claimed that we superseded them altogether. We are also very close to Islam, but we don't know it. Until you look at the Koran and begin to see that Mohammed assumes that there are people called Christians and Jews about. He doesn't quite agree with them, but he has at least some openings for contact with them. All that is there, and there *is* quite a lot going on. I am not hopeless about that because just as [in] the beginning of Christian unity [we were asking] "What on earth are the Catholics telling the Baptists? or Baptists telling the Catholics?" We thought nothing good could come out of that, but a lot of good came out of it. And a lot can come out of the other. We need to be encouraged and obviously *we all need to enter more deeply into the inner sanctum of ourselves.* Yes. Yes. To be seeking the face of God *there*. It is only in that *deep* framework that we shall be able to be open in a creative way.

KELLER: Would you say more about the relationship of our inner personal experience with God and how that enables us to live in the midst of what is now a very complex and violent world? You mentioned that there are things opening up that we never would have dreamed of, which indicates to me there is something happening that is almost transpersonal. Would you say more about how our inner life relates to our relationships with other persons?

ALLCHIN: Yes. I believe there is something transpersonal that is opening up. One of the things that has really fascinated me in the last year or two, and has rather been a kind of relief from the conflicts inside the Anglican communion (which has been painful for Anglicans) is this sense in our secular society of wondering now if society is as secular as [we think] because there *seems* to be a rediscovery of the arts in relationship to the sacred. Sacred music, and people wanting to find out—very creative work. This is totally unexpected, in a way, because any kind of inner transformation, surely requires letting God put the different bits of us *together*: the intellectual, the emotional/feeling, the imaginative, the thinking/calculating—they all need to be together inside us in relationship to God, so that the grace of God can work in bringing us into greater wholeness.

KELLER: In an informal conversation earlier today, you mentioned that human transformation takes place in the context of a *whole* person. That is what I hear you saying in different words now. Say more about how the world perceives itself as *secular* and at the same time it may be more deeply spiritual than it realizes. Are you saying that the boundaries between sacred and secular are really artificial?

ALLCHIN: Not entirely artificial, but they are often exaggerated or misunderstood. There needs to be distinctions. If the mystery of the Trinity is at the *heart* of things, then things can be distinct but not separate. This in general is a characteristic of a functioning and a developing *human* life. The things that appear to be separate and different in fact need one another in order to complement one another. This goes on at all kinds of levels, and is beginning to happen. We are starting to understand it better. The kind of project you [David Keller and Emily Wilmer] are involved in here [i.e. trying to integrate contemplative experience of God into the lives of people who live very busy and responsible lives] is a very interesting example. [It] is taking rather secular examples of inquiring—as in commerce or in industry, or in scientific questions—in order to think through these inner questions which we have left either hanging in the air or we have left [them] in formulations made a thousand years ago (which may have been good ones, but they are very old now, and so we need new ones to correspond more to where we are now) Your own project is a part of the stirring that is going on.

KELLER: One of the things that I am hearing is that you are talking about personal experience, your own journey, and how others have influenced your experience of life and guided you. This led to things that have happened that you and others could not have dreamed of. In your remarks I am sensing that there is indeed not only a *sense* of mystery but also a deep dynamic or some activity going on. How would you describe this context of mystery in your own human journey and relate it to, for example, what is our *shared* human journey? How does transformation relate to your journey and to how you participate in the wider human journey?

(Interviewer's note: In response to this question Donald describes the influence the Christian monastic tradition has had on his spiritual formation. This personal influence led to the emphasis in his teaching and writing on the need to recognize and revive the integral role of monastic life and values in the wider Christian tradition.)

ALLCHIN: I have thought about this since [our conversation at] lunch, and I have recognized something that I've known about myself. Since I have really reflected about it, as I say when I was fifteen or sixteen, I met one of the members of the Society of St. John the Evangelist. I heard him preach a retreat [in which he] very much pushed us when we were teenagers towards a life of prayer. That was very hard. As I said, I was delighted to discover that there were monks. I had read about monks in history, but I didn't think there were any [at that time]. All my life I have been quite closely related to monastic communities. I have never joined one, [I was] not particularly moved by God to do that. But I have felt very strongly that for any kind of balanced human or balanced Christian life, the kind discipline and constant worship of a monastic community is absolutely invaluable. This is something I could have never have survived without, as a Christian. I discovered it, with a little house of prayer that our Anglican Franciscans had, and still have. It was like a more contemplative house where the novices went for a time. I used to go and spend some time there. It was there that I was first hit by one of Merton's books. I read *The Sign of Jonas*, the one about his first years as a monk. I had this experience which people describe (long before I met him) [of] a vivid experience like he was in the room talking to me. I was living in a little tiny House of Prayer. He was in a great big monastery—about two-hundred people packing themselves in at that moment. He was writing [with] such an authentic human quality—with such humor, but also such depth about the discovery of the life of prayer and life of God.

I suddenly realized [more about monastic life] when I became a Canon of Canterbury [Cathedral]. I was living close to France and the [Roman Catholic] Benedictine community at Bec had close links to Canterbury Cathedral. That gave me a link to *them*—as a very well-established, rather typical French Benedictine community. Also I discovered through more personal contacts a Cistercian Abbey [and the writing of] Andre Louf and his book on prayer which many have read, and some of his other books, too. I had the enormous privilege and gift that they gave me from that monastery. They invited me (when I had time and need) to just live along side them. I lived in the Guest house, but apart from that, I lived almost entirely with the community. I received communion with them every day. This was all done with the approval of the bishop. There I wrote the book on Mary (*The Joy of All Creation*) and the *Participation in God* book. It was a place where it was possible to write about those kinds of things because I was living in a community of people who were *living* those kinds of things. In terms of my Anglican existence, I was for almost twenty years what in England we called the "warden" [of a religious community of women]. [When the] first communities of sisters were being re-founded in the Church of England the bishops were very suspicious of them. The community elected a priest who had a certain status in the church as the warden, someone who would be their advisor, but also their representative to the Episcopate. In a way that is no longer needed because the communities are now totally accepted in our church. The bishops themselves are deeply related to them. I did that for about twenty years for the community [The Sisters of the Love of God in Fairacres, Oxford]. I have done it for the last twenty years for a smaller community, but a very profoundly alive community in South Wales—a place called Tymawr. So I have been feeding off the grace and the gift and the discipline of religious sisters who I have worked with and have tried to serve. They have served me much more than I have served them.

I have gained much more from their contact. But I have been able to solve certain problems.

KELLER: You have mentioned consistently the importance of monasticism from your very early life until now. You have used the phrase "those kind of things" in reference to what you were experiencing with the monastic community. Could you be more specific about that and also your phrase "life of prayer"? Could you tell more about those kinds of things, and (this is my phrase) those things "that were giving you life"?

ALLCHIN: First of all, monasticism takes many forms at the present time. Partly through my contact with the Sisters of Tymawr who had contact with the community of L'Arche and the communities of handicapped people. There has been quite a new experience—profoundly praying community. Both mentally and physically handicapped people lead a life of intense faith (not because they don't have the intellectual problems of others), [but] perhaps because you are living a life where you are in some sense marginal to the world [and] where much of your early experience was probably being [in] a world of rejection. There is a wounded-ness in you which need the grace of God and feed on it. That helps others of us who are not so obviously wounded to recognize our own wounded-ness and find help from them. We've had a lot of contact with L'Arche communities. The small Roman Catholic Benedictine community of Kent is close to the community of L'Arche. Quite a number of the women who have become nuns have in fact been people who were working with them.

So there are all *kinds* of communities which have a monastic flavor to them. At the same time, most people in this country, particularly the Church of England, see all our religious communities are dying out. Some of them *have* died out, but some are quietly growing, a little bit. They are very deeply rooted. This is not just a question of organization. It is very striking about the Community of Tymawr in South Wales. There are relationships with associates and "along siders" and groups who are linked with them—people who are living a deep life of prayer in the world. All of those relationships have become more realistic than they used to be. That is something I find very encouraging in the Church. A big thing is that the Cistercian Order in the Roman Catholic Church, from the time of St. Bernard until about thirty to forty years ago, one of their rules was "We don't have people called Oblates or Tertiaries; we are just *ourselves.*" But in the last thirty years, *lay* Cistercian communities have been founding themselves. We have to accept these people [and enable them to] share our life. As I remember Merton saying: "I think we need to have smaller communities than this one—[we need] communities that are more closely linked to the world outside." And he said probably we need more intermediate communities between [traditional monastic communities] where people can pass more easily in and out. If you've been a monk for twenty years, especially in a contemplative community, you've got a great deal of "inner" activity going on which you need to express. Go and express it. Perhaps you will do it for [the rest of your life], or perhaps you will do it for five years and find your way back [into the rest of society]. We must be more flexible. In our Christian world, we have had very rigid institutional lines. I am very much struck by the way in which young people who visit a place like Tymawr often take it for granted. They have been using Buddhist mediation techniques. We now have a number of Buddhists in the monastic communities in this country. A lot of people go and spend some time with them. There is a kind of exchange going on at that level in a way that, surprisingly, sometimes people have jumped into things without fully enough thinking. On the whole, my anxiety is overcome by my delight in seeing the people feel drawn to that kind of experiment, and that kind of searching. A lot is going on in your country [the USA] in that way.

KELLER: Yes. I can speak from my own experience in my years at St. John's Benedictine Abbey in Collegeville, MN. They have hundreds of Oblates. They have an annual retreat for Oblates who can come to the Abbey. They have a process of study before becoming an oblate. While, as in your words, they are not monks, yet they are living an intentional monastic way in the world.

ALLCHIN: Yes. This is one of the things you, personally, have been looking at historically both in relation to the Desert Fathers and in relation to the early Celtic monastic [life]. There always was a distinction, but it wasn't a separation. Again, it is this question of Trinitarian theology. Things can be distinguished and also united. Distinguished in order *not* to be separated. There are ways in which married people who are bringing up children, with all the responsibilities of married life, can live as very close members of a monastic community. For people living in the monastery, that is an enormous affirmation and an enormous strength. Obviously, you have seen it in your experience in the Egyptian desert. Forty or fifty years ago, most people would have said that the monastic life has died out in the Coptic Church. Certainly seventy years ago [it had atrophied]. Before World War I, people thought monasteries were dying out, just as people [thought] when I first went to Mount Athos in the 1950s and 1960s; the monasteries there were all declining in numbers, and becoming older. Suddenly, in 1970s and 1980s, one or two of them began to grow, and they've gone on growing. They are the real kind of old fashioned Orthodox fundamentalists—they only believe in rigid Orthodoxy. I had a young man from Romania who just finished his doctoral thesis on Father Dumitru Staniloae, who was perhaps the most open of all Romanian Orthodox theologians, almost the most open of all Orthodox *theologians* that I know of, in his relations with other Christians. Stefan Toma has been writing a doctoral thesis on Father Dumitru as an Orthodox theologian in contact with the West and churches outside Romania. He said he had done his thesis in Greece, and he was sent by his institute. An awful nuisance to do it in Greek, but he got to know Mount Athos. I asked him "What do they think about Father Dumitru on Mount Athos?" He said that one of the younger monks said that "we regard him as our spiritual Father. We read his books and they are already our spiritual food." I am sure there are *some* monks who are not doing that, but it is clear that there are quite a lot who are. Therefore, there is a kind of openness and mutual giving.

I think quite a lot of our thinking about how our inner life develops inside us is too *literally* "inner." Because actually the inner life needs to be fed with relationships with other people. The inner life has [an] aspect of the recognition of God as beauty. The whole aesthetic side of our nature, which so often, in our Western world, we put in a separate little box called "Art." Some people get into it, some do not. Some kinds of art are very high brow. The whole notion that the beauty of the world [is] being expressed not only in natural beauty but in various kinds of human beauty is something we desperately need to recover. This would be a part of recovering the art of prayer and meditation. This is one of the things where this can grow. We need to see how to let God put things together.

KELLER: That is a good place to start our second interview. In your statement, "We need to let God put things together?" I am hearing something significant about the nature of transformation. Also, in our next interview I'd like to follow up on some of your comments about the Trinity. You have mentioned the Trinity several times along with the understanding of "separateness yet togetherness" and diversity and intimacy. You have also made inferences that one of the marks of transformation is how our lives as human beings become similar to God's Trinitarian reality and that this similarity is almost one of the *reasons* for transformation or one of its fruits or goals.

ALLCHIN: Our life may conform to that. As a Christian, I *say* that because I *believe* that. I can say that it is one of the most fruitful and sanctifying parts of our tradition: to let the doctrine of the Trinity come to life. [Now] that is going to be heard by certain kinds of Hindus and Buddhists [who will] say "yes, we have very similar doctrines." I don't yet hear people from the Islamic world saying that. In a way, they started as a kind of reaction against something. We need to think through how we were expressing this [Trinitarian] doctrine. Their fierce re-assertion of absolute oneness of God is also something we've got to listen to. These are many things that we can follow in our next interviews. The crucial need to communicate what is deepest in us, in our experience of God and our experience of transformation. Perhaps next time we can look at what are some of the concepts or images that are important to us. How can we communicate to our *own,* but also listen to others, and communicate who we are to others?

KELLER: Thank you very much, Donald.

ALLCHIN: Thank you for listening.

All Things Shout "Glory"

An Interview with Donald Allchin:
Part Two of Three, July 12, 2007

(Interviewer's Note: This was the second of three hour-long interviews over a three-day period (July 11–13, 2007). In this interview Donald reflects on the mystery of human transformation in the Christian tradition, showing that transformation, spirituality, and contemplation "all stand together." He emphasizes the role of worship, liturgy, the sacraments, and prayer in the process of human transformation. In doing so, Donald approaches transformation from an ecumenical point of view referring to Anglican, Protestant, Orthodox, and Roman Catholic perspectives. He mentions contributions from the Welsh spiritual tradition, the Danish Lutheran theologian N. F. S. Grundtvig, the Wesleys, the Anglican Christian Divines, the Oxford Movement, Orthodox prayer practices, and the role of the arts. Donald links transformation with deification and insists that transformation is an integrative process involving the whole person and every aspect of society and the natural world. The interview begins with a reference to an article from the Pentecost 2007 edition of the *Sewanee Theological Review*.)

Allchin: I was interested that the editor said at the beginning of this issue that the main themes are about transformation. A secondary and related theme is contemplation. We'll get back into that. You [David Keller] suggested that we might talk about the relation of spirituality and particularly of contemplation (*contemplative* spirituality) to a more general term like transformation which I suppose has the New Testament Transfiguration [of Jesus on a mountain] lurking in the background. Looking at this particular number of *Sewanee Theological Review* you see [that] spirituality, contemplation, and transformation all stand together. For the editor, transformation is the overarching thing. Perhaps for Thomas Keating, it is contemplation or meditation, which is the central and obvious thing. Partly because Thomas [Keating] is a life-long Cistercian monk and a Cistercian abbot [it is] absolutely natural for him that the heart of the whole thing is meditation. He takes it for granted: there is [both] the liturgical practice of the church, and also an understanding of and learning of the doctrines of the church, very often through worship. Worship is one of the great ways in which we do begin to understand the doctrines. There is not a difference between [the article in *Sewanee Theological Review*, an Anglican journal] and, [Thomas Keating] but they start from different places. One is starting from an Anglican place—in which the term contemplation is not known much. The other is coming from a Roman Catholic and monastic life in which meditation, the reading of Scripture, and the prayerful reading of Scripture is absolutely at the center of things. It is seen almost without question, in relation to the whole monastic office which is said every day, and the monastic Mass, the Eucharist, which is celebrated almost everyday at most monasteries. The whole liturgical setting of it is in a way presupposed. I would want to hold these things together—as an Anglican and as a person living in the world in the beginning of the twenty-first century.

The words "transformation" and "transfiguration," taken in relation to the whole patent of Christian worship and the worship of the people of God, does provide the kind of setting for this more inward, special work of meditation and contemplation which may lead to a more personal depth which in general the other [corporate worship] doesn't lead to. We can never really be sure about that, because a great many people are not very articulate, [yet] in fact [we see this] through their faithful worship in the congregation and their faithful carrying out of basic Christian obligations and virtues. *Liturgy* means "the work of the people" in Greek and that means it is [both] the corporate offering of the church and the practical offering of the individual Christian and work of the people. I don't know if this is too simple or too Anglican—wanting to have the best of both worlds [i.e. corporate worship and personal contemplative prayer]. I am not doing enough justice to the obvious dynamism behind a man like Thomas Keating and what he is saying and feeling. I do greatly value the contemplative element in life and I do see how much it is lacking in great part of our society and in a great part of the church. The church doesn't realize that it ought to have a contemplative heart. I am not complaining about this, I am saying there are two underlying issues coming out of these interesting and valuable articles.

Keller: It is quite an extraordinary issue. I want to support what you are saying. I agree that contemplation is a language for entering into the dynamism of transformation. So carry on.

Allchin: When I say *liturgy* I imply sacramental liturgy in every sense of *sacramental*. This is where these ancient Celtic words, Welsh words—which came into the Welsh language in about the year five-hundred or six-hundred like "bydysawd," which is the ordinary word in modern Welsh for "universe," which the dictionary tells you means "that which is baptized" or "ready to be baptized." The universe *becomes* the universe by being plunged into the death of Christ and the rising of Christ—the two things together, not one or the other. Baptism is dying and rising with Christ. Three words [are used] in [a] very early Welsh poem in praise of the Trinity. A verse on the Father speaks of the worlds as *presen*—meaning God's presence to us. The verse about the Son speaks of the worlds as *bedydd*—that which is baptized (exactly the same notion as the more general word). The third verse, doesn't actually mention spirit, but we know it must be the Spirit. There God is spoken of as the elements, in Welsh *elfydd*. I think it is referring to an Irish term for God—the pre-Christian Irish term for God [meaning that] God is the Lord of the elements. It carries with it in relationship to the Holy Spirit the sense that the world in which we are involved, and of which we are a part, is very gifted with all kinds of different elements in it, but it needs to be brought together into unity by the Spirit. That is true about the ecological problems of the world at the moment, and also true about the psychological problems inside a lot of people now. Only as we go further into contemplation and interior silence, [do we see] the necessary value of that [i.e. the unity of all things]. That reveals to us all kinds of things in ourselves which otherwise we are unaware of. So that is my kind of opening.

Would it be interesting if we talked about [the Danish Lutheran theologian] Grundtvig? . . . Grundtvig, was a great nineteenth-century Danish Lutheran who in some ways is a contemporary of the Oxford movement. [His] difference from the Oxford movement is partly that he is from a Danish Lutheran background, and that he has much more of a social conscience of a man like F. D. Morris, or one of the early Christian socialists. He is a kind a combination of a great hymn writer and preacher and is known in Denmark by the public as the originator of People's High Schools—an educational move in the nineteenth century—to distribute the land amongst the peasants who had been landless until about 1800. As a result, Denmark became this country of peasant proprietors who took part in these curious schools—which were residential groups of people living, working, talking, singing, and praying together. The main way you learned the language well and learned to read and write, and history and gospel, was in a very living context. That old way of doing things is very much [in contrast to] the present time, with the whole of our terribly technological understanding of education, how it is done, and the importance of getting the economics of it right. Making the students do as much as they can as quickly as possible because they are like machines, and must be as efficient at possible. Anything less Grundtvigian you could hardly imagine.

Grundtvig has this sense of transformation: that God has created a world in order that it may be transformed by God's love—and at the heart of it, by the mystery of God's suffering on our behalf in Christ. This [happens] in such a way that out of [the] suffering the whole of the resurrection comes and the whole gift of the Spirit comes and the creation is fulfilled through the coming of the Spirit. This is the context in which we want to put meditation and contemplation. I don't want to get away from those things. I think as you do that they are very important. They must be put into that kind of context so as not to fall into a false kind of inwardness which has been characteristic by a good deal of pietism. It is fairly easily known that [some] pietism has become so ebulliently aggressive in its new modern neo-conservative Christian evangelical way. The old inward term of pietism is still there in lots of people and groups. The other one, which is turned outward, is so lacking in the *inner* understanding which would come from a little more contemplation, meditation, and a little more self inquiry. It is in desperate need of it [and] it seems to me that fundamentalism is very rigid. It is not overtaking us, in a way we would have thought twenty-five years ago. Only parts of the evangelical movement have turned into this negative, *anti-everybody else* point of view. This wasn't the way Anglican evangelicals were—on the whole.

Keller: One thing I am hearing you say, Donald, is that human transformation is not an entity on its own, but it is linked to and part of the transformation of all of creation. I am also hearing you say that not only is human transformation part of the transformation of all creation, but that human transformation brings with it a passion to be involved in the transformation of the world.

Allchin: Absolutely right. [Transformation is] a passion to be concerned and involved in the healing of human sin and suffering and in the healing of societies which are dysfunctional. But also of human beings who are dysfunctional—people who got into the drug world, the alcohol world, or various kinds of psychological entrapment. It is also concerned about the ecological. These two things can't quite be separated. These extraordinary worldwide days of jazz to raise consciousness about these things may be naive, but there is something very moving about them. It is an attempt to help young people become aware that they are a part of a human family and that they all like the same pop music—which I don't like, but that doesn't matter. Many of the pop musicians are themselves deeply aware of the way we are mistreating the material world and the living world. All of that comes together into this. I am saying that the particular aim of encouraging people to go further into an inner, silent contemplative prayer is something which has relevance to the whole of their individual lives and the whole of society. This is why we may find glimmers of light and hope and also intuition to our understanding the central reality better from things going on *outside*.

I think that the whole recognition of the aesthetic element in human experience—the experience of beauty—is part of prayer but we have left it out for so long. We have made prayer terribly utilitarian. When you go back to the earlier centuries of Christianity (and all religions), we must ask: Why have all religions produced such beautiful buildings and places? This we just recognized about them. The British Museum now has a whole exhibition to show Christian and Islamic art side by side. This a very interesting thought. The present curator for the museum is a far-seeing person. I would guess the curator is a man of a real spiritual conviction. I don't know if he is actually a confessing, practicing Christian, but I wouldn't be surprised if he is. What is clear, and what has been written about in the papers, is that people go there and are astonished because they discover that this religion of the book with supposedly no images [i.e. Islam]—the books themselves are a kind of image. A great many things in Islam are not exactly *literal* icons but other kinds of icons. This helps us understand our icons better.

Keller: Donald, you have spoken about the contexts for transformation. You've mentioned Grundtvig. One of the things I became more aware of when I first read *Participation in God* is that this understanding or practice of the dynamism of transformation was referred to in the early church as theosis and divinization. This was also a rich part of the spirituality of some of the early Anglican Christian Divines—such as Hooker and Andrewes. How did they articulate this?

Allchin: They articulated it in a position where there was already conflict within the Christian world. Andrewes and Hooker are writing in the 1570s and 1580s, very soon after the break between the Church of England and the Church of Rome. They find a wholeness in the early church Fathers—both of them in different ways are enamored with the early Christian tradition. This is the place where we can find some resolution of these quarrels which are making people kill each other and burn each other at the stake. We've not yet begun to think about how is it, that in the sixteenth century, Christians were so happy not only to kill one another, but to kill one another in the most appalling ways specifically because they had made doctrinal mistakes.

In the seventeenth century there are four remarkable poet theologians: John Donne, George Herbert (the central one), Henry Vaughan, and then Thomas Traherne. One thing interesting is that we seldom discuss this. Is it too difficult? Are we nervous about it? John Donne's family was originally from Wales. John Donne himself did not have much contact with Wales. George Herbert's family was one of the great Welsh families, and he grew up as a child in Wales, and spent the rest of his life in England. Herbert is clearly very deeply influenced as a poet and as a believer by something out of that Celtic tradition. Henry Vaughan is bilingual. In his poem, we can see he is showing a whole vision of a transfigured world [that is] related to earlier Celtic poetry. Traherne, as always, is rather an enigma. He lives just on the edge of the speaking world, in Herefordshire. He was born in Hereford. Certainly in Hereford market days you heard a great deal of Welsh spoken as well as a great deal of English. I was talking with the Archdeacon [of Hereford] last night at supper. I've know him quite well for a long time, and we began to talk about this. He said of course he must have heard Welsh spoken. The servants and peasants spoke Welsh. Traherne wasn't a grand person; he was in touch with these people. On the other hand, Traherne also begins with these beautiful meditations—the *Centuries of Mediations*, which begin with a kind of childhood vision of the world. There's a lot of questioning and argument and thought and meditation about how that [vision] is lost in the growth of human life, as a child grows up, and then how you try to rediscover it. These writers are for one reason or another to be very much attracted by [the early church] Fathers, especially by the Greek Fathers—partly because of this ancient Christian heritage which is hidden in the Western side of the British Isles and partly because they were sufficiently close to people like Erasmus and the more humane part of the Reformation itself.

Hooker is really more influenced by Aquinas, but also very influenced by the Fathers, too. The whole notion that, yes, the Christian religion is precisely about God entering into the whole of our human situation in order that we can be lifted by him into God's situation. That is quite clear. Hooker is very cautious about using that language but he does sometimes. He is saying it in a great variety of ways. This is not to say that Andrewes isn't cautious about using that language, because it becomes quite normal to him. He is deeply into the Greek and Latin fathers, both in his private prayers and in his preaching. At the same time, they are living in this late-sixteenth-century and early seventeenth-century world, and a brilliant very detailed study of Andrewes keeps making the point that he is living in Shakespeare's London. Peter McCurrach doesn't say that a bishop could not have gone to one of the theatres in London in the 1560s or 1600s, but he could easily have seen Shakespeare's plays performed in front of the royal court or in the house of a nobleman. Even without seeing them performed, you are aware that you are in a society that is extraordinarily alive intellectually and aesthetically. Looking back, we notice more the secular bits of it more than the religious, but the religious bits are there. We have a constant discussion going on in the literary journals in the last ten years about whether Shakespeare is a secret [Catholic]. A lot of Catholics, Roman in particular, read the plays and finds all kinds of hints. Shakespeare was very close to the people who suffered for their fate.

If you carry that forward into John and Charles Wesley, and start to look at Charles Wesley's Eucharistic hymns, and his preaching, they were really inheriting that [earlier patristic perspective] in the eighteenth century. They were expressing it in eighteenth century language. The sacramental depth of all that gets somewhat lost in the eighteenth century, but it is still there in the eucharistic hymns.

Keller: Could you be more specific about what they were saying in terms of transformation?

Allchin: There is a beautiful Wesley hymn which came to me in the middle of the night that more or less says "God is taking our nature on him in order that he may give us his nature." Some of the Wesley's hymns are extraordinarily direct in saying that. A verse came to me in the middle of the night; it may come back later today.

Keller: One thing I hear, as you speak, is that Hooker had a very organized mind and approached the [English] Church in that way. Then you have Andrewes who has these amazing prayers within his personal life but he is also an extraordinary preacher. Then there are the poets, Trahearne and Vaughan and Herbert, especially Herbert expressing a similar perspective. So you have the pattern of an organized theologian expressing transformation in the context of the way he looks at the church and at life. Then you have Andrewes expressing it in a very personal way but also in a public way through preaching. Then you have Herbert who is an amazing poet as is Vaughan and the others doing the same thing.

Allchin: Herbert also writes that book *The Diary of a Country Priest*, that small book full of what a county priest actually must do day-by-day. He must visit the people when they are not well, he must do all kinds of simple and down to earth things. So that rather elaborate poetry is rooted in the practice of pastoral care. Rowan Williams [has a] little book called [Donald can't remember the title]) This little book was published three or four months ago; its [content is] addresses given all of Holy Week in Canterbury Cathedral. Hundreds of people came. He manages to be very simple sometimes and he ends quoting two or three bits from George Herbert in particular, including the ending of *Love Bade Me Welcome*. He actually says it was one of the finest poems written in the English language. He doesn't often commit himself as plainly as that.

[I was] working away on Traherne, and reading the prose of Traherne—much of it had never been published before. It had never been *available* before. These writers' works—Traherne in particular—have been hidden. For some divine reason, the manuscripts have not been looked at; we don't understand, why. The biggest manuscript was found on a burning rubbish dump by a man who was looking for spare parts for his motor bike. He found this big old leather-bound book and took it home. He kept it three or four years, and then he went to Canada to get a job as builder. In Toronto, while working on the windows of a house, he looked in and saw a man with a table covered with papers and books. He says "I've got an old book at home. Would you like to have a look at it?" He takes it in, and the man says "We've got to take this to the university library straight away—to the history department. It is a seventeenth-century manuscript—I don't know what it is." He knew it was something very important—an equivalent of the Dead Sea scrolls. It had been hidden for over 300 years. *Sewanee Theological Review* has an article about Trahearne which is talking about the spaciousness of Traherne. I think that it is true of all of them. Because they were living in a world of conflict, in the middle of the seventeenth century, and there had been a civil war. Because our civil war was fought like the thirty years war in Germany, it wasn't *so* brutal, but it was pretty horrid. The king had his head cut off, and a lot of others were executed. In that very conflicting time, they did manage to discover a way of holding together. One of the best recent books about George Herbert has said that when you look at underlying theology of these poems, you find sometimes he seems to be a Calvinist, and sometimes not. He was seeing that there was truth on both sides. I would want to say [that] this is why I feel so desperately sad about the kind of fight that goes on between Anglicans at the present time. Our particular vocation *is* to recognize the conflict and discover what God is saying through it. That's what the great seventeenth-century poets did.

Keller: Would it be true to say that part of human transformation is vision? Being able to become aware of God's presence in conflict, in differing opinions?

Allchin: Yes! The saints of God are on the whole people who were very balanced. The saints are of many kinds. They were extremists. You wouldn't want to say St. Francis was balanced. Yet when you think of the different aspects of his vision with the animals and the natural world and the lepers [he is] also dealing with humans of every kind and is especially drawn to those most damaged, but [at the same time] he has this extraordinary kinship with the animal world.

Keller: Would you call "Integration" a key word about transformation.

Allchin: Yes. Transformation leads to integration. The more we take [a] Trinitarian [point of view], the more we [understand] the doctrine of the Holy Spirit and [the more we realize that the Spirit] speaks in our own tongues. All of these different languages [are] being spoken together [yet] one message comes through—the paradox of many languages with one message. That is part of the paradox of how God is. The third person—the Trinity in particular. As in St. Paul—the body has many members but they all belong together. The Spirit works in the whole body, the whole creation.

I think that if we commit ourselves to the inner work in any kind of traditional Christian language, this [becomes] basically a way of reading and praying the Scriptures, the Bible. It is at the heart of Thomas Keating's understanding of [the relationship between contemplative prayer and listening to the scriptures.] Or if you think of the place of the Jesus Prayer. This [prayer that has its focus on the name of Jesus] is very strong in Christianity. There are similar prayers in Islam, and in Buddhism. [In the Jesus Prayer] it is the divine *name; the name of God made man. We enter into that name, but we find ourselves being united with the whole creation though that name. Evelyn Underhill says she had a conversation with [the Orthodox theologian] Father Sergius Bulkakov. I'm convinced [they met] at a Sergius conference in 1935. I want to write a little bit about that because it is as interesting example of Anglicans being willing to learn from Eastern Christians.

Keller: You have mentioned Vladimir Lossky and other Eastern Orthodox writers. I know you have read theologians like Maximus the Confessor, Gregory Palamas, and other earlier theologians and mystics like Gregory of Nyssa. You describe them as speaking of human beings being created in the image of God and that our life's journey is to move along from the image in us to expressing the likeness of God in the way we live.

How do you relate that simple statement to your understanding and your experience of human transformation? Is that a good encapsulation?

Allchin: Yes. In thinking about some of the questions, I have never really thought about the way this word "liturgy" which we know originally means "the work of the people." In classical Greek, it is a public thing like paying income taxes. In Christian terms, it is the work of the whole people of God being caught up into baptism or Eucharist—hearing the word of God and responding to Him with faith. But it is also in Christianity [that] it also has the sense of caring for the most needy, lonely, wounded people, and also taking care of ordinary daily chores—a thing that is actually rather beautiful. I would have thought that almost all the great mystics are very down to earth. Julian of Norwich sees the world like that. Sees little tiny things in which people see God and find God and grow into God through daily life.

Keller: You just mentioned the phrase "the little things." That reminds me of St. David, the patron saint of Wales and his final exhortation to the people prior to his death.

Allchin: Yes! Be joyful! Keep the faith and do the little things. Isn't that amazing? Joy, keeping the faith, and doing the little things. You've a whole life picture: keeping the faith (that is the structure, the given thing) and then doing the little things. But in the middle of it all: "be joyful!" That's just the purpose from the beginning.

Keller: You've raised the issue of the presence of joy and the need for joy. Many people today including myself are being bombarded, literally as well as figuratively, with violence, with contentiousness, and difficult polarities between people and nations. Sometimes it is hard for me and others not to become cynical. Would it be true to say that one of the fruits or one of the consequences of human transformation would be to see beyond these tensions or *into* . . . ? [Allchin interrupts the question . . .]

Allchin: Yes! And I haven't begun to read the first part of a book by David Ford—it just came through the post about ten days ago. The first two or three chapters are all on the Book of Job. *Cries* to God. *Cries, cries, cries,* to God. The righteous man who is crying to God out of great tribulation. It is the cry of Jesus on the cross, so the very heart of redemption. However we think of it, there is the fact that God himself has entered into all of this. That's where the healing comes from. It is so difficult for us to enter into that by ourselves.

Keller: It is hard work.

Allchin: Yes, it is hard work and threatening. And is taking us into a very unknown world. And looking back on church history we can see so many times when it has got distorted and there Christianity itself has been made into a kind religion of suffering, as if the suffering was an end in itself. But it is [in] a way, isn't it?

Keller: Yes. As you were talking, I was thinking of the place in John's Gospel where Jesus exhorts those in prayer to "Remain in me as I remain in you so that your joy may be full . . . ." Jesus was saying that his hope is that they may experience the joy he was feeling. How does that fit into what you sense is this path toward transformation—the joyfulness part of it? Could it be said that joy is one of the fruits or manifestations of a life that is being transformed?

Allchin: Yes I think so, and [Jesus'] joy has come because [his] life has been so very vulnerable and an honest life. So it has not [been] hidden from the elements of darkness and sadness and disillusionment and pain. It is accepted that [those aspects of his life] are really there, but somehow that is not the end. In and through our faith and in and through our inner life, suddenly out of that comes a fulfillment or a kind of resolution—the joy implies a new vision. This is a resolution of conflict, and suddenly a feeling that God is great and the world is just joyful. Creation has [been] given back to us, in a sense. Those gifts are the gifts of God. What do we mean by Grace? I don't know.

Keller: It reminds me of your book *Praise Above All* about the Welsh spiritual tradition.

Allchin: I did have a great compliment just after breakfast [today]. The man who is one of the leading three or four librarians of the national library in Wales said "Oh yes, we've never met, but I read your book about praise." I never had a Welsh person [make comments] about [my book], especially a person academically qualified in the way he was. I was glad to see it that way.

Keller: Thank you. This has been a rich conversation. I am grateful.

Allchin: Thank you for raising these questions. Divine providence is very odd. Who knows what will come into our lives between now and the third interview?

All Things Shout "Glory"

An Interview with Donald Allchin:
Part Three of Three, July 13, 2007

(Interviewer's Note: Donald Allchin begins this interview with a more detailed response to an earlier question about the process of human transformation in Christ. Throughout the interview he points out that transformation has both inward and outward dimensions, involves the whole person, is related to God's presence in creation, takes place in the liturgies and sacraments of the church as well as personal prayer, brings forth an awareness of the unity of all things within a rich diversity, and results in involvement in society rather than a self-centered relationship with God. Donald emphasizes the presence and influence of the Holy Spirit in transformation. He speaks of the influence of Evelyn Underhill on his understanding of spiritual transformation as well as several Orthodox theologians and spiritual writers. Donald mentions the importance of the Jesus Prayer and centering prayer. He relates transformation to the Incarnation and describes the inner life as "a meeting of the human and the divine." To sum up the interview Donald says, "Therefore, the development and transformation into a deeper inner life is not something that will make a life narrow but may have exactly the reverse effect. It is also not to cut a person off from other people.")

Allchin: One of the principal ways in which I think of transformation, in the sense of growing into the life which comes from God, is in relation to unity and diversity. The real transformation is that God brings us together into one. In doing so we don't become monolithic and rigid. On the contrary, our different gifts and our capacities for relating to other people all develop too. It is always with transformation a matter of both unity and diversity; that is my fundamental answer to the term. That could lead us to Evelyn Underhill.

As I've been reading pages of Evelyn Underhill I want to quote sentences of hers about the Jesus Prayer. I think that we've been right in Western Christendom in the last thirty to forty years that we've terribly neglected the inner life and the contemplative aspect of Christianity. But have we jumped too suddenly from Western activism and intellectuality into Zen and Buddhism and various kinds of Eastern religions too quickly? People have talked about the Jesus Prayer, but there is a whole Eastern [Orthodox] tradition which is very much in-between the Eastern religions [such as Buddhism] and Western Christianity. We've still got a great deal to learn. You yourself [David Keller] are doing this in a beautiful and practical way—your description of being with the monks in the Coptic monasteries. You have taken it very seriously.

We are starting with transformation, yes? Yes. It is a very, very wide term. For me, it starts with the thought that with the whole Christian life, the human is being transformed by the Divine and the Divine is gradually transforming the human. Our inner life is involved in a meeting of the human and the Divine. Two makers of Christ to put it in doctrinal terms. Heaven and earth and time and eternity are meeting. In that meeting, something new is coming into being. A characteristic of one of the new things coming into being is although it is one, it is also very varied. This is because the nature of transformation in spiritual life and in the inward life of a person is a kind of unification which doesn't take away all the diversity. In fact, human beings are not only very diverse as between one another, but all of us are diverse in ourselves because we've all got different gifts. Some gifts in the course of our lifetime have developed and some have not. There is a lot there in people that is just lying fallow and hasn't been developed, because we've had sense that Christians want to be terribly delimited and defined. We can't deny it to be true. We have [a] real doctrine of the Holy Spirit, who is clearly in St. Paul's and St. John's understanding of it in the New Testament, the one who brings unity and who reconciles—and the one who brings different gifts to each one. So there is this constant thing that the actual activity of God the Holy Spirit in the human life and human society and in the human heart is to create unity and diversity at once. I would want the transformation to allow for both of those things to be happening.

That would mean that there are [several] ways of thinking about the inner life. These are reformation ways of thinking—the openness and diversity of the inner life is a bit hidden. [It is possible to have] a strict hand and disciplined way of meditating [or using] lectio divina. There is a great [need to] set things aside in order to go to the *one thing*. That is very good, but if that gets out of proportion it leads to a rigidity, which is obviously one of the things that has kept people in Western Christendom out of sympathy with a good deal of old fashioned traditional spiritual writing. The fundamental aspect of Christian transformation has to do with integration of different elements and this is often very much inside us. I don't think perhaps in our thoughts about spiritual life [that] we have enough allowed the fact that the grace of God will bring out the gift which we have been encouraged to suppress or simply left to one side. Therefore, the development and transformation into a deeper inner life is not something that will make a life narrow but may have exactly the reverse effect. It is also not to cut a person off from other people. *There* I think there is an enormous amount to be learned from modern psychology and the fact that some [persons] are temperamental. Some are more inward looking, some more outward looking, some more imaginative and some more intellectual, and [there is] a whole group of people who are practical people establishing new business and new movements. [They are] bringing people together and organizing people. That is also part of what needs to be transformed. It is a very great gift, but perhaps some are a bit shy and can learn something from these people, [who in turn] can learn from the shy people. The development of the inner life is always to have in mind in the background this double thing.

This relates to some of the theologians—I think of Vladimir Lossky—who influenced me quite beyond anything that was easy. To him, of course, person and individual are not the same. *Person* is always the unique person that God had created in relationship with everyone else and with God. The *individual* is the person whom God had created, but shutting himself off and pushing others away. Specifically, you establish yourself by being different from other people and getting the better of them. Obviously, the transformation is not that. [It is necessary to] understand the transformation in relationship to the diversity as well as to the agreement of human society. [In that context] I go back to an eleventh- or twelfth-century Welsh poet who says, "Lord we thank you for making a world that is not uniform." This is sometimes quoted to people who are experts in scholastic medieval theology. They say "You can't *really* have that in a theological text!"

Keller: Let me stop you a minute there, Donald, because there are two things I've heard that I want to clarify. With regard to transformation, I hear you saying that there is a part of us which may not even be known to us and that in the process of transformation the Spirit begins to reveal that dimension to us—latent things; things that have not been personally identified.

The second thing you said was that we must be careful in our praxis not to use things such as contemplative prayer or lectio divina as if they were ends in themselves, but to let them be part of a process or . . . . [Donald interrupts David here.]

Allchin: It's the gift of the light. The light may come to us. Going back to the first thing about people becoming aware of the aesthetic capacities they may have, the imaginative capacities. A common thing in the discovery of spirituality in the general sense says: "We live in this very busy world where we work so hard and try to organize ourselves but we have allowed machines to take over so many things. We've all got to discover that we love beautiful things." I understand where the reaction to a certain sentimental spirituality comes from. At the same time, that instinct in the attempt to rediscover spirituality is I think a sound one because it *does* reflect there is something inside people that tells them the world and society we've created is too mechanized and too busy and too much a matter of words, ideas and definitions. The whole of that more reflective side, seeing the beauty of the countryside, and sitting and looking at something for a half hour. This is an aspect which is very precious and it is important. How do we sell these things to the world? This is one of the ways we can begin to sell it. It is very interesting and encouraging. In this country [the UK], for example, the man who did the stained glass windows in Hereford Cathedral, Tom Denny, is in his 40s and has been doing stained glass windows in a relatively small area—here in Herefordshire and Worcestershire and Gloucestershire. He's known as a man who loves to do very imaginative and unexpected windows for churches. The public response to these four windows was remarkable this year. [The windows] were not very big, but were specially planned by the Dean [of the cathedral] and the artist to be a place where people could sit and be quiet and look. One of the great gifts in Anglican worship in England [is the] tradition of cathedral music. In Hereford it is absolutely superb. The Dean himself has a master's degree in music. He is also a man who has clearly developed the whole aesthetic side of his understanding of things. He said Tom Denny is the man we needed for the stained glass. I saw the sketches and I couldn't think of what they'd be like. Especially with original pieces of artistic work; you don't see it until you see it in the place where it is meant to be. That's a little of how we "take this out to the world." In this county, a lot of things in the last thirty years, from the point of view of church and our society, has been pretty depressing. Our society gets more and more secular and strongly anti-religious in Britain. It is much stronger than in the States, but I can't judge your situation—but our situation has changed. Also, not so obvious, is the way in which suddenly people write poetic plays to perform in church. They begin to make new kinds of music, new kinds of stained glass. There is a whole sense of the liturgical life of the church beginning to express and relate itself to various contemporary [artistic expressions]. This is encouraging because it is part of the transformation. There is an inner transformation we see in the life of prayer which is secret and silent and goes with lectio divina and with centering prayer. But there is also the liturgical thing in a wider sense [that relates] to society as a whole and brings worship into that context. There, I think great things are happening.

Keller: Thank you. What you just said relates to an experience I had last evening. The sun broke through the clouds in front of St. Deiniol's Library [now Gladstone's Library]. I walked out to get some air. There was a holly tree alive with colour. I walked up and spent about fifteen minutes looking at a bee on a holly leaf.

Allchin: Absolutely lovely. We all had [similar] experiences on Sunday because it has been so damp. The trees are like springtime and here we are in July. The trees when the sun shines are gleaming as though it were May and not July. Everybody felt that. Coming back [to Hawarden] from the train station in Chester [I noticed] the sunlight on the hillside and mountainside was so beautiful. I just sat and gasped.

Keller: I'm hearing you say transformation is a fundamental human vocation yet not limited to theology and personal contemplative prayer. It is also awareness of the venue or context as well as the transformation itself. It can take place in sunlight coming through a stained glass window, in music, in looking at a bee, or looking at a hillside. Something is actually taking place—not just a nice view.

Allchin: I am sure the same thing is taking place when a family is growing up happily. [It could take place] in a caring community looking after old people—or ill people. [When that happens] you've created a place that is full of gifts of the Spirit. It involves people of different capacities and different temperaments.

Western Christianity *has* neglected the third person of the Trinity. The Holy Spirit. In the book of Revelation [we find] the seven spirits. These [are] lamps which are burning before the throne of God. The Holy Spirit did not just give seven gifts. God himself was seven-fold because God himself is infinitely varied [and] has created a world that is infinitely varied and has created human beings that are infinitely varied. This is where I remember a great saying from [the Romanian theologian] Dumitru Staniloae. [It is] not to do with the question of homosexuality. But one can see it [in the context of] our present controversy about [human sexuality]. [Father Dumitru and I] were walking at ten o'clock at night through Bucharest back to this hostel and I am sure he was talking [about] Maximus the Confessor. He had spent years studying both as a theologian and a spiritual writer. [Father Dumitru and I] had been talking about the variety of human beings. He said, "But you see there are as many kinds of love as there are human persons." I said "Do you mean there is an infinite number of humans beings?" and he said "Oh no. Not infinite human beings. *Indefinite*. Only *God* is infinite." This was a real theologian—indefinite, not infinite. I'll always remember being corrected by him on this one. And there are as many kinds of love: the love of a mother for her child, of a father for a child, the love of brothers, and people who are working together—all those many different kinds of love. We make it like there are two or three but there are many. I thought about this a great deal in relation to the same sex love. It would have been fascinating to have asked him straight out about that. There was a wonderful time once when coming back from Sevier in Transylvania—sitting in a first class carriage. We were talking to each other on one side and talking in French and on the other side were husband and wife or just a man and woman in love with each other. Enjoying one another. Near Bucharest he said "Two lots of lovers in the same carriage!" (laughter)

Keller: Earlier you mentioned that Evelyn Underhill has influenced you.

Allchin: Evelyn Underhill wrote a book [that influenced me] in 1935 in her sixties. She wrote forty books in her life—[an] incessant writer; most quite small practical books about prayer. Some of the basic medieval mystical writers [were] being published [by her] for the first time like Julian of

Norwich or Walter Hilton. She was very fond of the early Franciscan spiritual writers. She did this big book called *Mysticism*. Still after a hundred years, it is a book people read to introduce themselves to Western Christian mysticism. *Worship* (1936) was not such a success; that was published twenty-five years later. *Worship* has to do with liturgy and personal worship. The editors of the series asked her to be as ecumenical from a Christian point of view as she could—and she did. Because she was member of the fellowship of St. Alban and St. Sergius but not usually able to come to the meetings and conferences, she suddenly had a whole new immersion that year, just in five to six days, into Eastern Orthodox worship. There she was sitting with Father Sergius Bulkakov who was at that moment in his seventies I suppose, and certainly absolutely an outstanding Orthodox theologian in the immigration in France—the head of the St. Sergius Institute in Paris. He was thought by many of the more rigid Orthodox, including a young Vladimir Lossky, as being far too liberal, but that is how he was. [Bulkakov and Underhill] hit it off. This is another lovely story which I enjoy and I do wish I'd asked Nicholas Zernoff more about it. Zernoff who was at that time, in the 1930s, a man in his late twenties or thirties, and a secretary of the Institute. A young member of the emigration and he spent his whole life teaching at Oxford. A great man. Nicholas told me that in a general discussion Evelyn Underhill got up. And at the end Zernoff said "Who was that little old lady? She can't know all that! She can't know that!" The two must have talked together a lot. In the book, *Worship*, she had two wonderful passages about the Trinitarian nature of the Eucharistic prayer—that the Eucharistic prayer begins with praising the Father, then the commemoration of the Son and the Last Supper, and then the whole thing is fulfilled in the Holy Spirit. In 1935 it is only Orthodox churches that keep this tradition now. The old Roman canon has almost nothing about the Holy Spirit. Nobody at that moment saw Vatican Two, the liturgical Trinitarian quality of Roman Catholic worship, nor had anyone seen the Protestant world in general. Largely through the BEM document (Baptism, Eucharist, and Ministry) that said very strongly that any Eucharistic prayer needs this Trinitarian quality. But Underhill also has a beautiful, quite a long passage on that. She also has a page on icons, which in the West, [at that time] were only just beginning to wake up to.

Then she comes on to the Jesus Prayer. Here is a quote: [Donald reads from Underhill] "A great reserve and a great freedom are characteristic of the personal life of prayer in Orthodoxy. Eastern orthodoxy is penetrated

by the conviction that the true Object of its worship transcends all definition. That which any one soul can apprehend is only a fragment and yet this
fragment implies the whole mystery of that which we adore." That implies
that the inner life is very personal but it is free. There is another story she
tells in a letter. At a St. Sergius meeting a young seminarian from a typical High Church had different kinds of intercession every twenty minutes
that morning and everything carefully worked out. Evelyn was thinking
"Isn't this lovely?" and suddenly a Russian boy stood up and said "I thought
we were going to talk about prayer." From this thing, each individual in
one sense has to find for themselves the centrality of the Jesus Prayer in
Orthodoxy.

I am interested [in] how much the term the "prayer of the heart" is
used in the centering prayer world. I appreciate centering prayer because
you do want to center. But in centering prayer the center is the heart. There
you mean "heart" in the biblical sense; not in the emotional sense. The
prayer of the heart, which is the Orthodox form, is remarkable because
it says that prayer is what goes on in the very deepest, inner-most part of
ourselves. It is where God is. If we found God there in the depths of the
heart and if we are silent with God in the depths of heart then the whole
transformation process [is at work].

[Donald Reads from Evelyn Underhill] "Prayer needs to descend into
the heart. This prayer consists in the unremitting repetition of holy name of
God, usually in the form of the prayer: *Lord Jesus Christ, Son of God. Have
mercy on me.* If the simplicity of its form is disconcerting, the doctrine
which underlies it is profound." She also says that this is a form of prayer
available to anybody—the simplest person. Almost any person can understand this and pray. On the other hand, the greatest theologian needs to be
praying it. Orthodoxy is penetrated by a conviction [that incudes] the need
and sufficiency of man [humankind] and the nearness and transforming
power of God. Therefore, its truest act of personal worship will be a humble
and ceaseless self opening to that divine transforming power which enters
with Christ into the natural order to restore and deify the whole world.
That is the whole purpose of the thing. It is deeply personal but absolutely
universal. That is what the meaning of incarnation is. Incarnation is taking
in the whole of humanity but also the world itself [which] is that which is
made to be baptized. The world was made to die and rise with Christ in
some mysterious way and that we celebrate as we go more deeply into this.
Then Underhill quotes a passage from a book about Orthodoxy: "The light

of the name of Jesus passes though the heart to eradiate the universe—a foretaste of that final transfiguration in which God shall be all and all." That is a wonderful way to sum up the full meaning of the Jesus Prayer. I know in practice Western Christians do use it and find it is extremely helpful with people of very different personal temperaments. I think it is a central part of Orthodoxy. [Especially in] the really difficult times in Russia in the 1930s with the Stalinist attack on everybody. Most churches in Russia were closed. By 1939, there were four dioceses out of 250 [that] were actually functioning [with only] about five bishops. When the Germans attacked Russia, there almost seemed to be Russian attempts to take their side. Stalin has to make concessions to the church in order to say "We stand for Russia!" and "Holy Russia." The patriarch then reappears. In the end, they can open about 20 percent of the churches. So many people say the faith and prayer and love of the Russian people never failed because they had the Jesus Prayer. People in their own secret lives lived on the Jesus Prayer. If Jesus is present in the heart in the prayer, then it is a very eucharistic prayer. I think that is the thing which is what we need to look *back* into.

Because I went so often to Romania during the communist time and saw how in Romania, partly because the communist regime went quite mad, it was a very nationalist kind of communism. A great deal of what was traditional in Romania (great old monasteries and buildings) had to be left. And when possible they left a small group of nuns or large group of monks at the monastery as a tourist place. In one sense the church did go on. [Referring to] the first patriarch after the revolution in 1947 in Romania, one of his clergy said to me "He has been fighting every day for the last twenty-five years with the representatives of the state trying to keep a whole space in which the church can exist. Sometimes he has been successful; sometimes he hasn't. We all know that he sits in his office and various important political people come to him." The Bishop of Gibraltar (an English bishop in continental Europe) went in to visit the patriarch and the patriarch said "You thought I was in prison, didn't you? but I am not yet." [laughter]

Keller: In the last ten minutes or so, as you've brought in the wisdom of Evelyn Underhill in reference to the Jesus Prayer and the heart. One thing I heard is that the process of transformation, while it is a very deeply personal activity, is not only about the person, it is the person *with* all of creation—with all of the other people. So would it be true to say that transformation, while it is a vocation of each person, is also part of a larger vocation?

Allchin: Absolutely. This is really where the Christology comes in and the doctrinal end. It is the thing which is very common. [Certainly] strongly in Augustine. Certainly with Gregory the Great. Perhaps a bit more explicit in the Greek Fathers. In the Incarnation, in taking humanity Jesus has really taken on the whole of humanity. In taking on the whole of humanity, he has taken on the whole of creation. The creation is sanctified by the Incarnation. Therefore, the whole of creation is caught up into these things. That is why the liturgy is so full of natural symbols. It surely is exactly the kind of Christian corresponding insight to things that you do see in Eastern religions. Both in Buddhism and Hinduism the inner act of worship is absolutely inclusive of the whole creation—they don't use this word. Everything leads. It is all gathered in. This is here. It is obviously something that is implied in Sufism. I think one reason why [Thomas] Merton in the last two to three years of his life was interested in Sufism. I always say that in the last five or ten years he was going through [a] non-disintegrating explosion. He was really interested in all the great religious traditions. At the same time what most people who write about him don't recognize is how much Merton was influenced by Russian theologians in Paris. And how much he was influenced by Vladimir Lossky. There are passages in his diary where someone has either given him a new book by Lossky or he's got hold of a book. He stops and says this is absolutely the real thing.

Keller: Donald, we have ten or fifteen minutes left. There are two things . . . .

Allchin: I want to say by way of my testimony, I didn't start as a small boy [appreciating] the Crusades. It is a very old fashioned evangelical thing for children. I didn't like it at all. I longed to go back to the church where there was music and where my mother also came. On the other hand, yes, it is very strange the [way] things happen to you—the fact that I got to know Merton via Dale Moody at the Southern Baptist Seminary in Louisville and I got to know Merton at a time when he had read all this material from the French Orthodox Diaspora in Paris. [Merton and I] shared an enthusiasm for the Shakers and wanted to know about who these people actually were. I could give Merton a sense of immediate relationship with these people.

In my school days I first met an elderly lady who had been a contemporary of Evelyn Underhill. Later when I was at Canterbury [Cathedral] there was old lady who had lived in precincts of Canterbury. Then in the 1930s, when Evelyn was getting bad asthma, a Mormon used to work with her and probably typed for her. Evelyn would say "I can't give this lecture because I can't speak. Will you go for me?" So I learned these things which I want to hand on because they are very personal. That is what I wanted to add. Even the thing about the one or two things in the Crusaders class have stuck with me in a sense, even though I did not like the atmosphere of it very much

Keller: One of the things you have said and demonstrated through the importance of the Jesus Prayer in the Orthodox Church is its simplicity; it is something that anyone can incorporate into their life. My final question for today is this: When we look around in the world today there many men and women who have tremendous responsibility and tremendous access to power and therefore of control of the masses and of nations. It seems that some of them, in the way they approach government and pursue their ideology, seem to be crossing into the dark side of what is possible. In what ways can we communicate to them the dimension of humanity you have described; one that is not simply personal but, as you say, embraces and includes the lives of everyone? How can that somehow influence this tendency we experience these days to darkness and violence?

Allchin: I suppose this is where the cross comes in. The cross is the place where the light of God meets the darkness and violence. This is where the Jesus Prayer is very much centered on that. It means that the people with immense responsibility need even more than they [ever] have before to be aware that the darkness can swallow up whole peoples. [The] willingness to think that we've got to fight the terrorists and the ultra [conservatives] is a terrible misunderstanding—a terrible error because we become just like them. We have invented Guantanamo Bay and we have invented Abu Ghraib. We are constantly treating middle eastern people, Arabic people, in a way which is humiliating them There is an extraordinary [article] in the *Guardian* [a British daily newspaper] today about one of the people who led the attack on London eighteen months ago. His wife, who is Arabic and a Muslim had no idea he was up to that. They were a law abiding couple, in the Muslim sense, so he had his friends and she had her friends. His friends did not meet her, and her friends did not meet him. She did not know he was involved in this plotting to set off bombs in London. She had a miscarriage for her second child the day before they set off all the things. She said she has been puzzled in trying to understand this. She said "I seemed to suffer for them before they actually did it." She has recently been trying to write a book to help. This is a long piece in the *Guardian* saying this is what she has said and felt. Some people are already critical of that saying, "We mustn't listen to her." [But] she doesn't represent wickedness [and] we *must* listen to her. We must try to understand Islam. Then there is this wonderful correspondence between Merton and Abdul Aziz, who was a civil servant in the Pakistani government. (Details are in transcript #1).

Keller: As I reflect on these three hours we have spent together, I want to thank you for all you have shared. This is a very rich gift you are giving all of us. It seems to me, in my mind and heart, you are saying that human beings are called to become like the one who made them, yet not to become God. We are to become manifestations of God. Is this what you have been saying?

Allchin: Manifestations of God's creative love.

Keller: What you are saying is that we must be truly careful to avoid things that will take us into darkness. Careful in the positive sense of being stewards of who or what we become. I am thinking of the Greek word *"askesis"* whose root meaning is "to care for."

Allchin: I found that in your foot note in that special number of the *Sewanee Theological Review* where you had an article on contemplative prayer—full of interesting articles. I began to read Tilden Edward's piece. Read it in the middle—where it was saying wonderful things. He is the first person to say "I want to study Celtic Christianity in Wales. Who can you introduce me to?" I met Tilden in New York and I sent him two names. I couldn't think of any other names at that time. And now, twenty-five years later, they are coming in scores. That is right. People are coming in scores. Setting themselves up on one side or the other.

Keller: Is there anything else you want to say?

Allchin: I am very grateful to you for asking me these things, and making me think about various things I don't usually think about. I perhaps should put some more of this down on paper. What I am very conscious of is that as you get older, it is very important to remember to put down more memories. I think perhaps I ought to.

Keller: I hope you do.

Allchin: One of the two old ladies [spoken about earlier] who did know Evelyn Underhill said, "She was very smart. She had a wonderful sense of humour. People make her sound so grim and solemn. I knew her when I was a young girl. She was delightful."

Keller: Thank you again, Donald. These conversations and listening to you speak is an authentic example of transformation and how the interaction of people manifests God's presence.

Bibliography

Allchin, A. M. "Abingdon Conference." *Sobornost Review* 3/6 (1949) 258–60.

———. *Ann Griffiths.* Cardiff: University of Wales Press and the Welsh Arts Council, 1976.

———. *Ann Griffiths: The Furnace and the Fountain.* Cardiff: University of Wales Press, 1987.

———. *Bernard Walke: A Good Man Who Could Never Be Dull.* Abergavenny, UK: Three Peaks, 2000.

———. "Can we do Wales then?" *The Merton Journal* 13/2 (2006) 2–10.

———. *Celtic Christianity.* A Cowley Audio Cassette Tape. Cambridge, MA: Cowley, 1989. Ninety minutes.

———. *Celtic Christianity: Fact or Fiction?* Bangor, UK: University College of North Wales, 1993.

———. *The Communion of Saints.* Oxford: SLG, 1975.

———. "Dumitru Staniloae." *Sobornost incorporating Eastern Churches Review* 16/1 (1994) 38–44.

———. *The Dynamic of Tradition.* London: Darton, Longman and Todd, 1981.

———. *Enlli: Cyrchfa i Bererinion.* Pwllheli, UK: Ymddiriedolaeth, Ynys Enlli, 1991.

———. "Foreword." In *Beyond the Shadow and the Disguise,* by Monica Weis, Paul M. Pearson, Kathleen P. Deignan, 5–9. Stratton-on-the-Fosse, UK: The Thomas Merton Society of Great Britain and Ireland, 2006.

———. *"The Gift of Theology": The Trinitarian Vision of Ann Griffiths and Elizabeth of Dijon.* Oxford: SLG, 2005.

———. *God's Presence Makes the World: The Celtic Vision through the Centuries in Wales.* London: Darton, Longman and Todd, 1997.

———. "The Hymns of N. F. S. Grundtvig." *Eastern Churches Quarterly* XIII (1959) 129–43.

———. *N. F. S. Grundtvig: An Introduction to His Life and Work.* London: Darton, Longman and Todd, 1997.

———. *N. F. S. Grundtvig: An Introduction to His Life and Work.* Aarhus, Denmark: Aarhus University Press, 1997.

———. "Grundtvig's Translations from the Greek." *Eastern Churches Quarterly* XIV (1961–62) 28–44.

———. *Heart of Compassion: Daily Readings with St. Isaac of Syria.* London: Darton, Longman and Todd, 1989.

Bibliography

———. "The Holy Spirit in Christian Life" *Sobornost incorporating Eastern Churches Review* 5/3 (1966) 170–81.

———. *The Joy of All Creation: An Anglican Meditation on the Place of Mary.* London: Darton, Longman and Todd, 1984.

———. *The Kingdom of Love and Knowledge: The Encounter between Orthodoxy & the West.* London: Darton, Longman and Todd, 1979.

———. *Landscapes of Glory: Daily Readings with Thomas Traherne.* London: Darton, Longman and Todd, 1989.

———. *The Living Presence of the Past: The Dynamic of Christian Tradition.* New Haven: Seabury, 1981.

———. *Looking at Celtic Christianity through Its Poetry.* Audiocassette Recording, recorded by David Keller, 2005. Available in digital format or compact disk: tycoedd@yahoo.com.

———. *Looking at R. S. Thomas and Ann Griffiths.* Audiocassette Recording, recorded by David Keller, 2005. Available in digital format or compact disk: tycoedd@yahoo.com.

———. "Merton and Traherne: The Two Thomases," Presidential address, *A Mind Awake in the Dark.* Abergavenny, UK: Three Peaks, 2002.

———. "Merton at Ninety." *The Merton Journal* 12/1 (2005) 2–4.

———. "Michael Ramsey and the Orthodox World." *Sobornost incorporating Eastern Churches Review* 10/2 (1988) 49–53.

———. "Our Lives, a Powerful Pentecost: Merton's Meeting with Russian Christianity." *The Merton Annual* (1998) 33–48.

———. *Participation in God: A Forgotten Strand in Anglican Tradition.* London: Darton, Longman and Todd, 1988.

———. *Pennant Melangell: Cyrchfan Pererinion.* Oswestry, UK: Pennant Melangell printed by Border Business Centre, 1994.

———. "Peter Hammond." *Sobornost incorporating Eastern Churches Review* 22/1 (2000) 50–56.

———. *Praise Above All: Discovering the Welsh Tradition.* Cardiff: University of Wales Press, 1991.

———. *Praying the Trinity.* A Cowley Audio Cassette Tape. Cambridge, MA: Cowley 1989. Ninety minutes.

———. *Remembering Merton.* A round table discussion between a few of Merton's friends—Tommie O'Callaghan, Donald Allchin, Jim Forest, and John Wu, Jr., chaired by David Scott at the Thomas Merton Society conference "Your Heart is my Hermitage," held in Southampton, 1996. http://www.thomasmertonsociety.org/panel.htm No pagination.

———. *Resurrection's Children: Exploring the Way towards God.* Norwich, UK: Canterbury, 1998.

———. *The Silent Rebellion: Anglican Religious Communities, 1845–1900.* London: SCM, 1958.

———, ed. *Solitude and Communion: Papers on the Hermit Life, given at St. David's, Wales by Orthodox, Roman, and Anglican contributors.* Oxford: Fairacres, 1977.

———. *Song To Her God: Spirituality of Ann Griffiths.* Cambridge, Massachusetts: Cowley 1987.

———. *The Spirit and the Word: Two Studies in Nineteenth-Century Anglican Theology.* no loc.: Faith, 1963.

———. "Spirituality and Welsh Poetry, 1930–80." in "Spirituality, Imagination and Contemporary Literature," Supplement to *The Way* (1994) 70–78.

———. ed. *The Tradition of Life: Romanian Essays in Spirituality and Theology.* Oxford: Fellowship of St. Alban and St. Sergius, 1971.

———. *Trinity and Incarnation in Anglican Tradition.* Oxford: Fairacres, 1977.

———. "A Vision of Unity in Diversity. In Memoriam Demetrios Koutroubis." *Sobornost incorporating Eastern Churches Review* 6/1 (1984) 73–78.

———. ed. *We Belong to One Another: Methodists, Anglicans, and Orthodox.* London: Epworth, 1965.

———. *The World Is a Wedding.* New York: Oxford University Press, 1978.

Allchin, A. M., and John Coulson, eds. *Rediscovery of Newman.* London: SPCK, 1967.

Allchin, A. M., and H. A. Hodges. *A Rapture of Praise: Hymns of John and Charles Wesley.* London: Hodder and Stoughton, 1966.

Allchin, A. M., and E. Wyn James. *Rhyfeddaf Fyth . . . Emynau a llythyrau Ann Griffiths ynghyd â'r byrgofiant iddi gan John Hughes, Pontrobert, a rhai llythyrau gan gyfeillion.* Gregynog, UK: Gwasg Gregynog, 1998.

Allchin, A. M., D. Densil Morgan, and Patrick Thomas. *Sensuous Glory: The Poetic Vision of D. Gwenallt Jones.* Norwich, UK: Canterbury, 2000.

Andrewes, Lancelot. *Complete Works.* Library of Anglo-Catholic Theology, 11 Vols. Vol. III. Oxford: Parker, 1841–54.

Andrews, Rhiain M., et al. *Gwaith Bleddyn Fardd a Beirdd Eraill y Drydedd Ganrif ar Ddeg.* Translation by Patrick Thomas. Cardiff: University of Wales Press, 1996.

Chadwick, Owen. *Michael Ramsey: A Life.* Oxford: Oxford University Press, 1990.

Church, Richard William. *Pascal and Other Sermons.* 1923. Reprint. Charleston, SC: Nabu, 2013.

Cobb, "Dr Pusey and Sister Clara." *The Fairacres Chronicle* 16/1 (1983) 4–15.

Coutts, James, ed. *Homage to Ann Griffiths: A Special Bicentenary Publication.* Penarth, UK: Church in Wales Press, 1976.

Cropper, Margaret. *Flame Touches Flame.* London: Longman, Green, 1949.

Damian, Peter. *Selected Writings on the Spiritual Life.* London: Harper and Brothers, 1959.

Daniel, Catherine. *Enlli: Porth y Nef.* Liverpool: no publisher named, 1995.

Davies, Morris. *Cofiant Ann Griffiths.* Denbigh, 1865. Whitefish, MT: Kessinger, 2010.

Evagrius. *Chapters on Prayer.* Translated by John Eudes Bamberger OCSO. Kalamazoo, MI: Cistercian, 1981.

Evdokimov, Paul. *Woman and the Salvation of the World: A Christian Anthropology on the Charisms of Women.* Crestwood, NY: St. Vladimir's Seminary Press, 1994.

Girard, René. *Deceit, Desire, and the Novel: Self and Other in Literary Structure.* Baltimore: Johns Hopkins University Press, 1976.

Gorodetzky, Nadejda. *St. Tikhon of Zadonsk.* Crestwood, NY: St. Vladimir's Seminary Press, 2003.

Griffiths, Ann. *Hymns and Letters.* London: Stainer and Bell, 1999.

Grundtvig, N. F. S. *Vaerker i Udvalg,* Vol. III. Gyldendal: København, 1940.

Hammond, Peter. *The Waters of Marah: The Present State of the Greek Church.* London: Macmillan, 1956.

Härdelin, Alf. *The Tractarian Understanding of the Eucharist.* Studia Historica-Ecclesiastica Upsaliensia, 8. Uppsala: Acta Universitatis Upsaliensis, 1965.

Hastings, Adrian. *A History of English Christianity.* London: SCM, 2001.

Bibliography

Hopkins, Gerard Manley. *Poems and Prose*. London: Penguin, 1953.

Kramer, Victor, A. "'A Very Disciplined Person' from Nelson County: An Interview with Canon A. M. Allchin about Merton." *Merton Annual* 17 (2004) 235–55.

Liddon, Henry. *Life of E. B. Pusey*, vol. IV. London: Longmans Green, 1898.

Lloyd, Nesta. *Cerddi'r Ficer: Detholiad o gerddi Rhys Prichard*. Translation by Patrick Thomas. Llandybïe, UK: Cyhoeddiadau, 1994.

Lossky, Vladimir. *The Mystical Theology of the Eastern Church*. Crestwood, NY: St. Vladimir's Seminary Press, 1997.

McCann, Dom Justin, ed. *The Golden Epistle of Abbot William of St. Thierry to the Carthusians of Mont Dieu*. London: Sheed & Ward, 1930.

Mascall, E. L., and H. S. Box, eds. *The Blessed Virgin Mary: Essays by Anglicans*. London: Darton, Longman and Todd, 1963.

———. *Saraband: The Memoires of E. L. Mascall*. Leominster, UK: Grace Wing, 1992.

Maximus the Confessor. *Philosophical and Theological Questions*, Vol. I. Introduction and Commentary by D. Staniloae.

Merton, Thomas. *Conjectures of a Guilty Bystander*. Garden City, NY: Doubleday Image, 1968.

———. *Dancing in the Water of Life: The Journals of Thomas Merton. Volume five, 1963–1968*. Edited by Robert E. Daggy. New York: Harper Collins, 1997.

———. *The Hidden Ground of Love: Letters on Religious Experience and Social Concerns*. Edited by William H. Shannon. London: Collins Flame, 1985.

———. *Learning to Love: The Journals of Thomas Merton. Volume six, 1966–1967*. Edited by Christine M. Bochen. New York: Harper Collins. 1997.

———. *The Road to Joy: The Letters of Thomas Merton to New and Old Friends*. Edited by Robert E. Daggy. London: Collins Flame, 1989.

———. *A Search for Solitude: The Journals of Thomas Merton. Volume three, 1952–1960*. Edited by Lawrence S. Cunningham, New York: Harper Collins, 1996.

———. *The Seven Storey Mountain*. Orlando: Harcourt Brace, 1948.

———. *Turning towards the World: The Journals of Thomas Merton. Volume four 1960–1963*. Edited by Victor A. Kramer. New York: Harper Collins, 1996.

Meyendorff, John. *Byzantine Theology*. Crestwood, NY: St. Vladimir's Seminary Press, 1974.

Miller, Charles. *The Gift of the World: An Introduction to the Theology of Dumitru Staniloae*. Edinburgh: T. & T. Clark, 2000.

———. *Toward A Fuller Vision: Orthodoxy and the Anglican Experience*. Harrisburg, PA: Morehouse, 1984.

Nouwen, H. J. M. *The Genesee Diary*. New York, Image, 1981.

Orford, Barry A., and William Davage. *Piety and Learning: The Principals of Pusey House: 1882–2002*. Oxford: Pusey House, 2002.

Pearson, Paul, M. "Donald Allchin and the Thomas Merton Society." *The Merton Journal* 18/1 (2011) 2–4.

Pelikan, Joraslav. *The Vindication of Tradition*. New Haven: Yale University Press, 1986.

Pryce, H. "A New Edition of the *Historiae Divae Monacellae*" *The Montgomeryshire Collections: Journal of the Powysland Club* 82 (1994) 23–40.

Rattenbury, Ernest. *The Evangelical Doctrine of Charles Wesley's Hymns*. London: Epworth, 1941.

Ramsey, Michael. *The Gospel and the Catholic Church*. Reprint. Eugene, OR: Wipf & Stock, 2008.

Bibliography

Roberts, Enid. *A'u Bryd ar Ynys Enlli.* Talybont, UK: Y Lolfa, 1993.

Roberts, Gomer Morgan. *Hanes Methodistiaeth Galfinaidd Cymru: Cyfrol 1—Y Deffroad Mawr.* Caernarfon, UK: Llyfrfa'r Methodistaid Calfinaidd, 1973.

Rowell, Geoffrey, ed. *A Fearful Symmetry? The Complementarity of Men and Women in Ministry.* London: SPCK, 1992.

Scott, David. *Beyond the Drift: New and Selected Poems.* Hexham, UK: Bloodaxe, 2014.

Staniloae, Dumitru. *Prayer and Holiness: The Icon of Man Renewed in God.* Oxford: SGL, 1996.

———. "Some Characteristics of Orthodoxy." *Sobornost incorporating Eastern Churches Review* 5/9 (1969) 627–29.

———. "Tradition and the Development of Doctrine." *Sobornost incorporating Eastern Churches Review* 5/9 (1969) 652–62.

———. *The Victory of the Cross.* Oxford: Fairacres, 1970.

———. "The World as Gift and Sacrament." *Sobornost incorporating Eastern Churches Review* 5/9 (1969) 662–73.

Taylor, Jeremy. *Selected Works.* Edited by Thomas K. Carroll and John Booty. Mahwah, NJ: Paulist, 1990.

Thomas, Patrick. *Brechfa and Beyond.* Llanrwst, UK: Gwasg Carreg Gwalch, 2009.

Thomas, R. S. *Laboratories of the Spirit.* London: Phoenix, 2004.

Thunberg, Lars. *Microcosm and Mediator: The Theological Anthropology of Maximus the Confessor.* Lund: Gleerup, 1965.

Traherne, Thomas. *Centuries of Meditation.* Edited by Bertram Dobell. New York: Cosimo Classics, 2007.

Underhill, Evelyn. *The Letters of Evelyn Underhill.* Edited by Charles Williams. London: Longmans, Green and Co., 1951.

Ware, Kallistos. "Obituary." *Sobornost incorporating Eastern Churches Review* 33/1 (2011) 37–46.

Ware, Timothy. *The Orthodox Church.* 2nd ed. London: Penguin, 1993.

Webb, Clement C. J., *The Religious Thought of the Oxford Movement.* London: SPCK, 1933.

Williams, Rowan. "The sermon preached by the Archbishop of Canterbury at the High Mass of Requiem for the Reverend Canon Dr. Arthur McDonald Allchin, St. Mary Magdalene, Oxford, 12 January, 2011." *Sobornost incorporating Eastern Churches Review* 33/1 (2011) 46–49.

Williams, Thomas Jay. *Lydia Priscilla Sellon.* 2nd ed. London: SPCK, 1965.

Williams, Waldo. *Dail Pren.* Aberystwyth: Gwasg Aberystwyth, 1957.

———. *The Old Farmhouse.* Translated by D. J. Williams. London: Harrap, 1961.

Yannaras, Christos. *The Freedom of Morality.* Crestwood, NY: St. Vladimir's Seminary Press, 1984.

Printed in Great Britain
by Amazon